FOUR

WHEELS

AND A

BOARD

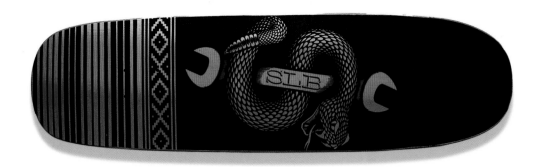

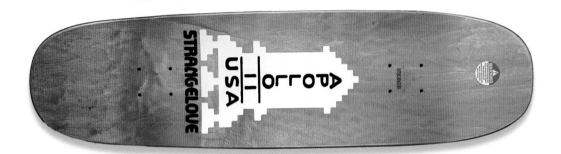

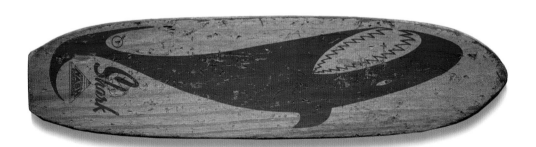

FOUR WHEELS AND A BOARD

The Smithsonian History of Skateboarding

Edited by Betsy Gordon and Jane Rogers

Foreword by Rodney Mullen

Directors' Notes by Anthea M. Hartig
and Cynthia Chavez Lamar

In Association with the National Museum of American History
and the National Museum of the American Indian

Smithsonian Books
Washington, DC

Published by Smithsonian Books
Director: Carolyn Gleason
Senior Editor: Jaime Schwender
Assistant Editor: Julie Huggins

Creative Director: Gary Tooth
Edited by Sharon Silva
Designed by Elise Crigar and Alex Barnes

Essays written by Ted Barrow, Jim Fitzpatrick, Eli Morgan Gesner, Tony Hawk, Kevin Imamura, Eric Jentsch, Mimi Knoop, Catharine Lyons, Dan Mancina, Rodney Mullen, Jack Smith, Rodney Smith, Miriam Klein Stahl, C. R. Stecyk, Bryce Wettstein, Cindy Whitehead, and Neftalie Williams

Oral histories by Salman Agah, Brian Anderson, Leo Baker, Matt Bass, Cara-Beth Burnside, Bob Denike, Skip Engblom, Richard Novak, John O'Malley, Judi Oyama, Bryan Ridgeway, Alexis Sablone, and Elissa Steamer from interviews conducted by Betsy Gordon and Jane Rogers

This book may be purchased for educational, business, or sales promotional use. For information, please write: Special Markets Department, Smithsonian Books, P.O. Box 37012, MRC 513, Washington, DC 20013

Library of Congress Cataloging-in-Publication Data is available upon request.

Printed in China, not at government expense
26 25 24 23 22   1 2 3 4 5

For permission to reproduce illustrations appearing in this book, please correspond directly with the owners of the works, as seen on pages 231–32. Smithsonian Books does not retain reproduction rights for these images individually or maintain a file of addresses for sources.

Case front, clockwise from top left: *S. L. Barbier 2022 deck; skate deck used by Mimi Knoop during the 2004 X Games; Schmitt Stix 2019 skate deck for the inaugural USA Olympic skateboarding team; Pocket Pistols 2021 Chuck Treece pro model reissue deck; Birdhouse 2016 Tony Hawk pro model skateboard; Santa Cruz 1999 memorial deck for Tim Brauch.*

Case back, clockwise from top left: *REAL 2019 skate deck painted with braille text; Powell-Peralta skate deck, ca. 1980s; StrangeLove 2019 Bohemian Grove skate deck; Native Skates 2008 Spirit Feather model deck; SHUT Skateboards 1989 Shark model deck; Native Skates 2008 Alcatraz model deck.*

Title page: *From a rare, limited-edition skate deck meant to be displayed on a collector's wall to a well-used skateboard ridden by three generations of skateboarders, the Smithsonian collection of skateboard history and culture contains a wide variety of artifacts.* **From top:** *One of twenty limited-edition hand-screened skate decks produced by Sal Barbier in 2022. StrangeLove Skateboards' Apollo Moon Landing deck issued in 2019 references the film The Shining. The yellow plastic California Free Former deck from the 1970s was commonly referred to as a banana board. The 1963 Nash Shark deck was a solid plank of oak shaped like a miniature surfboard. Three generations of the Conner family of Virginia used this mid-1970s Caster skateboard before donating it to the Smithsonian.*

Opposite left: *Marty Grimes was the first Black professional skateboarder and the first to have a pro model deck. This 2020 reissue Hall of Fame Panther skate deck includes the panther that was originally designed by Angela Grimes for Marty's first pro model from the mid-1970s and was redesigned by Raith Grimes for Marty's family-owned skateboard company, HoodWood Skates.*

Opposite right: *This 2019 Bohemian Grove deck was part of a trio of conspiracy theory–themed skateboard graphics issued by StrangeLove Skateboards in 2019. Bohemian Grove, a campground in Monte Rio, California, hosts the annual gathering of the Bohemian Club, a San Francisco–based all-male private club that spawns conspiracy theories in some circles.*

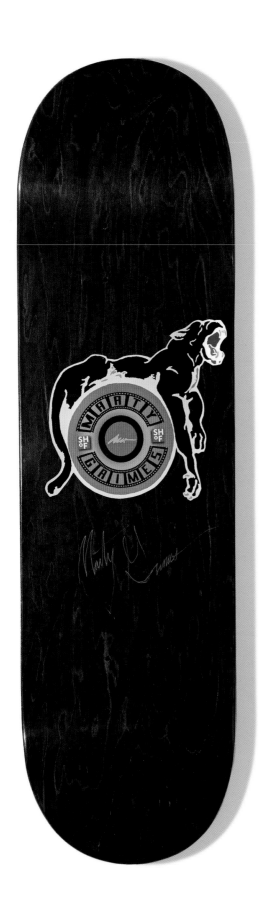

CONTENTS

Foreword Rodney Mullen 8

Directors' Notes Anthea M. Hartig
and Cynthia Chavez Lamar 10

Introduction Betsy Gordon and Jane Rogers 12

CHAPTER ONE '60s
**Surfboards, Airplanes, and Roller Stakes:
The Birth of the American Skateboard**

Introduction Betsy Gordon and Jane Rogers 21

Timeline: The 1960s 26

"The Last of the Surfs Is America" C. R. Steyck 28

What Is That Thing Called? Skip Engblom 32

The Never-Ending Endless Summer Eric Jentsch 33

Buster Wilson's Garage Jim Fitzpatrick 35

Skating in Europe Jim Fitzpatrick 37

East Coast Skating John O'Malley 39

Chaz Bojórquez: From Tagging to the Smithsonian
Jane Rogers 40

From Punch Line to Life Lesson Betsy Gordon 43

CHAPTER TWO '70s
**There's a Great Future in Plastics:
Technology Changes Skateboarding**

Introduction Betsy Gordon and Jane Rogers 45

Timeline: The 1970s 54

Women's Skateboarding Cindy Whitehead 56

From Creative to Cadillac Jane Rogers 60

The Rise and Fall of the Legend of Dogtown Skip Engblom 62

The Beginning of a Skateboarding Dynasty Richard Novak 66

From Black Hill to Signal Hill Jane Rogers 69

Magazines, Catalogs, and Skateparks Bryan Ridgeway 71

Pushing across America Jack Smith 73

My First Skateboard Tony Hawk 74

Carving a Path in Skateboarding Judi Oyama 76

So You Want to Collect a Skateboard? Jane Rogers 78

The Beginnings: Carlsbad Skatepark John O'Malley 80

Expatriating Skateboard Heritage Betsy Gordon 82

CHAPTER THREE '80s
Vert, Street, VHS, and Zines

Introduction Betsy Gordon and Jane Rogers 85

Timeline: The 1980s 92

Powell-Peralta Deck Donation Tony Hawk 94

Thanks for the Skateboard, Tony! Jane Rogers 95

No More Skateparks and the Rise of the Zine
Bryan Ridgeway 96

We Were Screwed Cindy Whitehead 98

Mail-Order Skateboards and the Ollie Brian Anderson 101

I Just Want to Skate Salman Agah 103

Pushing across America, Take Two Jack Smith 105

The History of Skateboard Graphics Matt Bass 106

SHUT Skateboards Rodney Smith 110

The Bones Brigade on the Road Jim Fitzpatrick 113

NHS: Surviving Skateboarding in the Late 1980s
Bob Denike 115

CHAPTER FOUR '90s

Not Just Guys and Not Just California

Introduction Betsy Gordon and Jane Rogers 117

Timeline: The 1990s 122

The Truth Lies between Style and Substance Ted Barrow 124

Rookie Skateboards Catharine Lyons 128

Florida Girl in a California World Elissa Steamer 132

The Island of Lost Children: Zoo York Eli Morgan Gesner 134

Skateboarding and Sneaker Culture Kevin Imamura 140

The Skateboard That Changed America Jim Fitzpatrick 147

From Skateboarder to Snowboarder and Back Again
Cara-Beth Burnside 148

Proud to Be a Skater Alexis Sablone 150

George Orton and the Rise of the X Games Jane Rogers 151

Turning Pro Brian Anderson 154

Skate Stoppers Betsy Gordon 156

CHAPTER FIVE '00s

Skateboarding Looks Back

Introduction Betsy Gordon and Jane Rogers 159

Timeline: The 2000s 166

Skateboarding in the New Millennium Ted Barrow 168

Tim Brauch and the Beginning of the Skate Collection
Jane Rogers 172

Skating While Blind Dan Mancina 174

Skateboarding as a Career Alexis Sablone 178

Fight for Fair Play Mimi Knoop 180

Native American Skateboard History and Culture
Betsy Gordon 182

Making a Living as a Pro Skater Leo Baker 186

CHAPTER SIX 2010s TO PRESENT

Diversity, Inclusion, and the Olympics: Skateboarding's Sixth Decade

Introduction Betsy Gordon and Jane Rogers 189

Timeline: The 2010s to Present 196

Exposing for the Shade: Skateboarding,
Gordon Parks, and Me Neftalie Williams 198

Brian Anderson: Skating His Way through Life
Jane Rogers 203

My Last 900 Tony Hawk 205

Making a Safe Space for Queer Skaters Leo Baker 207

An Electric Push Jack Smith 208

Coming Out to the Guys in the Van Brian Anderson 211

Pave the Way Skateboards Miriam Klein Stahl 212

From Apollo 11 to *The Shining* Betsy Gordon 214

Leo Baker's Journey Jane Rogers 216

Paisley Grabs Back Betsy Gordon 218

The Olympics—Are You Kidding Me? Alexis Sablone 220

Olympic Dream Bryce Wettstein 223

A Post-Olympic Future Betsy Gordon 224

Collecting the Olympics Jane Rogers 229

Acknowledgments 230

Photo Credits 231

Contributors 233

Index 236

FOREWORD

My aunt had dirt-eating cravings so overwhelming that even holding a potted plant made her salivate. She wasn't alone, either. Geophagy is relatively common in the southern United States and Central Africa, particularly among pregnant women. Doctors reckon their bodies generate cravings that override choice when they sense needed minerals. That we can be driven by an inexplicable awareness—a knowing— of our own essence and needs in the raw, uncomely sustenance of the soil merits some probing. If true, how often are we drawn to what we need without understanding why? It may be more meaningful—and, indeed, more common—than we think.

This visceral congruence between knowing and feeling is rooted in our design. One reason is that the same neural wiring in our heads extends throughout our body. For example, we've got 100 million neurons in our bellies alone, so whether by gut feelings or otherwise, *knowing takes more forms than we think*. Geophagy reflects this yet skateboarding exemplifies it. We endlessly create, adopt, and adapt new tricks by tuning the sensory integration between our body, board, and terrain through nuances of feel that correspond to physics with an algebraic precision. If our senses are off, we get hurt. The more advanced we become, the complexity and risk necessitates a oneness with our boards—a knowing we cultivate and trust. This shapes us individually and as a community.

Picture a kid learning about tone and tempo, trying to play a melody. Now, imagine Beethoven: the notes and scales were textured so palpably that he composed master-pieces, even as a deaf man. Skaters do this too. By coordinating feelings, we parse movements into pieces that combine syllabically according to their mechanics; these are compiled into a lexicon of tricks through which we not only convey an essence but actually speak. Today, any trick can be named with such denotative rigor that every nuance of motion will be understood, regardless of native tongue. Together, we have constructed a language from expressions of who we are, which forms a strong bond. Even the US State Department, through its skateboarding sports envoys, recognizes our community as a bridge to unite people across every race, culture, and class.

Each generation of skaters produces its standouts because they leave behind not only new ways of seeing and doing things but also parts of themselves. In other words,

Top: *For this 2016 image,* Rodney Mullen: Liminal, *Steven Sebring utilized his unique camera system: one hundred cameras arranged in a ring within a dome-like space that can simultaneously capture subjects in a 360-degree rotation.*

Bottom: *When Rodney Mullen visited the Smithsonian for the first time in 2012, he skated on this signature deck, made by his company, Almost Skateboards, that same year.*

their character embeds into the tricks they create and gets painted out by the way they do them. This is why authentic individuality and the deftness of its rendering make a more indelible mark than contest records ever could, which is one of many reasons why skating is more art than sport. Winning cannot endow a sense of belonging—our contributions do. In this way, what we *give* crystallizes into who we *become* and remains alive by what we leave behind.

When I was ten, my father wouldn't let me skate because he said I'd grow up to be a bum. I got what he saw. Yet what *I* saw were misfits who thrived on their individuality and the freedom to express it, who risked breaking their bones and smashing their teeth to make their mark through their distinctiveness—by being and thinking different. Through some quirk of fate, I was allowed to skate, but only "temporarily." As those years unfolded, my dreams lay prone to whim and threat as the stress further perforated the fabric of what we called home. This forged parts of me for the better, yet seared others for the worse. It also left holes. To this day, I struggle with belonging.

I have been a professional skater for more than forty years. Most of my life and friendships have been built around it. The same goes for my peers. It is hard to express what it takes to earn and sustain a good name in our community, which is why no amount of fame can compare with even a nodding acknowledgment from the few who know. This constitutes the core yet permeates our ethos as a kind of soil into which our identity is rooted and cultivated. Even as a kid, I craved it; I was drawn by a visceral sense of my own elemental nature in its unadulterated form of expression. I look back and find that nothing can compare to the intrinsic value of witnessing my own tricks adopted and furthered by my peers. This makes me part of what they build, which imbues a greater sense of belonging and permanence than I could have ever achieved on my own.

—**Rodney Mullen**

Rodney Mullen stands atop the mini ramp installed at the Smithsonian's first Innoskate public program in front of the National Museum of American History in June 2013.

DIRECTORS' NOTES—

CUCAMONGA DREAMING

There was nothing I wanted more. It didn't need to be fancy. In the mid-1970s, it wouldn't have been—maybe a blond-wood Dogtown cruiser with two-color wheels. Already loving roller skating at the tiki-themed Roller City along Route 66 (Foothill Boulevard in Cucamonga, California), a skateboard seemed the ultimate in cool freedom for a thirteen-year-old. My athletic, perceptive uncle gifted me the object of my desire for my birthday in, I'm thinking, 1977 or so. I was over the proverbial moon. I can still feel it beneath my feet as I rolled down my grandparents' concrete driveway. My euphoria was short-lived, however, as my overprotective if loving mother made me give it right back. My cool days evaporated before my teary eyes. I could still envision a future wearing Hang Ten shirts and OP shorts but not on a board.

It is thus a multilayered joy to bear witness to Betsy Gordon and Jane Rogers's pathbreaking *Four Wheels and a Board: The Smithsonian History of Skateboarding*. This accomplishment highlights the Smithsonian's more than six-hundred-object collection with keen interpretations of the cultural phenomenon of skateboarding. With its emphasis on the dynamic and varied intersections of boarding culture, beginning with its Hawaiian origins, it captures the American obsession with the art, lore, design, innovation, and daring of boarding.

One of the key—and critical—strengths of their work lies in the telling and honoring of the indigeneity of the sport so many of us love. From reservations to reservoirs, teens to elders, skateboarding has not only a history but also a series of interlocking spaces that, when conveyed through the people and their objects, reflects a powerful and lasting cultural impact. Moreover, this important work doesn't shy away from the ways in which issues of identity, race, ethnicity, class, and gender have played out and continue to roll out. Finally, Gordon and Rogers understand how boarding and boarders have been marginalized and even criminalized in contestations of space and design.

It is an honor to see this book and this collection come forth.

Anthea M. Hartig
Elizabeth MacMillan Director
National Museum of American History

NATIVE BEGINNINGS

Skateboarding is an Indigenous sport. The modern skateboard, or "deck," owes its heritage to the *papa he'e nalu* (surfboards) and *papahōlua* (land sleds) of Native Hawaiians. As skating has grown from its Native Hawaiian beginnings to America's mainstream and into a worldwide industry, the skating community has come to include people of all ages, genders, and cultures.

One of the most popular sports on tribal reservations, skateboarding has inspired Native communities—American Indian, Native Hawaiian, and Alaska Natives—to host skateboard competitions and build skateparks to encourage their youth. Native entrepreneurs own skateboard companies, sponsor community-based skate teams, and use evocative Native art and design to educate skaters about tradition, history, and life. Native artists and filmmakers, inspired by their skating experiences, credit the sport with teaching them a successful work ethic. As tribal support strengthens, a strong intertribal skate community has developed, uniting reservation, urban, and suburban skaters.

The National Museum of the American Indian first delved into skateboard culture and history in 2009 with the *Ramp It Up* exhibition exploring Native youth as participants and innovators in a quintessential American pastime. The exhibition then traveled for four years through the Smithsonian Institution Traveling Exhibition Services, and its stories were featured on the Smithsonian Channel's *Skateboard Nation*. The exhibition brought skateboarding to greater visibility within the Smithsonian and continued to foster collaborations, acting as a catalyst for collecting initiatives at the National Museum of the American Indian and the National Museum of American History. Those connections also helped to launch the Lemelson Center's Innoskate public programs that highlight innovations in skate technology.

Skateboarding is an exciting intersection of diverse cultures, which makes it an especially rich topic for the Smithsonian to collect and document. More than a physically demanding sport, it has driven technological innovations and exerted strong cultural influences on design, graphic art, filmmaking, and music. The richly woven cultural tapestry of skateboarding is what draws Smithsonian focus to the sport, which comes to life in its many aspects in *Four Wheels and a Board: The Smithsonian History of Skateboarding.*

Cynthia Chavez Lamar (San Felipe Pueblo/Hopi/Tewa/Navajo)
Director
National Museum of the American Indian

INTRODUCTION

Despite the many No Skateboarding signs posted at its entrances, gardens, and pathways, the Smithsonian Institution has collected skateboard artifacts for more than thirty years. The collection is diverse and varied, ranging from a handful of skateboard gags found in Phyllis Diller's huge joke file to the first skateboard Tony Hawk rode as a child, and from a children's lunch box to a pair of well-worn Vans skate shoes.

The Smithsonian recognizes skateboarding as being unique among other physical or athletic activities because it was largely invented by youth. As C. R. Stecyk, historian, writer, photographer, artist, and omnipresence in all things skateboarding, infamously wrote in 1975, "Two hundred years of American technology has unwittingly created a massive cement playground of unlimited potential. But it was the minds of 11-year-olds that could see that potential." All over America, young skateboarders took a simple wooden board with four wheels and made it their own. They made up the names of all the ways they were riding their skateboards, known as tricks, and used whatever available form of asphalt and concrete they could find. Appropriating bits and pieces from surfing, roller skating, downhill skiing, and

gymnastics, they dared one another to go faster, spin longer, ride upside down, and hop over limbo sticks. Without the accoutrements of organized sports—teams, coaches, regulated playing fields—they made up their own rules (which was more or less not to have any rules) and held improvised neighborhood contests. In the span of sixty years, what started out as unsupervised play somehow became a multibillion-dollar industry and eventually an Olympic sport.

After skateboarding's premiere in the 2020 Summer Olympics in Tokyo, a new global audience saw skateboarding for the first time. Because the Smithsonian has a comprehensive collection of skateboard history and culture in

Above left: This 1978 tin lunch box by Aladdin Industries features two girls and one boy skateboarding, evidence that skateboarding was not originally thought of as being a "boys-only" activity.

Above right: Stephanie Person, the first professional Black female skateboarder, came up during the 1980s, when female and Black skaters were few. Wearing these Vans, Person gained sponsors through self-advocacy and became pro with no sponsorship. She skated internationally through the 1990s and retired from skateboarding after a knee injury.

its collections, it felt timely to share the Smithsonian skateboard collections with the public. The Smithsonian is the only museum and research complex of its kind that collects, preserves, and interprets skateboarding as a vital part of the American narrative. These stories not only illuminate the impossible physical achievements of gifted champion athletes but also offer glimpses into the everyday life of anonymous citizens across America. They are stories of play, invention, innovation, creativity, competition, identity, social justice, and political protest. Our goal is not to possess only the most rare and famous but to assemble a broad scope of artifacts from amateurs and professionals, from kids who

Oscar Loreto Jr. was born without a left foot and hand and without four fingers on his right hand, the result of a congenital birth defect. Adapting quickly to a prosthetic as a child, he created a skate team while in high school and soon became active in the adaptive skate-boarding scene. Loreto is an athlete representative for USA Skateboarding, the national governing body for skateboarding in the United States. Shown above are the Vans shoes, Void skateboard, and prosthetic leg used by Loreto in the 2019 Summer X Games in Minneapolis, Minnesota.

used backyard DIY skate ramps to those who competed at the X Games.

For this book, we have selected the objects and archives that can uniquely demonstrate the depth and breadth of the skateboarding collection. Because the collections at the Smithsonian are so vast, they frequently cross traditional academic boundaries and cohabitate in several research areas. Born out of surfboards and children's toys, commodified by adults and industries, and used by advertisers to sell a range of products from tampons to energy drinks, skateboarding has always struggled to define its identity. Is it a sport, an art, a lifestyle, or something that continues to defy categorization?

The skateboard collection at the Smithsonian focuses on artifacts from people and places that are not often represented in the traditional timeline of skateboard history. They tell stories that challenge stereotypes of racial identity, add to recent discussions about traditional gender binaries, and illustrate national dissent movements. There are skate artifacts that document skateboarding's past, comment on current events, and offer a different perspective on American history.

As of 2022, the skateboard collection at the Smithsonian numbers just over six hundred objects. Until recently, most of these objects were not collected in any focused effort to form a comprehensive collection of skateboard culture. The first donations were collected for their innovative use of materials, specifically aluminum and fiberglass. In 1987, Powell Corporation founder and aerospace engineer George Powell and art director C. R. Stecyk donated three objects: two 1977 Powell skateboards ridden by pro skateboarder Stacy Peralta and a 1966 fiberglass surfboard shaped by Stecyk and manufactured by Dave Sweet Surfboards. These objects were included in *A Material World*, an exhibition that attempted to show how America had changed from a nation built by natural materials to a country dependent on polymers, plastics, and other synthetics.

More than ten years passed before the second skateboard donation occurred. In 1999, after the untimely death of their son, pro skateboarder Tim Brauch, the Brauch family generously donated over thirty items that mapped their son's skate legacy. Brauch's short career epitomized 1990s skating—his rise through the California amateur contest circuit, his early

sponsorships by Vans and Independent Trucks, his early pro deck by Santa Monica Airlines, and the establishment of his own shoe and clothing brand.

In 2004, Brauch's skateboard was displayed in the National Museum of American History exhibition *Sports: Breaking Records, Breaking Barriers*. This show sought to tell the stories of both well-known and little-known US athletes, focusing on

Above left: *This 1977 Powell Corporation skateboard for Stacy Peralta was part of George Powell's 1987 donation to the National Museum of American History, marking the first time skateboards had been collected by the Smithsonian. The unusual construction of the deck, which combined a formed aluminum core with an aluminum honeycomb skin and epoxy to close out the edges, was short-lived. According to Powell, "The decks were changing monthly during this era, and we had to accommodate the rapidly evolving style of skating, which quickly went from streets to ditches, to pools and skateparks."*

Above right: *In 1990, Tim Brauch won this award at the California Amateur Skateboard League (CASL) competition for finishing fourth in the mini-ramp contest. A volunteer-run organization, CASL, commonly referred to as the Little League of skateboarding, has been holding amateur skate contests for over thirty years.*

their significant accomplishments and the social contexts that inspired them. Brauch was one of over thirty-five athletes featured in the show, which included such sports superstars as Babe Ruth, Muhammad Ali, Billie Jean King, Mia Hamm, and the 1980s "Miracle on Ice" Olympic men's hockey team. Brauch was the only skateboarder included in the exhibit partly because he was one of the only skaters represented in the collections at the time, but primarily because the curator recognized the importance of skateboarding as a growing impetus on American culture and sought to include this aspect of sport in an otherwise traditional sports exhibition.

Despite their inclusion in two exhibitions, skateboarding and skateboarders were still not seen within the context of a unique, youth-defined American culture until the 2009 exhibition at the National Museum of the American Indian, *Ramp It Up: Skateboard Culture in Native America*. The goal of *Ramp It Up* was to show skateboarding as a means to discover and express Native American identity. The skate decks were not presented as examples of a sport or a specific technology, but rather as contemporary cultural artifacts from Native American history. While many skateboard history narratives begin with a metal scooter or a two-by-four with roller skate wheels, *Ramp It Up* declared that skateboarding had Indigenous roots by placing its origin within Polynesian surfing culture. The show proved to be popular with visitors, attracting people of all ages who had never seen skateboarding in any museum. After closing in 2010, the exhibition traveled throughout the United States until 2015, making stops at ten additional museums and cultural centers.

In addition to Native American skate decks and photographs, the show contained a number of generic skateboards from the 1960s to the 2000s to give visitors a short overview of American skateboarding. Aiming to balance Native American artifacts with the rich collections of other Smithsonian museums proved to be virtually impossible. Within the Smithsonian's 155 million artifacts and specimens, there were very few examples of American skateboard history. The artifacts in *Ramp It Up* had to be borrowed from private donors or purchased off eBay.

All of that changed when the Smithsonian received an email from the Tony Hawk Foundation in December 2011. The staff of the foundation had seen a 1980s Tony Hawk model skateboard in *Ramp It Up*, a deck that was purchased from eBay specifically for the show, and wanted to know if we were interested in a 1980s skateboard that belonged to him. There were two caveats included in this donation offer: we had to allow Tony to skate this skateboard one last time before he gave it to the Smithsonian and we had to travel to Florida to pick it up from Tony in person.

Tony was to be skating in the Quiksilver All '80s All Day Vert Challenge, a 1980s-themed skateboard demonstration at the Surf Expo trade show in Orlando, Florida. Although the name indicated a focus on surfing, Surf Expo included a robust presence of skateboard companies and events. The organizers of

Above left: *This 2008 prototype skate deck designed by Native Hawaiian Lawrence "Larry" Kaaua Mehau Bertlemann for Gravity Skateboards pays tribute to Bertlemann's legacy in both surfing and skateboarding. His surfing style inspired generations of skaters, especially the Z-Boys, who coined the term* Bert slide *for their low, crouching skateboard stance that imitated Bertlemann's surfing maneuvers. The shape of the deck replicates Bertlemann's signature fishtail surfboard. In true Hawaiian spirit, Bertlemann signed the deck "Aloha Smithsonian," before adding his signature phrase, "Everything is possible."*

Above right: *The graphic for this 2008 Native Skates Spirit Feather model deck is by Traci Rochelle Rabbit (Cherokee Nation of Oklahoma). By mixing the traditional Native symbol of an eagle feather with the contemporary beadwork Native Skates logo, Rabbit shows the fluidity between traditional and contemporary Native culture.*

the expo wanted to publicly showcase the donation to the Smithsonian by having Tony hand off his skateboard to Smithsonian curators at the bottom of the halfpipe.

Accompanying us was Jeffrey Brodie, deputy director of the Smithsonian Lemelson Center for Invention and Innovation. Located at the National Museum of American History, the Lemelson Center explores the role of invention and innovation in the United States, particularly its historical context, and how that history relates to current events. Brodie had been exploring ways to connect skateboarding with the mission of the Lemelson Center. He had a strong hunch that there was a connection between skateboarding, invention, and innovation and that showcasing that intersection could result in a dynamic Smithsonian public program.

In addition to receiving Tony's skateboard that day—a watershed moment for the Smithsonian—another pivotal event occurred during the All '80s All Day Vert Challenge that had immeasurable consequences for the Smithsonian skateboard collection. At the end of the event, Brodie turned to us on the escalator leading out of Surf Expo and declared, "I have an idea ...

I could invite a bunch of skaters to the Smithsonian and have them talk about being inventors. I think I'll call it Innoskate!"

After the arrival of Tony's skateboard, the National Museum of American History began a collecting initiative to explore the story of skateboarding and document the tremendous impact it has had on global culture. As a result of this initiative, the Lemelson Center for Invention and Innovation began to explore skateboarding's impact on technology. In 2013, true to Brodie's prediction in 2011, the interactive public program called Innoskate was born. This event, which combined professional skateboarders with artists, academics, designers, museum professionals, and others, created tremendous collecting opportunities for the permanent sports collections at the National Museum of American History. Many Innoskate

Above left: *Tony Hawk hands his 1984 skateboard to Jane Rogers, curator of sports at the National Museum of American History, with Jeff Brodie, the deputy director of the Smithsonian Lemelson Center looking on.*

Above: *Professional skateboarder Chris Haslam skates the mini ramp during the 2013 Innoskate program in Washington, DC.*

participants graciously donated their personal skateboard artifacts to the Smithsonian, significantly augmenting the existing collection but also establishing a large network of personal and professional relationships between the Smithsonian and the skateboarding community.

During the inaugural Innoskate public program in Washington, DC, Tony Hawk made another donation: the first skateboard he ever rode, a 1976 Bahne hand-me-down from his brother, Steve. This moment was broadcast on a Times Square electronic billboard, resulting in millions of media impressions. Throughout the Innoskate weekend, Hawk joined skateboard icon Rodney

Above: *Skateboarders (from left) Robin Logan, Mimi Knoop, Laura Thornhill Caswell, Patti McGee, Di Dootson Rose, and Cindy Whitehead with their donations to the National Museum of American History during the 2013 Innoskate program.*

Right: *Push to Heal is an organization that studies the effect of skateboarding through neuroscience. Therapy is used to see "how skateboarding can heal the human brain and contribute to our capacity for learning new skills." Studies have shown that skateboarding helps kids develop social skills and learn to deal with stress better.*

Mullen in standing-room-only panels that explored their legacies in skate history. Skating on a mini ramp built in front of the museum, skaters showed off their prowess and demonstrated tricks for the crowds. Lines of autograph seekers and skateboard fans formed in front of the National Museum of American History. Skateboarding had arrived at the Smithsonian in a big, big way.

Reading this book and looking at the images will take you through the past six decades of American skateboard history. Focusing not only on the artifacts in the collection but also on sharing the insights, memories, photographs, and words of some of skateboarding's most insightful ambassadors, it presents both the well known and unknown. It also speculates on what may be ahead. Trends include the increase of serious, peer-reviewed academic research into skateboarding, the global increase of skateboard-related nonprofits and NGOs, the proliferation of skate brands and skate media for queer and nonbinary folk, the making of intentional skate spaces for women and nonbinary participants, the threat of real estate development to DIY skateboard parks and terrain, the collaborations between skateboarders and skate brands with haute

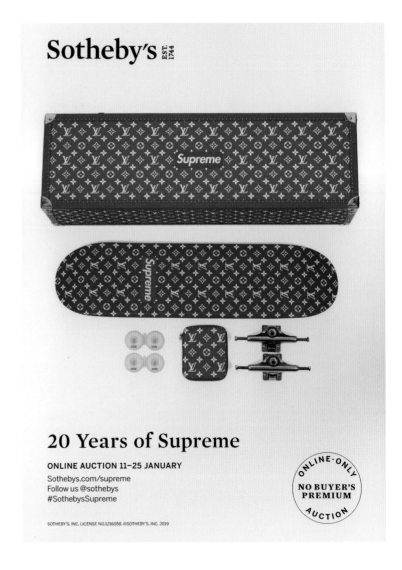

couture fashion houses and non-skateboard consumer goods—the list could go on and on.

What we can't see, however, is any resolution as to what defines true or core skateboarding. In fact, after sixty years of skateboard competitions, magazines, brands, and media attempting to define and commodify skateboarding, there still isn't a single consistent way to become a professional skateboarder. It used to be you won skate contests as an amateur, got sponsored by a skateboard company, joined its pro team, started winning professional skateboard contests, got your own signature skate deck, or shoe, or wheels, and voilà, you were a pro. Today, we have skateboard brands without any sponsored team and pro skaters who don't compete in any contests, aren't a part of any team, and don't have a line of signature products. To many, the inclusion of skateboarding in the 2020 Olympic Games in Tokyo didn't add any clarity or definition to whether skateboarding is or is not a sport. Likewise, the presence of skateboards in the art auction sales of Sotheby's and Christie's didn't convince everyone that skateboarding had arrived as an art form.

Be it fashion or a competitive sport, artistic expression or athletic achievement, skateboarding will always be funda-mentally improvisational. Instead of sticking to a script, it will always ad-lib. Skateboarders will continue to find new ways and new places to skate, redefining and expanding the lexicon of tricks and terrain. They will always be pushing available technology to find different ways to document and distribute their skating. They will continue to form unconventional collaborations to occupy spaces once thought of as being squarely in the No Skateboarding zone. The conundrum over what is core to skateboarding history and culture will never be solved. In other words, the kids are still making it up as they go along.

—Betsy Gordon and Jane Rogers

Above left: *Cher Strauberry was the first transgender skater to have their own pro model. Olivia Gibb provided the artwork on this 2018 deck, but Stevil Kinevil's brand, All Hail The Black Market, was the catalyst for creating the deck to celebrate the growing LGBTQ skate community.*

Above right: *This card from the Sotheby's 2019 auction of 248 Supreme skateboard decks documents the growing interest in skateboard culture of the fine-art auction house. The lot was purchased for US$800,000 by seventeen-year-old Carson Guo of Vancouver, British Columbia, Canada.*

Four wheels attached to a plank of wood, a makeshift ramp in a parking lot and a kid—here, nine-year-old Briel Weingartner of Redondo Beach, California—having fun just to have fun—a scene as true today as it was six or more decades ago.

BE
THE
FIRST
TO
FALL
IN
LOVE
WITH

COLUMBIA PICTURES presents

GiDGET

co-starring

SANDRA DEE   CLIFF ROBERTSON   JAMES DARREN

ARTHUR O'CONNELL   with MARY LaROCHE JO MORROW   and THE FOUR PREPS

CinemaScope   Screenplay by GABRIELLE UPTON · Based on the novel by FREDERICK KOHNER   in EASTMAN COLOR
Produced by LEWIS J. RACHMIL · Directed by PAUL WENDKOS

CHAPTER ONE
'60s

SURFBOARDS, AIRPLANES, AND ROLLER SKATES: THE BIRTH OF THE AMERICAN SKATEBOARD

Despite popular belief, skateboarding was not invented by a group of Southern California surfers in the 1960s on a day when the waves were flat. Polynesian surf culture, materials science and engineering from the aerospace industry, roller skates, an Olympic swimmer, and kids with free time on their hands all contributed to the first skateboards commercially manufactured in the United States in the early 1960s.

Surfing played an important role in facilitating the birth of the modern skateboard. The first skateboards resembled miniature surfboards and sported names such as Olympian Surfer and Sidewalk Surfer. Surfing gave skateboarding a ready-made network of practitioners, retailers, print media, and competitions. The first skateboard teams were largely comprised of surf team members. What is not as obvious are the unseen influences in skateboarding's bloodstream, what it inherited from surfing on the cellular level.

Although many Americans associate surfing and skating, few recognize the material connection between airplanes and surfboards, which eventually trickled down to skateboards. Surfboard makers have a long history of experimenting with materials borrowed from the aerospace industry, such as balsa wood and fiberglass and other polymers. What worked for an airplane in terms of adding strength and stability while decreasing weight also proved advantageous to a surfboard.

Opposite: *Both Southern California surf culture and teenage romance are promoted on this poster for the 1959 film* Gidget.

How did surfing and airplanes find each other? Like many things, it was the result of the unforeseen intersections of industries and personalities. One commonality was early twentieth-century California, where abundant sunshine, ocean water, good weather, and flat land attracted surfers, motion picture studios, and aviation factories. At the nexus of the surfing and aerospace industries was Duke Kahanamoku, an Olympic swimmer, surfer, movie star, and friend to aviation pioneers. Duke and his friends surfed in a time when surfboards were becoming similar to airplane wings. The salvage lots of 1920s aviation factories provided the earliest surfers with a plethora of scrap wood and composite materials for their experiments in making lighter and more buoyant boards. The US military need for a strong air force in World War II fueled aircraft innovation and invention, producing more and better scrap materials with which surfers could experiment.

Fast-forward to the 1960s, when a postwar baby boom created another comingling of industries and personalities that provided the perfect landing for American skateboarding. It was a decade of extreme contrasts between a buoyant sense of optimism and intense social and political turmoil. Beginning with the 1960 presidential election of John F. Kennedy, the decade ends not only with a man on the Moon but also with a three-day festival of love and music called Woodstock. Sandwiched between these milestones are the elections of two additional presidents, the Vietnam War and the mass protests against it, the Civil Rights Movement, the Beach Boys and the

Beatles dominating the pop music charts, and the assassinations of John F. Kennedy, Malcolm X, Robert Kennedy, and Martin Luther King Jr.

Given the grave problems of racial inequality, resistance to the Vietnam War, and the reverberations from four assassinations of political leaders, how did Americans find time to fall in love with a small wooden toy? How is it that against this tumultuous national backdrop the first commercially manufactured and mass-distributed skateboards appear along with skateboard teams, skateparks, skateboard magazines, skateboard contests, and an Oscar-nominated skateboard movie?

Blame it on the baby boomers. Between 1950 and 1960, the number of children in the United States under the age of eighteen increased from 47.3 million to 64.5 million. This surge in the youth population resulted in an unprecedented increase in the need for new housing, schools, and consumer goods. Businesses, especially those in the entertainment industry, began to steer their products specifically toward young people. With the success of films such as *Gidget* and songs like "Surfin' USA," Americans began to see an increasing number of products that emulated the surfer style portrayed in the media.

Those living near a surfing town had likely already seen surfers using homemade skateboards between surfing sessions. Surfers had made their own skateboards for years, long before the 1960s craze hit America. They were cheap and practical: cut a roller skate in half, nail the halves to a two-by-four, and you have a new form of transportation within an hour.

Unlike the Beach Boys and Gidget, not everybody had an ocean. What they did have, however, were concrete sidewalks and driveways in new suburban neighborhoods and plenty of asphalt in new schoolyards. After newspapers and magazines

Left: *Made of solid oak, shaped like a miniature surfboard, and with graphics on the top surface and no griptape, this shark-emblazoned 1963 deck made by Nash typifies the early commercially produced skateboards.*

Above: *Sandra Dee is held up on a surfboard by a group of surfers in this scene from the 1959 film* Gidget.

Before—and even after—skateboards were manufactured for sale in toy and sporting goods stores all across America, many skaters made their own, using roller skate wheels, nails, and scraps of wood. This 1969 rocket-shaped board shows the influence of President John F. Kennedy's space race on popular culture.

in the early 1960s started featuring a novel fad called "sidewalk surfing," it was just a matter of time before entrepreneurial manufacturers saw a vast concrete ocean of opportunity and began to produce inexpensive skateboards for landlocked youth.

From 1960 to 1969, more than forty independent brands produced and sold skateboards across the United States. Names ran the entire scope of the alphabet, from the Adolph Kiefer McNeil Corp. in Northfield, Illinois, to Val Surf in North Hollywood, California. Toy stores, bike shops, surf shops, department stores, hardware stores, and pharmacies peddled skateboards in varying shapes and sizes. Some brands, like Val Surf, Makaha, and Hobie, were rooted in the surf industry and sold skateboards as a supplemental product line. Others, like Roller Derby of Chicago, Illinois, and Nash Manufacturing Inc. of Fort Worth, Texas, expanded into producing skateboards as a way to sell more of their roller skate wheels. Still others were just trying to cash in on what they perceived as a profitable opportunity.

The 1960s saw the first skateboard contests that established how skateboarders competed against one another. In 1963, surf and skateboard manufacturer Makaha held what was widely considered the first skateboard contest, in the parking lot of Pier Avenue Junior High in Hermosa Beach, California. As more skateboard contests were organized, two forms of competitive skateboarding appeared: freestyle and slalom

racing. Combining elements from gymnastics and ballet—spins, handstands, and balancing—freestyle was performed on flat ground. It was judged qualitatively and assessed on its aesthetic merits as well as the perceived difficulty of the maneuvers. Slalom was adapted from downhill skiing and consisted of skaters racing down an incline or steep hill as they darted around cones. Judging was quantitatively based, with the fastest skater the victor. The participants were divided by gender—boys and girls did not compete against each other—and age.

In addition to hosting the first competition and supplying members of his skateboard team to compete in the event, Makaha owner Larry Stevenson was the publisher of the most widely read surfing magazine, *Surf Guide*. It frequently featured articles on skateboarders (mostly members of the Makaha surf team), advertised Makaha skateboards for sale, and covered the results of skateboard competitions. Stevenson set a template for other skateboard manufacturers to follow: make a product, sponsor a team, host competitions to showcase your team and products, and own the media that promotes your team, products, and contest results.

In these early years of skateboarding, girls didn't face the overt bias of skateboarding being a "boys' sport." Although never in numbers equal to the boys, girls such as Laurie Turner, Wendy Bearer, Collen Boyd, and Patti McGee were members of

the Hobie, Makaha, and Bun Buster teams. In 1965, Patti McGee was featured on the cover of *Life* magazine, and Wendy Bearer rode her skateboard on the *Smothers Brothers Comedy Hour*. When ABC's *Wide World of Sports* broadcasted the first international skateboarding competition in a sports stadium in Anaheim, California, Boyd and Turner were shown competing.

But it's all fun and games until someone gets hurt. What was initially touted as innocent fun became increasingly characterized by local and national news as a serious danger to health and well-being. Newspapers across the United States ran stories about skateboard accidents that resulted in injuries and sometimes even deaths. Letters to the editor from concerned citizens urged city officials to ban skateboarding, much to the displeasure of the young skateboarders.

The truth is, sidewalk surfing in the 1960s really wasn't all that much fun, or safe. The metal wheels and rigid trucks gave a stiff, slow, and merciless ride. Skaters couldn't turn, and any amount of speed resulted in bone-rattling vibration from the ankles to the jaw. If you hit a small pebble or a crack in the concrete, the skateboard seized up, hurling the rider onto the hard pavement. Some changes to trucks and wheels in the mid-1960s attempted to create a better riding experience for the skateboarder. The newer double-action trucks added two rubber cushions to the metal kingpin—the vertical bolt that attached

the wheels to the baseplate—to prevent the metal components from rubbing against each other. This allowed for a minor increase in the turning maneuverability. Clay composite wheels, made of a mixture of paper, plastic, walnut shells, and other materials, gave a slightly smoother ride but wore out quickly and needed frequent replacement.

Thanks to surfing, better technology and materials were available to skateboard manufacturers, but no one could utilize them and still make a profit at $1.49 a unit. Cheap materials severely limited the variety of tricks possible on a skateboard. Too often, initial enthusiasm quickly became boredom as kids found easier and less painful ways to play outside.

As cities all over the United States began to ban skateboarding, skateboard companies found themselves with unwanted inventory. By the end of the 1960s, formerly thriving companies, such as George Cooley Co. and Skee-Skate, declared bankruptcy and held liquidation sales of unwanted skateboards. Only a few companies, like Val Surf, Hobie, Nash, and Roller Derby, were still in business, largely because their original product lines (surfboards or roller skates) were still profitable. As the decade ended most skateboards wound up forgotten in garages and basements across America.

—Betsy Gordon and Jane Rogers

The 1960s

1778
- Charles Clerke, credited as the first European to document surfing in Hawaii, writes in his diary, "Upon this they get astride with their legs, then laying their breasts upon it, they paddle with their hands and steer with their feet."

1885
- Three Hawaiian princes, David Kawananakoa, Edward Keli'iahonui, and Jonah Kūhiō Kalani-ana'ole, introduce surfing to North America in Santa Cruz, CA.

1946
- Surfer Pete Peterson, with Douglas Aircraft Company plastics engineer Brandt Goldsworthy, creates a 100 percent fiberglass surfboard.

1956
- Dave Sweet begins to sell the first polyurethane foam surfboards in Santa Monica, CA. These lightweight boards allow a new generation, especially young girls, to surf.

1962
- Val Surf in North Hollywood, CA, partners with the Chicago Roller Skate Company to produce wheels for its own Val Surf skateboard model, becoming one of the first shops to sell skateboards.

1963
- The first known organized skateboard contest, sponsored by Makaha, is held at the Pier Avenue Junior High School in Hermosa Beach, CA.

- Surf legend Hobie Alter partners with Val Surf to produce the Hobie Super Surfer skateboard.
- Larry Gordon and Floyd Smith of Gordon and Smith Surfboards produce the G&S Fibreflex skateboard, which combines Bo-Tuff (a fiberglass-reinforced epoxy) with a wood core.

- Surfboard shaper Don Hansen launches the first women's signature skateboard for pro surfer Linda Benson.
- Lyndon B. Johnson is elected the thirty-sixth president of the United States.

- The Randolph Rubber Company of Randolph, MA, introduces the first skateboard shoe, the Randy "720," which is named the official sneaker of the National Skateboard Championships.

1966
- The National Organization for Women is founded.
- Jim and Paul Van Doren open Vans, a shoe factory in Anaheim, CA, and quickly put to work all they had learned about rubber-soled canvas shoes while formerly employed by the Randolph Rubber Company.

1906
- Thomas Edison sends cameraman Robert Bonine to Hawaii to film. His "Surf Board Riders" and "Surf Scenes" are thought to be the earliest footage of surfing.

1930
- Pacific Ready Cut Homes (later Pacific System Homes) of Los Angeles, CA, begins producing surfboards in its prefabricated housing factory, becoming the first American mass-producer of surfboards.

1959
- Albert Boyden applies for US patent no. 3023022A for a skateboard-like device. In 1963, Boyden teams with John Francis Humphrey to mass-produce and distribute the Humco Surfer skateboard. As of 2022, there have been more than one hundred thousand patent applications using the word *skateboard* within the title or description.

1960
- Four African American college students in Greensboro, NC, refuse to leave a Woolworth's "whites only" lunch counter after being denied service. The Greensboro Sit-In sparks similar actions throughout the country.

- Approximately 250,000 people take part in the March on Washington for Jobs and Freedom. Martin Luther King Jr. gives his "I Have a Dream" speech.
- President John F. Kennedy is assassinated.

1964
- The Civil Rights Act of 1964 passes. It prohibits discrimination in public facilities and accommodations and makes employment discrimination on the basis of race, ethnicity, religion, or gender illegal.

- *Sports Illustrated* publishes "The Skateboard Might Prove as Big and Giddy a Fad as the Hula Hoop" in its May issue. The article focuses on Larry Stevenson and the Makaha skateboard team, with Stevenson declaring that he will produce four thousand skateboards in that same month.

1965
- Patti McGee is featured on the cover of *Life* magazine. The headline beside her reads, "The craze and the menace of skateboards."
- ABC's *Wide World of Sports* airs the National Skateboard Championships, the first broadcast of a skateboard competition.

1969
- Larry Stevenson files US patent no. 3565454 for a "Skateboard with an inclined foot-depressible lever," an early precursor to the kicktail.
- Adidas debuts the Superstar, the world's first leather basketball shoe.

- Astronaut Neil Armstrong walks on the Moon.
- Woodstock, a three-day music festival in upstate New York, attracts more than four hundred thousand people.
- In November, five hundred thousand demonstrators participate in a Moratorium march in Washington, DC, against the war in Vietnam.

"THE LAST OF THE SURFS IS AMERICA"

C. R. STECYK

He kulana hee nalu o Farini,
He hu'a o ka nalu o Maleka,
He ika no ka nalu o Rusini,
He paean na ka nalu o Beretane.

A place to surf is France,
The last of the surfs is America,
The force that carries the surfs along is Russia,
The place where the surf lands is England.

—*Excerpted from Queen Emma's surf chant*

In 1969, I got a Screen Actors Guild card out of the standout theatrical production *Gidget Grows Up*. My line was, "Hey gang—Gidget's back." The assistant director schooled me on my motivation: "You're surprised and ecstatic that the Beach Queen has returned." Two takes later, I was officially a Malibu method actor.

By the time the Beach Queen had returned, surf culture had thoroughly saturated the America psyche via the non-maritime means of film, television, and music. However, thirty-five hundred years before the beach movie genre appeared, the Polynesians set out on their voyages of discovery from

somewhere near New Guinea. Surf riding was an activity that they took with them. From Samoa through Tonga, Tahiti, Hawaii, and finally New Zealand, Polynesian culture was spread further solely by maritime means than any other culture. Surfing was documented in the late nineteenth century by Mark Twain, in the early twentieth century by Jack London, in the 1920s by Olympic swimmer Duke Kahanamoku, in Depression-era advertising films for Chevrolet by Jamison Handy, and even in the cover of a 1938 issue of *Vogue* shot by Toni Frissell.

By the debut of *Gidget Grows Up*, surfing had transformed from an Indigenous cultural practice to an American money-making marketing bonanza, and the nascent skateboarding industry, which was born out of a child's homemade toy, was on the same path. The 1960s saw the advent of so-called sidewalk surfing, the younger, landlocked version of what Twain had witnessed in Hawaii in 1872. In addition to the obvious similarities between surfboards and the surfboard-shaped skateboards of the 1960s, surfing's DNA is deeply embedded in the history of skateboarding.

Contestants in the Pacific Coast Surfboard Championships, held in Corona del Mar in August 1928, show off their surfboards. Third from the left is aerospace engineer Gerard "Jerry" Vultee with the board made for him by Duke Kahanamoku.

Left: *In this ca. 1915 photograph, famed Hawaiian surfer Duke Kahanamoku stands before his surfboard. Known as the Godfather of Surfing, Duke Kahanamoku was a multi-medal Olympic swimmer, celebrity, and entrepreneur and served thirteen consecutive terms as sheriff of Honolulu.*

Below left: *Queen Emma, wife of King Kamehameha IV, was an influential figure in Hawaii's history, establishing the Queen's Hospital in 1859 and St. Andrew's Priory School for Girls in 1867, just a year after sitting for this 1866 portrait studio photograph, taken when she was thirty years old. Her surf mele, or chant (see opposite), predicted the international rise of surfing.*

Duke Kahanamoku is at the nucleus of the surf-to-skateboard genetic transfer. He is best known as the surfing ambassador to the world, having traveled to California, Australia, and New Zealand to demonstrate his prowess on hand-shaped wooden surfboards. Duke won three gold and two silver medals in three consecutive Olympic games: 1912, 1920, and 1924. He introduced a new style of swimming to the world with his flutter kick variation and powerful, rhythmic looping strokes. As an Olympic champion, Duke toured the globe giving both swimming and surfing demonstrations to thousands.

After his 1912 Olympic wins, Duke moved to California, where his Olympic celebrity served him well, allowing him to appear in a number of Hollywood films in the booming motion picture industry. The inexpensive land and abundant sunlight that drew early film production to the state were the very same things that made California appealing to the emerging aviation industry—large swaths of flat land allowed for airstrips, and lack of rain, snow, and other inclement weather ensured optimum visibility for flying. Hollywood, aviation, and Olympic champions made an extremely attractive mix. Duke was frequently photographed with Charlie Chaplin, Douglas Fairbanks, and Amelia Earhart. He surfed with aeronautical engineer and designer Gerard "Jerry" Vultee, who designed Charles Lindbergh's Lockheed Sirius *Tingmissartoq*, Amelia Earhart's *Little Red Bus*, and the record-breaking Lockheed Vega *Winnie Mae*.

In 1928, Duke shaped a solid redwood board on the beach at Corona del Mar, California, for Jerry Vultee using a piece of redwood similar to the traditional Hawaiian koa. At the same time and place, Tom Blake, a young surfing friend of Duke's, entered the Pacific Coast Surf Board Championship in Corona del Mar and won the paddling race with a modified Duke-style redwood board. Holes were drilled in Blake's solid wood board to make it lighter, faster, and float higher in the water. Losing to Blake in the race at Corona del Mar was Vultee, who had just designed a revolutionary airplane wing for Lockheed's Vega, a hollow wing sheathed with plywood over wooden struts, resulting in a much lighter aircraft that utilized fuel more efficiently to fly longer and farther.

No one knows if Blake and Vultee ever spoke to each other about their similar attempts at making airplane wings and surfboards lighter and faster, but we know Blake had ready access to most of the materials and production experiments being utilized by Vultee and his contemporaries.

In 1931, Blake applied for a patent for a "water sled," a hollow surfboard that used sheets of plywood over wooden struts. After gaining the patent, he teamed with aeronautical contractor Thomas Rogers, a fabricator of airplane wings, to produce his Hawaiian paddleboard. Blake went on to write the first book on surfing, *Hawaiian Surfboard*, in 1935, and devised the first waterproof camera housing, which allowed him to take photos from angles previously seen only by surfers. The May 1936 issue of *National Geographic* featured his work in Waikiki.

Another friend of Duke's, Preston "Pete" Peterson, formed an important friendship with an aeronautical engineer. In 1946, Peterson built a hollow, 100 percent fiberglass surfboard, the first such vehicle in existence. During the revolutionary process, he was advised by his longtime friend Brandt Goldsworthy, an active surfer and a member of the Palos Verdes Surfing Club. Goldsworthy worked as a plastics engineer in Douglas Aircraft's Project Engineering Group, pioneering the use of cast phenolic resin combined with fiberglass to produce some of the first fiberglass-reinforced laminated tools in the industry. During the war, Brandt had substantial contacts with both Owens-Corning and Dupont, the respective 1936 originators of fiberglass and polyester plastic. In 1947, Goldsworthy designed the 850-pound flying car for Consolidated Vultee Aviation, the aviation company founded by Jerry Vultee.

The influence of the emerging aviation and automobile industry on the surfboard's engineering, design, and material composition mirrors the technological advances adopted by the skateboarding industry in the 1970s when a number of skateboard manufacturers experimented with and appropriated materials—resins, plastics, and fiberglass—from the aerospace industry to create the modern skateboard. The pioneering work of Brandt Goldsworthy resulted in the ability to pultrude fiberglass into sheets. Skateboard companies from the 1970s such as Sims and Santa Cruz used pultruded fiberglass to create their first skateboard models. Kent Sherwood, stepfather of Zephyr skate team member Jay Adams, worked as a supplier to the surf and defense industries with his patented Foam Matrix system. It was Sherwood, with his background in plastic-injected molds, who first produced the skateboards for the Zephyr skateboard team. He went on to create Z-Flex skateboards as well as fins for Pegasus rockets. George Powell, an aeronautical engineer with a degree from Stanford University, used his knowledge of urethane, fiberglass, and aluminum to create his composite Quicksilver skateboards. He later teamed with skateboarder Stacy Peralta to form the skateboard brand Powell-Peralta and to master the correct chemical formula to create Bones wheels.

The legacy starting with Queen Emma continued to the 2020 Summer Olympics in Japan, as surfing and skateboarding made their debut. Utilizing technology honed over hundreds of years from the ocean to the airplane, Native Hawaiians Carissa Moore won gold in women's surfing while Heimana Reynolds represented Team USA in men's park skateboarding.

This solid redwood surfboard, shaped by Duke Kahanamoku for Jerry Vultee in 1928, is over nine feet long. Its winged V design was later incorporated into the logo for Vultee's aircraft company, as seen in the above lapel pin made in the 1930s.

Above left: *In 1932, Tom Blake (shown in a ca. 1922 photo) patented his design for a hollow surfboard, a ca. 1940s example of which is pictured left. It revolutionized surfing by making the boards significantly lighter than the two-hundred-pound solid redwood boards previously in use.*

Above right: *Toni Frissell was a renowned photojournalist whose broad subject range stretched from fashion to combat. This 1938 image for Vogue magazine depicted women surfing, a rarity for both fashion and sports photography.*

WHAT IS THAT THING CALLED?

When I was ten or eleven, I would get up early and go mat riding at the beach before the crowds showed up. One morning, I saw this guy coming from Santa Monica Pier, knee paddling. I found out later it was Pete Peterson, a big-time surfing champion from the 1930s. This wave came and, all of a sudden, he stood up and rode it. At that second, I knew what I wanted to do with the rest of my life. I became obsessed with trying to figure out what that meant, and no one could tell me. I would try and explain it to people, and they'd look at me like I was speaking a foreign language. No one could tell me what it was.

One day at school, a film was being shown, and soon after the flickering light of the 16 mm projector started, *Surfboard Riding in Waikiki* flashed across the screen. I jumped up and shouted, "That's it—it's called surfing!" and disrupted the class. The nun grabbed me and took me to the office. I had never been on a surfboard and was already in trouble for being a surfer.

From that point on, I would ride my Schwinn bike from Hollywood to Santa Monica Pier, because I knew if I went down Santa Monica Boulevard, I'd eventually hit the ocean. The ride would take me hours. It's about fourteen miles, and I'd ride my bike all the way down next to the pier and look out at the ocean.

I really love the ocean. I love being in the water. When the Hollywood Boys Club put a pool in, every lap was a certain distance, so you could count the laps to swim from California to New York. I was the only person who ever did it three times. That was because I just wanted to swim. My mom eventually found out that I was riding my bike fourteen miles a day to get to the ocean, and the next thing I know, we're living one block off the sand in Venice Beach.

Now I'm by the ocean and sand, and I know the name of this thing. My first surfboard was balsa wood with a foam nose and tail, a weird hybrid that surfboard manufacturers were creating at the beginning. It was the end of balsa and the beginning of foam. It didn't matter—I was on my way.

—*Skip Engblom*

Top: *Preston "Pete" Peterson, captured in this ca. 1930 photo, was one of the most celebrated and influential surfers of the 1930s, winning more competitions than anyone during a single season.*

Above: *The Santa Monica Pier, the birthplace of California beach culture, in 1958. Skip Engblom frequently trekked fourteen miles to visit the pier and look out at the ocean.*

THE NEVER-ENDING ENDLESS SUMMER

ERIC JENTSCH

The Endless Summer, producer-director Bruce Brown's love letter to the sport and spirit of surfing, follows two laid-back dudes, Mike Hynson and Robert August, as they chase the world's gnarliest curls. The surprising 1966 blockbuster documentary introduced authentic surfing to audiences around the globe, forever shaping perceptions of the sport and the lifestyle it celebrated. The artifacts collected by the Smithsonian that relate to the film represent a dynamic moment in American identity when the mainstream embraced surfing subculture—inspiring innovation, influencing art, and expanding minds.

Brown had to get creative to film in remote locations on a limited budget of $50,000. One solution was to use a fiberglass surfboard designed to fold at its center, allowing it to fit in an airplane's overhead compartment and save on shipping. The folding model was quickly discontinued, as it proved unstable on big waves.

Brown also struggled to find a distributor for his feature-length documentary. Encouraged by the positive reception the film received at US schools and cultural centers, he rented the Kips Bay Theatre in New York City in 1966 to demonstrate the documentary's commercial viability. Brown thought if an audience could be found so far from surfing's West Coast epicenter, distributors might take a chance on the film. To

satisfy audience demand, Brown had to extend the original two-week engagement to a year. That convinced Cinema V and Columbia Pictures to release the film to theatergoers worldwide.

A massive hit earning $20 million globally, *The Endless Summer* rode perfectly along the zeitgeist of changing times. Counterculture audiences connected with the film's promise of free-spirited fun, rejection of materialism, and link to the natural world. The movie's surprising success not only propelled the surfing ethos into the limelight but also changed perceptions of documentary filmmaking, proving that the didactic medium could be profitable and well received by general audiences.

Top: *To get the shots he needed for* The Endless Summer, *filmmaker Bruce Brown, camera in hand, rode the waves alongside his "stars," as shown in this ca. 1964 photo.*

Above right: *Made by Dusters in 2015 to commemorate the documentary's fiftieth anniversary, this longboard is autographed by the movie's director, Bruce Brown, and its two surfer-actors, Robert August and Mike Hynson. Additional signatures are from legendary surfers Greg Noll, Paul Strauch, and Fred Hemmings.*

Above left: *Made in 1963 by Hobie Surfboards for the film* The Endless Summer, *this bi-sect surfboard was designed to fold in half at the center, which allowed it to fit into an overhead compartment of an airplane. This innovation demonstrated the global appeal of surfing and the use of air travel as the preferred choice of surfers in search of the best surfing sites. The board was made for only a limited time, however, as it tended to bend and flex in big surf, becoming unstable.*

Above right: *In this original 1964 poster for* The Endless Summer, *artist John Van Hamersveld's use of silhouetted surfers against a neon pink, yellow, and orange landscape created one of the most iconic surfing images of the 1960s. Since its appearance, it has been reproduced over the decades on countless items.*

One of the most enduring legacies of *The Endless Summer* is its poster art. Artist John Van Hamersveld's Day-Glo image of three relaxed surfers remains ubiquitous in American popular culture. Van Hamersveld connected *The Endless Summer* to the alternative pop art of the 1960s, reaffirming surfing's connections to the counterculture. After receiving acclaim for the poster, he became one of the rock era's most influential designers, producing iconic album covers for the Beatles' *Magical Mystery Tour*, The Rolling Stones' *Exile on Main St.*, and the Grateful Dead's *Skeletons from the Closet*.

Like the film it advertised, the poster continues to evoke the spirited and simple lifestyle surfing represented in the 1960s. The image, found on all manner of merchandise, including housewares, clothing, and accessories, was reproduced on the skateboard on page 33 to recognize the fiftieth anniversary of *The Endless Summer*. Representing the shared history of skateboarding and surfing, it reflects the two sports' entwined aesthetic and values.

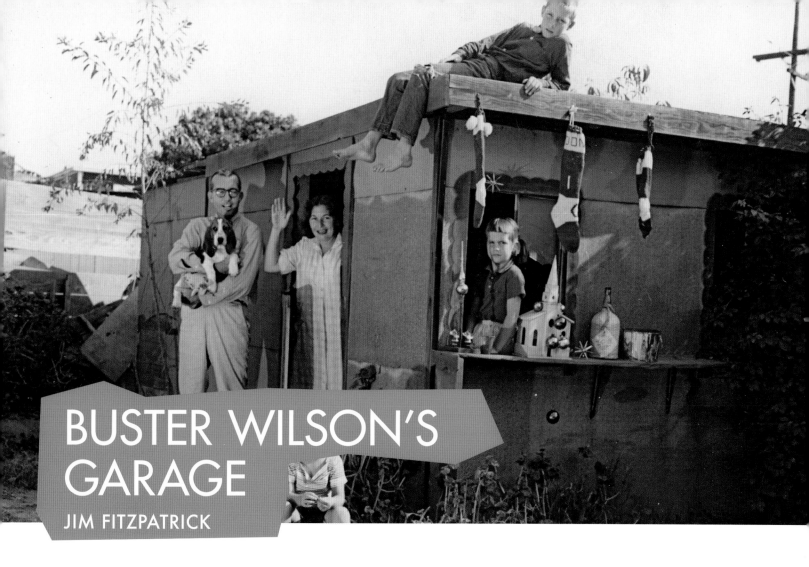

BUSTER WILSON'S GARAGE

JIM FITZPATRICK

Skateboarding came into my life during the summer of 1957, when I made my first skateboard with my dad, Fitz, and his buddy Buster Wilson. In the mid-1930s, when they were growing up in downtown San Diego, they had made their own skateboards. The reach of skateboarding in the 1930s never left their neighborhood, but the concept and the word itself, *skateboard*, had been part of their childhoods.

At the Wilsons' Point Loma, California, home, there were five Wilson boys ages two through eleven, seventeen bicycles, three dogs, five or six Jaguar automobiles in various stages of repair, bows and arrows, baseballs and gloves, basketballs, and seemingly every other article in the world meant to keep boys happy and engaged. Except on this particular day, Scott and Steve, the two oldest Wilson boys, and I hadn't settled on any

one activity, and we clearly exasperated my father and Buster as they worked beneath the chassis of one of the Jaguars.

I recall Buster rolling from beneath the car and growling something like, "Here! Do this!" We watched as he marched into the garage, opened a footlocker, pulled out several steel-wheeled roller skates, and then hauled down a few lengths of two-by-fours from the rafters. "Cut these! Pound these flat . . . get some nails . . . nail these on here like this . . . let's see what you come up with!"

My first skateboard struggled into existence, but the act of skateboarding arrived within an hour. The noise was incredible. The grinding of the steel wheels drowned out most conversation. Yelling and shouting were the only forms of communication. The Wilsons' two-story craftsman-style home was well positioned as a starter house for runs downhill leading toward Lindbergh Field. The driveway opened to the cross street, which allowed us to push and push and push while getting our balance, and then gradually turning to begin our downhill ride.

Above: *This Fitzpatrick family Christmas card dates from 1958. At the time, the family lived in the small, seaside community of Bird Rock, where Jim introduced skateboarding to the other kids in his neighborhood.*

Left: *The metal wheels of roller skates, like those on the 1925 clamp-on roller skate shown here, were often used for the first skateboards.*

The rush wasn't so much from the speed, because we didn't go very fast as we ground our way down the street's rough cement surface. Rather, it was from the sense that we'd done something we'd never done before: We'd made our own skateboards! And we were skateboarding down the hill!

That afternoon, I carried my skateboard and my enthusiasm back to our home in Bird Rock. Skateboarding's reach had extended fourteen miles. Within a day or two, I'd shown our neighborhood what we'd created. In less than forty-eight hours, skateboarding had expanded from six to ten skateboarders!

I kept tinkering with my board and skates, which fell off nearly every time I rode any distance. Nails vibrated loose, the steel wheels ground into pieces on the rough cement, and the inevitable small stone or stick would bring me to an immediate halt. That first summer I made at least a dozen different skateboards: longer boards, shorter boards, wider boards, one-by-four rather than two-by-four, different skate wheels, longer nails, shorter nails. Sewing-machine oil squirted under the little hubcap things covering the wheel bearings helped the wheels spin faster. We had a shed in our backyard with tools strewn

about: hammer, screwdriver, old coffee cans with assorted screws and fasteners, nails of all sizes. My creative impulses didn't necessarily help create a better skateboard, but every one was different. Each board took the experiment to a new level.

Summer vacation faded into flag football and then basketball, which was followed by baseball. My skateboards were always there but not necessarily used until summer vacation began again. La Jolla Shores, the public beach near Bird Rock, was known for its tennis club and nine-hole golf course, but it also became a destination spot for beginning surfers. I surfed an inflated mat and occasionally would talk someone into loaning me their balsa longboard to catch a few waves. The beach parking lot was enormous, and some areas clear of beach sand provided large expanses of asphalt for skateboarding.

That routine became the new standard for me. Surf. Skateboard. Fix the skateboard. Reassemble the skateboard. Surf. Eat something. Repeat. The following summer would be my last in La Jolla. My skateboards, though still steel wheeled, were longer lasting between rides, and I was mostly board surfing when our family moved to a house on Topanga Beach in Malibu, just west of Los Angeles.

I had my baseball glove, two steel-wheeled skateboards, a basketball, and the promise from my father of a "new foam surfboard as soon as we figure it out." My twelve-year-old world had changed its location, but as anxious as I was, I didn't know the best was yet to come.

Top: *In 1960, the Fitzpatrick family moved to Topanga Beach, California, where Jim Fitzpatrick took up surfing. Here, just two years after the move, he is already an accomplished rider.*

Above left: *Smithsonian donor Michael Savage recalls buying this ca. 1958 handmade wooden skate deck from "the old man who lived down the street," in Redondo Beach, California. The man made custom surfboards and occasionally made skate decks for the neighborhood kids.*

SKATING IN EUROPE

JIM FITZPATRICK

In 1962, Larry Stevenson was putting together prototypes of the clay-wheeled Makaha skateboards he thought could become popular with surfers. The next year, he founded both Makaha Skateboards and *Surf Guide* magazine. He hired Bill Cleary as editor of the magazine and tasked him with getting Makaha skateboards into the hands of young skateboarders to popularize skateboarding.

That same year, I was skateboarding as a Makaha Exhibition Team member on a Makaha skateboard at the opening of a new supermarket in Santa Monica. Those gathered for the ribbon-cutting ceremony may not have understood the connection between the supermarket opening and skateboarding, but they did seem to appreciate my efforts on my Makaha.

The Makaha Exhibition Team continued to develop, and in 1964, Makaha sent me to Europe with twelve Makaha skateboards and some brief instructions: "Skateboard wherever you can and give skateboards to kids who seem to really want them." So after two weeks of surfing and skateboarding in Biarritz, France, I traveled throughout Europe, stopping to skateboard every chance I had. What I hadn't realized was how difficult it would be to find places to skateboard. Cobblestones are a terrible surface for skateboarding! On my way to the French Riviera, I stopped in Madrid, where outside the Prado Museum I discovered a car park with a skateable surface. No one noticed. No one cared. It was unlike Paris, where, before heading off to Biarritz, I'd skated beneath the Eiffel Tower while hundreds of people applauded and shouted, "Encore!"

This 1964 Makaha skateboard (wheels not original) was used by Jim Fitzpatrick, a member of the Makaha surf and skateboard teams.

After spending time on the Riviera, I made my way to Italy, stopping in Florence and Venice, and then on to Austria and across France to Calais for the ferry to Dover and London. Piccadilly Circus provided cemented streets and sidewalks. While skateboarding across one of the pedestrian crosswalks, a uniformed bobby reached out and stopped me. Uh-oh, I thought. His interest, however, wasn't in incarcerating me. He asked, "Wutsit-ya-'av-der?" Despite my assurances, he wouldn't put the Makaha on the ground for a try. "Oh no, sir!" he said, "Tha's na-for-me, tha's for you to 'njoy. Go on wid it!"

In fact, one of the best skateboarding experiences I had during two months of travel was a few days later at the Stranraer Harbour ferry terminal, where I waited to make the crossing to Ireland. Enormous parking lots and staging areas were asphalted, and I took full advantage, skateboarding for nearly two hours before driving onto the ferry. A week later, when I was back in Paris for the return flight to the States, I once again took advantage of the asphalted area beneath the Eiffel Tower. Traveling in Europe with my Makaha skateboards changed the course of my life. I am forever grateful to all those who provided me the opportunity.

Top: *In 1964, Jim Fitzpatrick (center) was sent to Europe on a Makaha surf tour. Flanking him are French surfers (left) Jean-Marie Lartigau, and (right) François Le Gremme.*

Above: *Surfboard manufacturers often created a skateboard team to publicize their skateboard products, reaching more potential buyers in a store parking lot than on a beach. This November 13, 1964, ad from the* Long Beach Independent *promises "daring stunts and tricks" by the Makaha team at the May Company in Lakewood, California.*

EAST COAST SKATING

From a very young age, I knew I wanted to be a surfer, which is odd because we lived inland in Nassau County, Long Island, and no one in my family was a beach person. I knew that dream wasn't going to happen anytime soon, so I began the apprenticeship stuff to be a surfer. The first thing I could do was skateboarding. My dad and I saw it on TV one day, and I had him immediately go down to the basement and help me build a skateboard out of a one-by-six and a roller skate.

As homemade skateboards go, this one was really nice. It was six inches wide instead of the usual two-by-four, and it had a rounded nose and a rounded tail. When that one wore out, I bought a skateboard with steel wheels, and then I got a good Hobie fiberglass skateboard—the best one that was available. Those were beautiful things. I bought mine from Emilio's Ski & Surf shop on Long Island. Emilio's had a warranty on the boards, and my old one would always seem to break just when I wanted a new one, so I'd take it back to Emilio's.

We lived on a cul-de-sac with new pavement, and I practiced freestyle every day. That's mostly tacking back and forth to give yourself momentum and tricks and nose wheelies and tail wheelies—the earliest freestyle repertoire. But from an early age, I can remember making skating surfaces out of anything. We had a little sand pit in the back, and I would make wave forms and ride them with a fingerboard (miniature skateboard "ridden" with fingers). I was always looking at a space and trying to transform it into a rideable surface.

Eventually I rode for Emilio's, which meant I was on the local Hobie team. There were contests and a final every year at a park in East Meadow, and we would all compete. This was in the mid-1960s, and I became the New York State champ one year. My parents really didn't get it. Surfing was accepted, but they didn't understand skateboarding in part because it was something brand-new. Once my friends and I were in high school and could drive, we would go out looking for good places to skate. We usually found crude banked asphalt surfaces and rode those.

—*John O'Malley*

Top: *Although East Coast-raised John "Jono" O'Malley, pictured with a surfboard in May 1970, dreamed of being a surfer as a kid, he ended up on a skateboard first, becoming a New York State champ in the 1960s.*

Above: *In this April 1965 photo, taken in a suburban New York community, a group of young bicyclists and others look on as their contemporaries ride by on skateboards, the latest fad sweeping the country.*

FROM TAGGING TO THE SMITHSONIAN

JANE ROGERS

I feel like skateboarding is as much of a sport as a lifestyle, and an art form, so there's so much that transcends in terms of music, fashion, and entertainment.

—*Tony Hawk*

This decades-long debate in the skate world, sport versus lifestyle/art form, is the enigmatic question that will probably never have a definitive answer. But if we were to try and define it, artist Charles "Chaz" Bojórquez makes a solid argument for lifestyle/art form over sport. His work can be found in many collections, including a substantial archive in the Smithsonian Archives of American Art, works in the Smithsonian American Art Museum, and limited-edition Vans and Chuck Taylor sneakers and an extensive portfolio in the National Museum of American History.

Born in 1949 in East Los Angeles, California, Bojórquez gravitated to the arts at an early age. He landed a scholarship to the prestigious Chouinard Art Institute, now the California Institute of the Arts, establishing himself as a painter and studying calligraphy under Chinese master Yun Chung Chiang, which served him well in his preferred art form, graffiti.

Discovering graffiti art from the 1930s and 1940s in the Los Angeles River sewer pipes when he was a boy, he became obsessed with this visual medium as a way to express his individuality and hone his style. He created his first tag in 1968 and soon began tagging in his Highland Park neighborhood, quickly earning the tag "CHAZ," which meant "the one who messes things up and likes to fight." His introverted personality found a freedom in tagging, and Bojórquez started using one of the oldest forms of graffiti, cholo style, invented by Mexican Americans in the 1940s. Marking their territory with lists of names, or roll calls as they were known, gangs would decorate the cityscape with this urban art form.

Bojórquez experimented with different mediums for his tags. Spray paint was under too much pressure, making it hard to control and causing drips and run off. His first tag was made from a stencil created with Christmas wrapping paper taped together, making it easier to get in and out quickly, a necessity when tagging. Combining his Chicano heritage and popular entertainment culture, he created a Day of the Dead Chicano skull wearing a fedora hat and fur collar, from the then-popular movie *Shaft*, with crossed fingers representing good luck. Señor Suerte, or Mr. Lucky, was born.

California artist Charles "Chaz" Bojórquez's 1973 pictographic tag Señor Suerte—"Mr. Lucky"—combines elements of his Chicano heritage with symbols of the popular entertainment culture of the time.

Right: *Bojórquez stands with the tools of his trade in this photograph by Castro Frank from 2016. Bojórquez brought his graffiti-style art to skateboarding, continuing the debate as to whether skate is a sport, a lifestyle, an art form, or maybe a bit of all three.*

Below right: *Both Vans and Converse used Bojórquez's graffiti art to adorn their products. The Syndicate line (pictured here) was introduced by Vans in 2005, bringing a higher degree of quality in an effort to compete with the popular Nike SB brand. Syndicate lasted ten years and brought together designers, artists, and skaters for some of the company's most popular styles.*

After ten years, Bojórquez quit his day job and committed to his art. His first painting, *Placa/Rollcall*, created in 1980, resides in the permanent collection of the Smithsonian American Art Museum. His personal papers spanning his career as an artist from 1956 to 2017 reside in the Smithsonian Archives of American Art.

Skate companies often reach out to artists for inspiration, and Bojórquez's talent made him an obvious choice. Throughout his career, he has produced collaborations with Disney, including T-shirts, baseball caps, keychains, and stickers, and with skateboarding brands Vans, Converse, and Zoo York. His Syndicate line of Vans shoes with a Sk8-Hi and a Slip-On model, which are ingrained in skate culture, include embroidered brushstrokes and his signature, in his distinctive tagging style. His portfolio includes hand-drawn and computer-graphic designs for these collaborations and his work with Disney, for which he created a graffiti version of Mickey Mouse.

His artistic free spirit and partnerships with skate companies lend credence to the idea that lifestyle is as important an aspect of skate history as its sport and competition side. So, is skate a sport, a lifestyle, or both and does it even really matter? As far as the National Museum of American History collections are concerned, skate is a sport, as it resides in the sports collections. But skate as a lifestyle is also recognized for its influence on society. One can argue that the collection includes both aspects of skate, so the debate goes on.

Perhaps Bojórquez sums it up best in a quote from *Chicago* magazine in 2012: "When I was tagging in the streets, I never thought that I would ever be designing products with my graffiti letters. You would think that doesn't fit the free spirit of graffiti or the artist life, but it does. It puts my work in the context of culture."

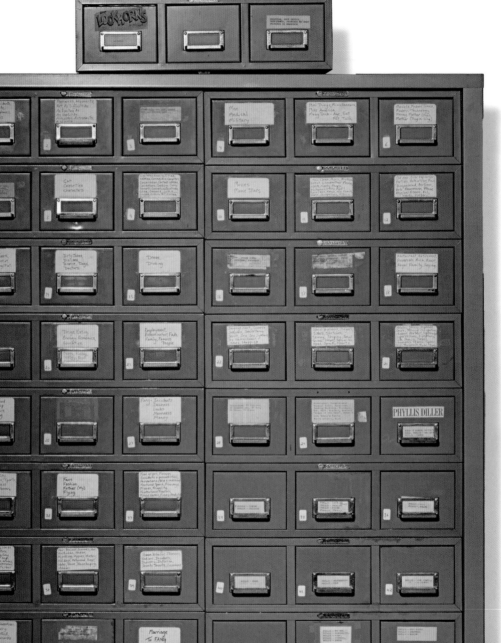

FROM PUNCH LINE TO LIFE LESSON

Sports - (Skateboarding)

```
Vic Grecco                March 25, 1966

1 King Size Skate Board (wheels included)
Accomodates a Family of 6...
```

AUTOS

```
Orben Gag                 August 2, 1967

I don't want to say anything about this car,
but if I used it to buy a skateboard, I'd be
trading up!
```

In 2003, legendary comedienne Phyllis Diller sent a letter asking if the Smithsonian might be interested in collecting memorabilia from her nearly six-decade career. In her typical self-deprecating fashion, her letter ends with, "Even if I end up in the zoo or with the mammals, I will be honored."

Diller's donation includes objects from her stage, film, and television career, including her entire joke archive. Housed in a large metal cabinet with forty-eight separate file drawers, the archive contains 52,569 three-by-five-inch index cards organized alphabetically by topic, with each card featuring a single typed joke. Twelve cards contain the word *skateboard*. Ranging in date from 1966 to 1981, these dozen cards appear in six categories: Accident, Auto, Fads, Sports, Teenagers, and Unknown.

Diller's early 1960s use of skateboarding in her repertoire shows her keen sense of American pop culture. Her cross categorization of skateboarding perfectly mirrors skateboarding's amorphous identity in its earliest decades—was it a teenage fad or a sport? For Diller, it was a punch line, an easy gag, something to laugh at.

In 2013, comedians Chris Rock and Jerry Seinfeld take skateboarding beyond the joke and add another definition: invaluable life lesson. In *Comedians in Cars Getting Coffee*, Seinfeld states, "I'll tell you one of the great activities is skateboarding. To learn to do a skateboard trick, how many times have you got to get something wrong before you get it right? And you hurt yourself.... You learn to do that trick, now you've got a life lesson. Whenever I see those skateboard kids, I think those kids will be alright."

—*Betsy Gordon*

Above: *Twelve cards in Phyllis Diller's joke file include the word skateboard. These are two of them, both from the 1960s.*

Opposite: *From 1962–94, Phyllis Diller used this metal cabinet to organize her jokes alphabetically. It holds 52,569 three-by-five-inch index cards, each with a typewritten joke or gag.*

CHAPTER TWO

'70s

THERE'S A GREAT FUTURE IN PLASTICS: TECHNOLOGY CHANGES SKATEBOARDING

The 1970s opened with the celebration of the first Earth Day and closed with the Sugarhill Gang releasing *Rapper's Delight*, the first hip-hop song to become a Top 40 hit on the Billboard Hot 100. Between those two events, Microsoft, Apple, VHS, and the *Star Wars* franchise got their start; the 1973 Paris Peace Accords ended direct US involvement in the Vietnam War; two oil embargoes limited the supply of cheap gasoline to Americans, which resulted in high prices and long lines at the pump; a US president resigned in disgrace; and the Iran hostage crisis began.

A severe drought in California in 1976 and 1977 emptied swimming pools and irrigation ditches, literally exposing new pavement for skateboarders to use and allowing sidewalk surfing to take to the air. Recovering from the moribund end of the 1960s, 1970s skateboarders took advantage of new inventions and innovations in plastic, wood, and metal and a proliferation of skateparks across America where competitions arise. The wooden toy of the 1960s becomes a potent symbol of adolescent swagger and cool.

The overarching skateboard narrative of the decade is an emphasis on ability and performance. The pendulum swings from adapting existing materials and borrowing skating styles from

Opposite: *By the mid-1970s, skateboarders had an impressive array of products to choose from, as this 41st Avenue Skateboards ad from the August 1976 issue of* SkateBoarder *magazine illustrates.*

other sports to inventing things specifically for skateboards and skateboarding. Although freestyle, downhill, and slalom racing resurface from the 1960s, new types of skating—bowl, pool, and, eventually, vert (short for vertical)—emerge. A highly competitive class of skaters forms, one that actively competes and needs up-to-date equipment to win. These skaters were the true inventors. Similar to their surfer and aviator ancestors, this generation of skaters acted as test pilots for the skate deck, wheel, and truck manufacturers. Their laboratories were the concrete and asphalt hills sprouting up in new housing developments, empty swimming pools, irrigation ditches, and asphalt banks in neighborhood schoolyards.

In the early years of the decade, the skateboard underwent major design and manufacturing changes: the integration of a kicktail, the adoption first of the urethane roller-skate wheel and later of the closed-bearing urethane wheel, and the invention of trucks designed specifically for skateboarding. Larry Stevenson's patented "inclined foot-depressible lever"—a kicktail—was adopted by most skateboard manufacturers. This changes the shape of the skateboard from a flat plank to a board that has a defined front and back—a nose and a raised tail. Skaters could now use the tail to lift the nose of the board up off the ground, allowing for better balance and turning ability. During this decade, plastics, specifically polyurethane and fiberglass derivatives, became more commonly used as skateboard materials. In 1972,

Frank Nasworthy noticed a pile of urethane roller skate wheels in the corner of Creative Urethanes. He attached the wheels to his skateboard and found that they provide a faster, smoother, and better controlled ride. Nasworthy used all his savings to create Cadillac Wheels and sells his urethane wheels to the surf shops still selling skateboards. In 1973, an excess of pultruded fiberglass originally destined to become surfboards is repurposed into skateboards, launching the brands Santa Cruz and Bahne.

Ron Bennett created the Bennett Hijacker in 1973, the first truck made specifically for skateboarding. With its signature red bushings (plastic inserts that act as a flexible washer to allow the trucks to pivot), it provides superior turning ability. In 1974,

Left: *In the 1960s and 1970s, Bruce Logan was among the top pro skaters, dominating in freestyle and downhill racing. This ca. 1975 Bruce Logan World Pro Champion skate deck was made by Logan Earth Ski, the skateboarding company founded by Bruce, his mother, and his siblings, Brian and Robin, in the early 1970s. Revising the sidewalk surfer description of skateboards, the Logan family decided to call their skateboards "earth skis," as seen on this ca. 1973 sticker (top).*

Above: *Unlike trucks adapted from roller skates, the Tracker Fultrack, which debuted in 1975, was designed using feedback and advice directly from skaters and was made exclusively for skateboards.*

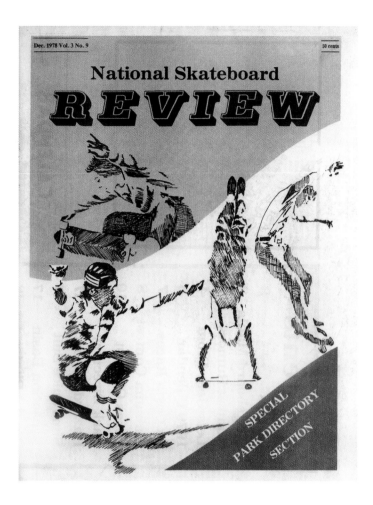

Dec. 1978 Vol. 3 No. 9   50 cents

National Skateboard
REVIEW

SPECIAL PARK DIRECTORY SECTION

Tony Roderick and NHS Inc. decide to combine a closed precision bearing found in copy machines with a urethane skateboard wheel. Unlike Cadillac skateboard wheels, which have open ball bearings that could fall out of the wheel, Roderick's Road Rider wheel has closed bearings that don't spill out onto the sidewalk. In addition to not having to chase a bunch of minuscule steel balls on the ground, a closed system prevents dirt from clogging the bearings. Less dirt results in faster-spinning wheels, giving the skater more speed. Skateboard wheels diversified quickly in size and hardness to respond to the performance needs of the skaters: smaller and softer for downhill racing, slalom, and freestyle; larger and harder for pool and wall riding.

Parallel to the innovations that occurred in skateboard wheels were the rapid developments in skateboard trucks and decks. In 1975, the Tracker Fultrack entered the market, followed by Gullwing, Independent, and a host of other manufacturers. Decks changed in size, shape, and material, ranging from short and slender solid wood or plastic decks with a kicktail (for freestyle and slalom); long wood, metal, or fiberglass composite decks with no kicktail (for downhill); and wide decks made of maple ply (for bowl or pool) to many other combinations of choices depending on the manufacturer.

By the mid-1970s, these updates in wheels and trucks allowed skateboarders to ride faster and turn more sharply, with more control and less propensity for wiping out. This brought out more skaters, which created more demand for skateboard product. More product demand created more skateboard companies. In short, skateboarding manufacturers became profitable again. Nash, Hobie, Makaha, and G&S rebound from their 1960s nadir, while a seemingly endless stream of new brands—Zephyr, Z-Flex, Logan Earth Ski, Sims, Powell-Peralta, and Alva, to name just a few—began claiming a share of the growing market.

In 1974, with both the number of skaters and the amount of product growing, surf and skateboard photographer James O'Mahoney created the United States Skateboard Association (USSA) and later the World Skateboard Association (WSA) to bring the world's skaters together via competitions. These organized contests provided a path to becoming a professional skateboarder. Unlike other sports, skateboarding has no high school teams, no intramurals, no Triple-A farm leagues. Skate shops and skateboard companies sponsor team riders, giving

This cover of the December 1978 issue of National Skateboard Review *included a "special park directory" inside to help skateboarders find skateparks around the country.*

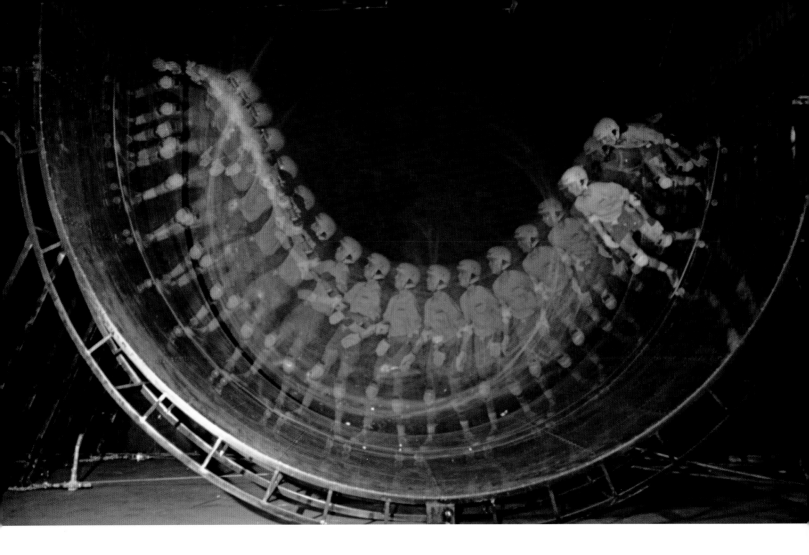

them skateboards, clothing, and other free equipment. Winning contests might attract more sponsorship, allowing skaters to trade up from local shop to national-level support and eventually from sponsored skater to professional with prize money and perhaps their own signature skate deck model.

With the industry flush with profitable product lines and skateboard competitions becoming popular, magazine coverage exploded. *SkateBoarder* was resurrected in 1975 to facilitate the flow of information from seller to buyer, followed by the introduction of *Wild World of Skateboarding* in 1976 and *Skateboard World* in 1977. Downhill slalom race organizer Di Dootson started publishing the *National Skateboard Review* in 1976 to cover the skateboard racing results from La Costa and other asphalt hills in Southern California. These publications were heavily illustrated, increasing the need for skateboard photography. Skateboard magazine photography launched the careers of teenagers James Cassimus and Glen E. Freidman, who began by documenting their skateboarding friends. Surf photographers Warren Bolster and Art Brewer quickly adapted to land photography to create some of the most iconic images of the era. In an effort to capture the complex series of movements created by a single skate trick, photojournalist C. R. Stecyk experimented with stop-action shutter speeds while Bolster employed strobe

lights. At the same time, the rise of affordable and readily available cameras, most notably the Japanese single lens reflex (SLR) models, put lightweight, easily portable cameras in the hands of teenagers everywhere to photograph their friends skating and submit the images to the skate magazines for publication.

With more maneuverable skateboards and taking advantage of a prolonged drought in California in 1976 and 1977, skaters found paradise in emptied reservoirs, drainage ditches, and swimming pools. Working with the geometry of an empty pool—flat bottom, sloping vertical walls, and tiled top edges (called coping)—skaters eventually discover how to "get air." They would propel their wheels off the edges of the pool and, for a few brief seconds, hover in the interstice of neither up nor down, floating weightless before gravity returned them to earth. In that liminal space, tricks were conceived and given names, such as frontside air, ollie, and lipslide. As a result, a distinctly different style of skateboarding emerged, one that did not emulate existing sports like skiing, surfing, or gymnastics. Each new trick acted as a

The demand from skateboard magazines for high-action images of skaters pushed photographers like C. R. Stecyk and Warren Bolster to invent new ways to capture their tricks. Here, Warren Bolster employs a strobe light to record the individual movements of a skater on a ramp.

building block to yet another never-been-done-before maneuver with a skateboard. There was no manual to follow, no coach or rule book. The kids made it up as they went along.

This sudden burst of energy in the pools and drainage ditches of Southern California would have become quickly forgotten if it weren't for the coincidental presence of C. R. Stecyk. Stecyk, an omnipresent fixture in a myriad of Los Angeles–based subcultures and industries, was associated with the shop Jeff Ho Surfboards and Zephyr Productions. From 1975 to 1980, he wrote and supplied the photos for a series of articles for *SkateBoarder* magazine under two pseudonyms, John Smyth and Carlos Izan. These essays, later known as the "Dogtown Chronicles," create a mythical aura around the Zephyr shop skateboard team skaters. The Z-Boys, as they were later called, acquired the intoxicating elixir of being "cool" and were irresistible to teenagers jaded by the war in Vietnam, Watergate, and tiresome gas lines.

Almost simultaneous to the beatification of the Z-Boys came a second wave of new venues: purpose-built skateparks. From the mid-to-late 1970s, more than three hundred skateparks opened across forty states, with the bulk of them located in California. The proliferation of skateparks across America was aided by two uniquely American things: the availability of large,

inexpensive parcels of undeveloped land and the promise of making a quick buck. Full-page ads touting the ability to make "tremendous amounts of money" with skateparks started to appear in the back pages of *SkateBoarder*. Skaters wanted replications of the perfect spaces they found in empty pools, drainage ditches, and schoolyard embankments. What they often got was rough concrete snake runs with moguls that imitated ski slopes and other gimmicks conceived by non-skateboarders.

Another form of purpose-built skate terrain emerged during the 1970s: the homemade ramp. Requiring no entrance fee or gas money, ramps sprouted up in backyards and driveways throughout suburban America as an attractive alternative to the skatepark. These plywood ramps were halfpipe or quarter pipe (half or quarter of a circle), with little to no flat transitional space between the curving sides, no coping, and no top platform for standing. Like many skateparks at the time, what they lacked in design sophistication, they more than made up for in social magnetism, providing a place where skaters could congregate and improve their skating prowess.

J. Grant Brittain had to step to the back of three other photographers to capture this memorable 1985 shot of Lance Mountain at Upland Pipeline Combi Pool.

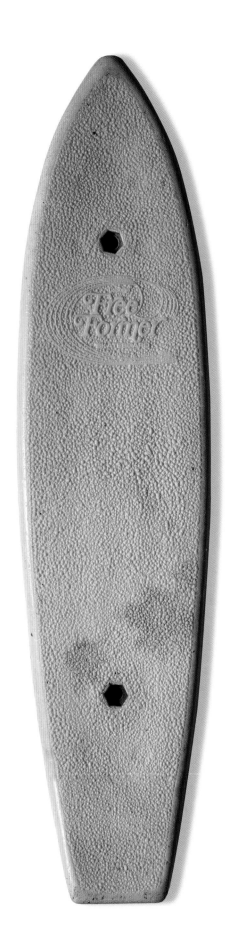

These early skateparks and homemade ramps served as the first social networks for skateboarders. Predating the Internet and cell phones, they were where skaters went to see the latest tricks; the newest decks, trucks, and wheels; and the stiffest competition. The change of pace was so rapid that skateboarding's existing mass media couldn't keep up. By the time the magazines landed in mailboxes, chances are the trick on the cover was already outdated.

An almost uncalculatable number of tricks were invented. As each new maneuver was successfully performed, it was simultaneously given a name that was either a shorthand description of the move, a riff on the skater's name, or a combination of the two. Although many skaters take credit for inventing a trick, it is doubtful that any one person singlehandedly performed a skate trick before anyone else. More likely is that whatever someone claims to have done "first" was probably being done at the same time by a number of skaters. What determined the association of the trick with the skater is how it was documented and how this documentation was distributed. A skater associated with a photographer used frequently by a widely distributed skateboarding publication was more likely to be credited as the "first" to invent something

Take the ollie, for example. In 1977, two Florida skaters, Alan "Ollie" Gelfand and Jeff Duerr, were both doing a no-hands aerial maneuver in which all four wheels of the skateboard flew above the edge of the pool or bowl. Jeff's friends called this a "due air," while Alan's friends called it an "ollie air" in homage to Gelfand's nickname. Gelfand caught the eye of Californian Stacy Peralta on a Powell-Peralta scouting trip to Florida. 1977, he was flown by Peralta to California to have skate photographer James Cassimus document the trick. Gelfand won *SkateBoarder* magazine's Most Spectacular Maneuver award in 1978 for the trick, though no photographs of it were published until January 1979. No matter who really invented it, the ollie became the seminal skateboard trick and reset the genome of modern skateboarding.

In the 1970s, freestyle and downhill racing are not inventing new moves as rapidly as the pool riders. The new in downhill or slalom is based on seconds shaved off an existing record. In freestyle, it is a few more 360s or a longer handstand ride. These new skaters are going higher, skating faster, and inventing new tricks every time they congregate. They exude energy and bravura, epitomizing the thrill of doing something that has never been done, the pride of having it named after you, and the swagger that comes after landing on a magazine cover.

As skaters increasingly turned to riding pools or bowls, skate decks and trucks grew wider to provide increased stability for speed and for grinding (sliding) along the coping. The flexibility provided by fiberglass decks (perfect for slalom racers)

Commonly referred to as a "banana board" because of its bright yellow color, this plastic skate deck, made ca. 1975 by California Free Former, represents a short-lived experiment in materials by the skateboard manufacturers of the 1970s.

didn't perform well in a bowl. The early 1970s experiments in using solid wood (Logan Earth Ski), plastic (Free Former), fiberglass (Bahne), and aluminum (Powell Corporation) gave way to using multiple layers (plies) of maple. By the late 1970s, maple ply became the de facto material of most skate decks. As the materials, sizes, and shapes of the decks changed, so did their surfaces. Griptape was applied to the top to ensure a nonslip surface. This coincided with skaters discovering that the sole of their shoe combined with griptape created the necessary bond between skaters' feet and skateboard to enable more time in the air. More time in the air allowed for the invention of more tricks.

The bottom of the skate deck changed as well. Initially an unseen space to place the manufacturer's logo, the undersides of decks became increasingly visible as skateboard magazines featured shots of skaters riding out of the pool or bowl. Skaters began to plaster the bottom of their decks with stickers from their wheel, truck, or deck sponsor, transforming their decks into billboards. Eventually, all sizes and shapes of plastic accoutrements appeared on the bottom of skate decks: long, thin rails to enable the skater to grab on to the bottom of the deck and protective covers for the deck's nose and tail. In 1977, Dogtown Skates introduced a totally new concept of corporate logo in which it covered the bottom of its decks with artwork by Wes Humpston.

It isn't until the late 1970s that skateparks were built with skateable pools and bowls. Until then, most skateboard competitions centered around freestyle and slalom racing, even though skateboard magazines increasingly featured pool and bowl riders on their covers. Skate competitions eventually modified their categories to include vert skaters. In 1977, the Third Annual Pro Hang Ten World Titles contest added a new category, freestyle aerials, to the slalom and freestyle events. In 1978, Henry Hester sponsored the first bowl-only competition, the Hester Series, at Skatepark Heaven in Spring Valley, California.

Above left: *Utilizing Bo-Tuff fiberglass epoxy over a maple core, the Fibreflex skateboard by Gordon and Smith (G&S) arched back and forth underneath skaters' feet, giving them the ability to pump during a slalom race. This cutting-edge technology, combined with the urethane skateboard wheel, propelled G&S into being one of the most profitable skateboard brands of the 1970s.*

Above right: *Targeting potential skatepark investors, and promising an opportunity to make "tremendous amounts of money," ads like this one, which appeared in the January 1978 issue of SkateBoarder, were in every American skateboard magazine in the late 1970s.*

Bowl competitions required a new way of evaluating the skater's performance. Unlike downhill and slalom where winners are determined by time, many of the tricks seen at the Hester Series had never been seen before by the judges. At the first Hester Series contest, the judging system was completely improvised by the skaters before the competition and used a point system from zero to one hundred to score every trick. At the next contest, they changed the judging system to include a forty-five-second time limit for each skater's run, followed by the same point system.

Mirroring the boom-to-bust cycle of the 1960s, skateboarding started to decline rapidly by 1979. Many skaters who started riding as teenagers in the early 1970s were now young adults with no real opportunities to maintain their sponsored or pro careers. Some, like Stacy Peralta and Tony Alva, were successful in shifting from contest skater to company owner. Many left skating to find employment or attend college. In addition to the decrease in interested participants, the gas shortages of the mid-1970s made it increasingly difficult and expensive to drive to skateparks, dramatically affecting attendance levels. Dwindling attendance cut into revenue, and many skateparks struggled to generate a profit. In addition, skateparks were getting sued by parents over injuries and could not afford the skyrocketing liability insurance policies. Skateboard companies were left, once again, with too much supply and too little demand.

Like at the end of the 1960s, many skateboard manufacturers and suppliers went out of business as the 1970s came to a close. However, skateboarding did not disappear entirely. The innovations in decks, wheels, and trucks allowed skateboarding to establish its own identity. The homemade skate ramp became even more significant as one of the few remaining places for skaters to congregate and skate vert. Perhaps even more significant is that skating in the 1970s becomes fun and transforms itself into being something cool. Fun and cool are hard, if not impossible, to completely extinguish, especially if they can be commodified to sell product. The spark ignited by the 1970s continued at a slower pace into the next decade.

—Betsy Gordon and Jane Rogers

Top: *This 1978 T-shirt was designed by graphic artist Pushead (Brian Schroeder) for Del Mar Skateboard Ranch, one of the last California skateparks to open before the mass skatepark closures of the late 1970s and early 1980s made skateparks a thing of the past.*

Left: *Native Floridian Mark Lake began his pro skateboarding career at nineteen with this 1977 signature pro model deck by Flite Skateboards. In 1985, he began skating for Walker Skateboards, where he designed his infamous Nightmare board (see page 89). Two years later, he left Walker to create his own company, Lake Skateboards.*

In 1977, the Powell Corporation, founded by George Powell, produced its first skateboard, this Quicksilver, which was ridden by Stacy Peralta that same year. Although its design of aluminum alloy skins epoxied to a hard maple core was innovative, the model was viewed as outdated within less than a year of its release, as other manufacturers strove to perfect the size, shape, and material composition of a skate deck.

The 1970s

- Twenty-eight Ohio National Guard soldiers fire at unarmed antiwar student protestors at Kent State University, killing four students and wounding nine others.

- *Ms.* magazine publishes its debut issue, becoming the first national magazine to make feminist issues available to the public.
- Jeff Ho, Skip Engblom, and C. R. Stecyk open Jeff Ho Surfboards and Zephyr Productions in Santa Monica, CA.

- Southern California surfboard manufacturers Bill and Bob Bahne team up with friend Frank Nasworthy and start selling pultruded fiberglass Bahne skateboards with Cadillac wheels. In less than two years, Bahne Skateboards becomes the largest skateboard company in the world.

- The US Supreme Court announces a decision in *Roe v. Wade,* which overturns state laws against abortion.
- The Arab oil embargo leads to fuel shortages and long lines at gas stations as gas suddenly becomes scarce.

- Downhill skateboard races are held at La Costa in San Diego County, CA. Using information gleaned from seeing the races, Larry Balma, Dave Dominy, and Gary Dodds produce the Tracker Fultrack, a wider truck designed for slalom racing.

- Bahne-Cadillac National Championships are held at the Del Mar Fairgrounds. This contest marks the first appearance of the Z-Boys, the Zephyr skateboard team.

- With design input from Tony Alva, Vans introduce the #95 (later known as the Era). This is Vans's first shoe marketed specifically to skateboarders.
- Jimmy Carter is elected the thirty-ninth president of the United States.

- Severe drought in California results in dry irrigation ditches and empty swimming pools, increasing the terrain opportunities for skaters.
- Jeff Ho closes Jeff Ho Surfboards and Zephyr Productions.
- Aerospace engineer George Powell founds the Powell Corporation.

- The Atari 2600 becomes the first successful home video game system, popularizing the use of microprocessor-based hardware and cartridges containing game code.
- VHS is introduced in the United States by RCA.

- Stacy Peralta joins George Powell to form Powell-Peralta. Powell utilizes his aerospace engineering degree to invent Bones wheels and patents the double radius design. In creating a wheel that curves on both side edges, Bones changes the way skateboard wheels ride and wear.
- Vans introduces the #38 (later the Sk8-Hi), designed specifically to protect a skater's ankle.

1972
- Title IX is signed into law, prohibiting discrimination on the basis of sex in any federally funded education program or activity.
- Five men are arrested for the burglary of the Democratic National Committee headquarters at the Watergate office complex in Washington, DC.

1973
- Northern Californian surfers Richard Novak, Doug Haut, and Jay Shuirman repurpose pultruded fiberglass meant for surfboards and begin manufacturing skateboards. Together, they form NHS Inc. to make and distribute Santa Cruz skateboards. NHS is now the oldest continuously operated skateboard company in the world.

1974
- James O'Mahoney creates the United States Skateboard Association (USSA), and then a few years later the World Skateboard Association (WSA), to bring the world's skaters together via skateboard competitions.

- In May, the House Judiciary Committee launches formal hearings in an impeachment inquiry against President Richard Nixon. In August, Nixon becomes the first US president to resign. Vice President Gerald Ford becomes the thirty-eighth president.

- Brothers Marty and Clyde Grimes become the first African American skateboarders to compete as pros. They are sponsored by Z-Flex.
- The Vietnam War ends.

1976
- The original Zephyr team leaves for other brands after less than nine months.
- Logan Earth Ski releases a Laura Thornhill signature skateboard.
- Ermico Enterprises Inc is founded by Fausto Vitello and Eric Swenson. They go on to form Independent Trucks and *Thrasher* magazine.

- Former Z-Boy Tony Alva leaves G&S and founds Alva Skates.
- Wes Humpston and Jim Muir form Dogtown Skateboards. Instead of using a company logo on the bottom of their skateboards, they use the infamous Dogtown Cross. This is credited as being the first skateboard graphic.

- The first home personal computer, the Commodore PET, is released for retail sale.
- *Star Wars* debuts in movie theaters.
- Elvis Presley dies in his home in Graceland at age forty-two.

1979
- Marty Grimes becomes the first African American to have a signature deck (Z-Flex) and to have a trick named after him, the Grimes slide.
- Stacy Peralta retires from professional skateboarding. He becomes a team manager and forms the Bones Brigade.
- The Three Mile Island nuclear accident occurs, the most catastrophic nuclear power plant accident in US history.

- The Iran hostage crisis begins. In the aftermath, a second energy crisis develops, tripling the price of oil and sending US gasoline prices over one dollar per gallon.
- The Sugarhill Gang releases "Rapper's Delight," the first hip-hop song to become a Top 40 hit on the Billboard Hot 100.

WOMEN'S SKATEBOARDING

CINDY WHITEHEAD

For women in skateboarding, the early 1970s were the perfect time to jump onto a skateboard and be accepted by male skaters and the fledgling skateboard media. Skateboarding was in its infancy, and there were no preconceived rules of gender in the skate world yet. Urethane wheels had just been introduced, and teenage girls in coastal California—from Venice to San Diego—were creating a distinct style in skateboarding.

In Venice, Z-Boys skater Peggy Oki adopted the low and smooth yet aggressive surf style that was an extension of who she was, in and out of the water. In the South Bay and down to San Diego, girls like Laura Thornhill and Robin Logan were favoring a more "toes on the nose" upright surf style, spinning endless 360s.

In addition to their surf-style sisters, another small group of girls brought a very different skill set to the freestyle competitions. In San Diego, "The Ellens," as they were collectively known—Ellen Oneal and Ellen Berryman—incorporated gymnastic maneuvers into their skateboard routines, creating a "feminine" and widely accepted look for women at the time.

The famous 1975 Del Mar Nationals contest showed the skateboard community just how different those skate styles could be. With Peggy getting low on her board, improvising all the way, and Laura and Robin Alaway's daffys and choreographed freestyle routines, the judges' personal preferences decided whose tricks warranted more points.

Being able to compete in many different types of skateboarding was key at these contests. Most of the women were competing in freestyle as well as slalom, high jump, and sometimes even downhill racing. These contest divisions were adapted directly from other mainstream sports like skiing, gymnastics, and track and field. Although many skateboarders preferred freestyle for its creativity, others liked slalom, racing, and high jump because of the level playing field. A stopwatch or a bar was all that was needed to determine who was the "best" on that given day.

Having female skaters up and down the California coast helped create a distinct, localized style indicative of each area. Santa Barbara's Edie Robertson and Vicki Vickers, who hailed from Texas originally, along with Northern California's Judi Oyama were all showing up at contests.

The "localism" in style also flowed into each region's skateboard teams. The teams, skaters, and media were all hyper-local—that included team uniform colors, skate style, and even magazines to some extent. You really didn't see anyone in *SkateBoarder* magazine from anywhere but California.

Shot by photographer Bruce Hazelton, this two-page spread of Cindy Whitehead skating the plexiglass 360 ramp at Fountain Valley Skateboard Park appeared in the June 1978 issue of Wild World of Skateboarding. *Whitehead was one of the first women skaters to have her own article and photographic feature in a skateboarding magazine.*

Skateboarder Cindy Whitehead, who turned pro at the age of seventeen, is shown in 1976 with her Sims skateboard (top). Whitehead later went on to become the only woman member on the Sims team in 1980, and wore this men's jersey (bottom) as part of her uniform.

Another great example of this localism is Di Dootson's *National Skateboard Review*. Although it tried to cover events all over the country, giving detailed competition results, you may not have had the opportunity to see it if you were anywhere other than San Diego. As an LA-based skater, I had never heard of Di's newspaper until I saw it in the Smithsonian in 2013 and was amazed that there was yet another publication I didn't have any knowledge of back then.

As skateboarding moved into the mid-1970s, flat-land freestyle became too sedate for many skateboarders. They turned to ditches and empty swimming pools, which were plentiful during the California drought of 1976–77. The banked walls provided a challenge for those skaters wanting to go further than freestyle routines and slalom. Girls like Laura, Robin, Peggy, Kim Cespedes, Vicki, Judi, and others thrived during this transition, while some of the ladies rode out the freestyle wave until those contests fizzled out.

In 1976, Carlsbad Skatepark opened, and many other skate-parks quickly followed suit. Soon skateparks dotted the land-scape of Southern California, and skateboarding had a huge boom in popularity.

As this shift took place, a number of manufacturers—primarily mom-and-pop operations—started creating useful articles of clothing and safety gear for skateboarders, who had been using volleyball kneepads and lightweight plastic Jofa hockey helmets in skateparks that now required safety equip-ment. While padded shorts and motocross-style jerseys with the skateboard team names on them came into fashion, the girls in skateboarding had to learn to make these items fit their bodies.

This first wave of female skaters was now moving toward adulthood, with jobs, college, and dating filling their time. Skateboarding was left behind, and, in some cases, it wasn't because they wanted to leave but rather because they financially had to. Male skaters who were winning contests and had endorsement deals could make a decent living, but unfortunately for the women that was not an option.

A new wave of female skaters gravitated to these skate-parks like bees to honey and could not get enough of the perfect manmade halfpipes and pools.

Girls like myself skated day and night at parks like Torrance, California's Skateboard World. Suddenly, we were not expected to do those highly choreographed freestyle routines to songs from the Beach Boys, the Steve Miller Band, and other popular music. Those were reserved for our skate demos at schools and shopping malls. At the skateparks , we could simply focus on getting as high as we wanted on vertical terrain.

There were contests at all the California skateparks —sometimes it would be in the manmade pools or halfpipe, and if you were lucky enough to compete at Upland, perhaps in the combi or the full pipe. The pro women now had their own division. Even though there was just a handful of us skating, we thrived on seeing one another at comps. It was a sisterhood that only a few belonged to.

Above: *This Laura Thornhill model skateboard, used by Thornhill herself, was made by Logan Earth Ski ca. 1978. Thornhill and Robin Logan were the only two women to have signature skateboard models in the 1970s.*

Right: *As skateparks began sprouting up all over California in the 1970s, skateboarders secured memberships to as many as possible. These membership cards for Skatopia Skatepark, Skateboard World, and Marina del Rey Skatepark, all in Southern California, were used by skater Cindy Whitehead from 1977 through 1979.*

Geographically speaking, we were a spread-out bunch, and the only way we knew what one another was doing was by word of mouth. It was like an intricate game of "telephone tag." Sometimes stories were spread just to freak the other girls out and make them wonder if their tricks were going to cut it at the next contest.

Skateboard magazines were of no help in keeping us informed of other skaters' skills and progress. As more women were abandoning freestyle, the magazines began to pull back on coverage of women. Freestyle was not seen as a threat, but girls shredding pools wasn't something most magazines wanted to show alongside guys doing the same. Some of us felt that it was due to adolescent masculinity, and showing girls shredding just like the guys wasn't great for some male egos. Since the photographers couldn't sell the images to the magazines, most didn't bother shooting the women. Because of this lack of media coverage, most women's late-1970s skate history is sparse.

The pay gap between men and women was huge. First place in the women's division was perhaps $100, but guys might get $3,500. In 1978, pro skateboarder Vicki Vickers spoke out about inequality in skateboarding in *SkateBoarder* magazine, saying, "Women deserved equal pay for equal skate." I did the same in 1978 when I scored a centerfold on the 360-plexiglass ramp and a two-page article in *Wild World of Skateboarding* magazine. At age fifteen, I let the world know that "you should listen to your own thoughts and don't give in to what people say is socially acceptable." Unfortunately, two teenage girls speaking out couldn't change the vast difference in the male-to-female ratio the magazines continued to portray; nor did it make a dent in the "equal pay for equal skate" department. We skated anyway because we loved it, and at some point, we were just glad we had our own division and no longer had to compete with the boys.

By 1978, things were starting to look good for bowl and vert skaters, as downhill and slalom were falling by the wayside. The Hester Series was created and was the biggest set of contests for bowl riding at the time. Although there were four contests in total—Spring Valley, Upland, Newark, and Orange, California—contest records only show results for women in the last two contests of the series.

By 1979, bigger challenges appeared that hindered our ability to skate. The United States had its second gas shortage, which meant gas was rationed—even- and odd-numbered license plates determined what day you could get gas. As skaters, we had to improvise so I'd "borrow" the plates off my grandmother's car and put them onto my Pinto station wagon. That way, I could have enough gas to drive everyone to the skatepark and still have a full tank.

We thought that was the worst skateboarders had to deal with, but then came the 1980s and things changed drastically.

In this 1977 photo by Warren Bolster, Southern California–born freestyle skateboarder Ellen Oneal is captured executing an arabesque

FROM CREATIVE TO CADILLAC

The skateboarding community is small but welcoming—even to two Smithsonian curators who don't skate but love its history. So when Betsy Gordon received an email from Smithsonian colleague Jeff Brodie introducing Keith Stephenson, a lifelong skateboarder who worked as a photo-journalist at *Thrasher* magazine during the 1980s and 1990s, it was kismet. Stephenson's friend Tom Heitfield is the son of Vernon Heitfield, who owned Creative Urethanes and was responsible for creating the very first urethane wheel for roller skates. Tom Heitfield was kind enough to donate to the Smithsonian the first prototype urethane wheel, complete with a handwritten tag from Vernon's wife, Ruth, explaining the provenance of this fascinating piece of skate history.

Creative Urethanes began to produce urethane for roller skate wheels in 1970. A batch of the wheels proved too slippery for the roller rinks, so the Heitfields had a huge unsold supply. A family friend visited the factory and thought the wheels would be perfect on a skateboard. That friend was Frank Nasworthy.

As most in the skateboarding world know, Nasworthy then went on to create Cadillac Wheels. The urethane wheels made by Nasworthy's company became the standard in skateboard wheels in 1973 and propelled the sport to a higher level, allowing skaters to glide faster and smoother and with better control of their board. The urethane wheel ushered in a new era of skaters and aided in the creation of the skatepark. But few know this backstory of the little family-owned business in Purcellville, Virginia, that started it all. Creative Urethanes would go on to manufacture urethane wheels for skateboards and also made skateboards, field hockey sticks, surfboard fins, and other non-sports-related urethane products.

—*Jane Rogers*

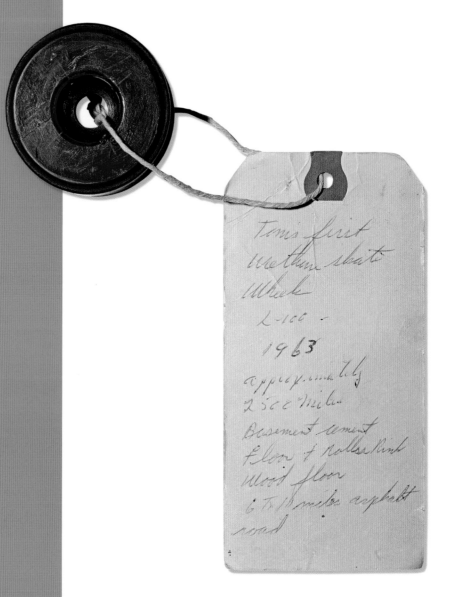

Vernon Heitfield, founder of Creative Urethanes, manufactured this original urethane wheel, which bears a label by his wife, Ruth. Heitfield created this wheel so that his son could roller skate on their concrete basement floor.

Top: *With the skateboard industry growing, Frank Nasworthy bought a load of Philippine mahogany from a US Navy chief in San Diego in 1974. He hired local carpenters to shape twenty-four-by-six-inch decks and had one thousand completes ready for Christmas sales, including this one.*

Middle: *Produced in 1975, the DK 38 model by Cadillac Wheels became the first high-volume production wheels made when Bahne and Cadillac joined forces. The thirty-eight-millimeter-wide wheel contained a precision bearing that simplified manufacturing but added cost, which skaters willingly paid for the smoother, quieter ride.*

Bottom left: *The color of this 1973 original "clear" amber Cadillac wheel is the unpigmented thermoset urethane, or the color urethane becomes when the viscous liquid hardens to solid material. This model had open bearings and, like most wheels of the time, was only an inch wide.*

Bottom middle: *The Da Kine model takes its name from the Hawaiian slang term da kine, meaning "the kind" or "the best." By early 1974, the diameter was reduced from two inches to less than an inch to avoid hitting the underside of the deck, allowing skaters greater maneuverability on their boards.*

Bottom right: *This DK 51 model is similar to the DK 38, though wider at fifty-one millimeters. Different wheel sizes gave riders greater choice depending on their ability and riding style.*

THE RISE AND FALL OF THE LEGEND OF DOGTOWN

SKIP ENGBLOM

Over the years, people have had the misconception that I am a surfboard shaper. I am not. I'm a surfboard builder. Shaping requires a certain discipline and takes a certain personality and ego because you put your name on everything. I don't want to do that. I just want to work on the boards, go home, and go to the beach. I'm a surfboard builder, a craftsman.

That may not seem significant, but it shapes my story and defines the beginnings of my role in what would become the Dogtown legend. It was January 1970. I had been hearing about Jeff Ho, but I didn't know him. A huge weather system came through California and rained out everything, and the parking lot at Bay Street in Santa Monica was under two feet of water. I was in my '49 Cadillac with Craig Stecyk, the photographer, artist, and skater extraordinaire. Craig looked at me and said, "That's the guy, Jeff Ho—you should go into business with him." At that time, Jeff was living in this '48 Chevrolet panel truck.

So I walked across the flooded parking lot, jumped onto Jeff's vehicle, and freaked him out. I said, "That guy next to me said that you need a surfboard factory and that we should go into business together. My name is Skip." He said, "Yeah, I know

who you are. Well, if you could find a factory today, we'll go into business together." We both climbed through the back window of my Cadillac and drove up to West Los Angeles. We turned on Armacost Avenue and saw a For Rent sign. I looked at Jeff and said, "What do you think?" We rented the building for $250 a month. We shook hands and that was how it started. He and I, we weren't friends. We didn't even know each other, and an hour after we met, we went into business together.

Now we were making Jeff Ho's surfboards, and we decided to make a cheap label. I came up with the name Zephyr, and it turned out that the cheap surfboards became high-performance ones by reducing some of the production steps. The changes made the boards lighter, and they worked better overall. Jeff designed the boards, I built the boards, and Craig brought an artistic sensibility and the ability to shoot photos and put together ads. It was a three-legged table: everybody was good at something. I didn't want to be the head guy, Jeff wanted his

C. R. Stecyk captures the early days of the Zephyr skate team in this group photo from 1975.

name on it, and that was good with Craig and me. I just wanted to make some stuff, and Craig looked at it like a great art studio.

Our factory location in West Los Angeles was going well enough, and we had Select Surf Shop in San Diego with its three shops. The owner of Select called and said that his Santa Monica location was closing and asked if we would be interested in looking at it. Since we had a cash influx from working part-time for Blue Cheer, another surfboard factory, we had the funds to consider his proposition.

No wonder the owner wanted to close the shop. It was in complete disrepair. There was not only lots of work to do to get it into shape but also 100 percent of the existing employees had to be replaced.

On January 1, 1971, at 12:01 a.m., Craig and I opened a bottle of Brew 102, put "Green Onions" by Booker T & the M.G.'s blasting on the turntable, and then closed the door and left. That next day, all the kids in the neighborhood started to hang out at the shop. Craig came up with the name "Dogtown" to describe the neighborhood, a rough patch in Santa Monica southwest of Lincoln Boulevard between Pico and Rose where the kids surfed at the ruins of the Pacific Ocean Park pier, or POP as they called it.

The big letters on the outside of the building read Jeff Ho Surfboards, and the small letters underneath read Zephyr Productions. When urethane wheels came out, these young surfers discovered that they could use skateboards to mimic surfing, and the Zephyr surf team transitioned into the skate

Top: *The Zephyr skate team, known as the Z-Boys, made its competition debut at the Bahne-Cadillac Del Mar Nationals, held in Del Mar, California, in 1975. Team members Peggy Oki, Jay Adams, and Tony Alva all won or placed in freestyle contests, which were skated on the course pictured here.*

Above: *In 1975, Jay Adams, the youngest member of the Zephyr skate team, placed second in junior men's freestyle at the Bahne-Cadillac Del Mar Nationals. A year later, he was skating for a new team and had his own signature skate deck, shown here, made by Z-Flex.*

team. We had the perfect subjects—Jay Adams, Tony Alva, and Stacy Peralta—three uniquely weird people who approached things three different ways. We also had Bob Biniak, Wentzel Ruml, and Peggy Oki.

Tony Alva was one of the most elegant, effortless skaters. It looked like he was still moving through time and space when other people were glued to the earth. Stacy Peralta was very smooth. His vertical performances are often discounted because he made them look so easy. Jay Adams had this internal gyroscope that was so different from everybody else's. He was computing equations in his head on how to get to a place in the terrain that other people hadn't even thought about.

And then the Del Mar skating competition happened, and the legend began. I had the entries for the Zephyr team, and I threw them on the sign-in table and said, "Here's our money; here are our entries; we want our trophies, now." People ask how I had the confidence to have that attitude with an unproven

During the severe California drought of the mid-1970s, former Zephyr team member Stacy Peralta skates in an empty swimming pool in Coldwater Canyon in this 1977 photo by Hugh Holland.

team, but back in the day, you developed a really thick skin. These were our opponents; these weren't our friends.

Not only did we have great skateboarders with swagger, but we also had Craig Stecyk, who could take incredible photographs and write articles about our skaters and make them rock stars. Every machine needs propaganda. Now you have a lot of young people who are rock stars.

But it all went south quickly. Suddenly, Zephyr becomes Z-Flex. Generosity is one of the greatest tools you can ever employ. The more you give away, the more is returned to you. I told Jeff Ho, "If you want to maintain this situation, to begin with we need to pay Stacy, Jay, and Tony. Because we're not doing that, they're doing other stuff."

Jay Adams and some of the guys went off with Kent Sherwood. Stacy was loyal and stayed with us. Tony Alva decided to create his own company called Alva Skates, but he first went to Logan. The reality is, it wasn't that we hated one another. It got white hot, and then people went in different directions in a matter of months. And there it is, the rise and fall of the Legend of Dogtown.

Right: *C. R. Stecyk's graffiti Dogtown Cross tag, photographed here by Stecyk ca. 1974, quickly became an iconic skateboard graphic.*

Below: *Founders (from left) Skip Engblom, C. R. Stecyk, and Jeff Ho are seen near their Jeff Ho Surfboards and Zephyr Productions shop in Santa Monica, California, in this 1974 photo by Anthony Friedkin. Their Zephyr surf team would soon spawn a highly competitive Zephyr skate team.*

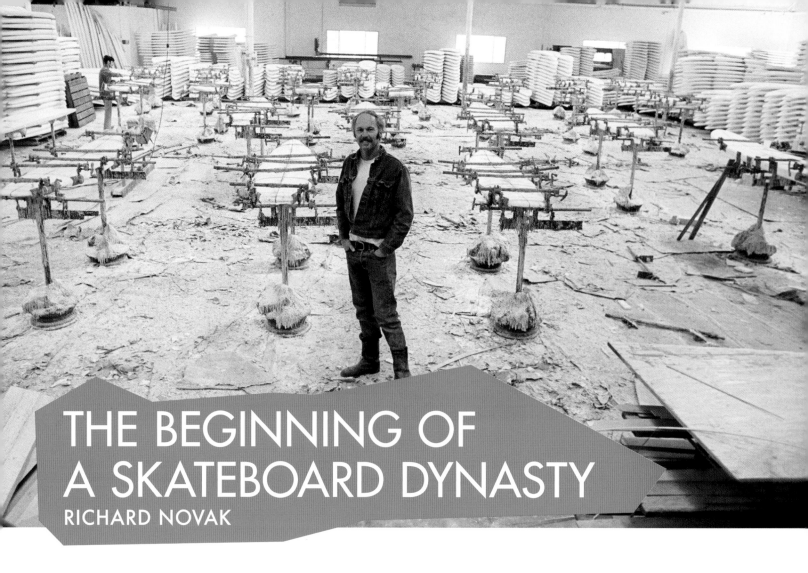

THE BEGINNING OF A SKATEBOARD DYNASTY
RICHARD NOVAK

If you surfed in the 1950s, when the waves were not cooperating, you skateboarded. Everyone who surfed had a two-by-four with roller skate wheels and trucks nailed to the bottom. As we got older—fifteen and sixteen—we tried to emulate surfing moves on a skateboard. The surfboards at that time weighed about forty pounds, so we weren't doing the maneuvers that you see on waves now. We were just hanging on to ride the wave. The skateboards were so rudimentary that when you tried to emulate a surf move on one, it usually ended in sidewalk disaster.

I started working in surf shops in Santa Cruz around 1957. We were working with a lot of composites, mostly reinforced plastics, foam, resin, and fiberglass, that people making surfboards weren't using at the time. When I would go down south with the older guys from the surf shop to surf, they would usually dump me off somewhere because they wanted to go out and drink, and I was underage. They would leave me in Laguna Beach with this guy named Gordon "Grubby" Clark.

Grubby happened to work with Hobart "Hobie" Alter, and they were experimenting with foam for a lightweight surfboard core, which they then wrapped in fiberglass and resin. Grubby was a physicist, and he realized I had an aptitude for math and figuring out how to build things. He started teaching me about chemicals. Ester-based polyurethane foam is what forms the core of a surfboard, and ether-based polyurethane was used

for skateboard wheels. The chemicals for surfboard cores and skateboard wheels have the same urethane base.

By the early 1970s, my fallback job was making surfboards. I had the knowledge from Grubby, so I pulled a couple of strings to get into the surfboard business. Grubby let me have the distribution for his Clark Foam surfboard blanks (uncut foam slabs before shaping and finishing) in Northern California. I did the experimental work for a surfboard resin called Shamrock 6908, and some friends and I decided to start a reinforced plastics company. We sold raw materials to people who built sailboats, race cars, fairings, agriculture tomato carriers—anything made with fiberglass. Buyers called in the orders, we'd deliver the raw materials in the morning, and then we surfed the rest of the day. It was a really cool job, but it was a low-margin business with a lot of five-dollar weeks, and my partner, Jay Shuirman, had a wife and two kids. We would pay everybody out first, and then we'd pay ourselves with what was left. We ran a double payroll deal: one of us would work and the other would collect unemployment, and when unemployment ran out, we'd switch roles. We kept bouncing back and forth in this tough business, but it just wasn't working for us. So finally,

Gordon "Grubby" Clark stands in his Clark Foam manufacturing warehouse in the mid-1970s. Beginning in 1961, Clark Foam dominated the surfboard blank market until its closure in 2005.

in 1973, Jay and I and another friend of ours, Doug Haut, formed the NHS Corporation (from the first letters of our surnames, Novak, Haut, and Shuirman).

We sold a guy a bunch of pultruded fiberglass sheet material who burned us by not paying for it, so we went back and picked it all up from him. At the same time, our friend Jimmy Hoffman was living in Hawaii, and while we were on a surf trip over there, the McCully bike shop people in Honolulu asked us if we could make and sell them some skateboards. We were making surfboard fins at the time, so it was easy for us to make some skateboard decks from all the leftover fiberglass material. We made five hundred skateboards with loose ball bearings, urethane roller-skate wheels, and roller-skate trucks, and they sold out immediately. We built another five hundred boards, and they sold out too. Overnight we were in the skateboard business.

Then, in late 1974, a guy named Tony Roderick came into our surf shop with the revolutionary idea of blending a precision bearing, used in copy machines, with a urethane wheel. He had originally walked into the O'Neill Surf Shop, which was nearby, and the people there told him to walk down the street to our shop. We liked Tony's concept, and we helped him tweak the wheel design so it would work specifically for skateboarding. That collaboration spawned the Road Rider wheel with precision bearings, an innovation that changed skateboarding forever.

But we had a problem. Precision bearings were very expensive—too expensive to use in skateboard wheels. So I started digging around inside old electric motors, as that was where precision bearings were used the most. I found out that the 608 bearing, which was a mass-produced size and style, usually had a 10 percent rejection rate because of noise deficiency within electric motors. I called up the IKS bearing company and told them I had a need for their noise-rejected bearings. We negotiated a bit, and I was able to get the price down from eighty cents to about ten or fifteen cents for each bearing.

With that settled, the plan started to come together in my head. Jay and I were able to double the price of a skateboard wheel because it was so innovative and it worked better than anything on the market. Our next hurdle was the seven-millimeter axle size on roller-skate trucks, which didn't work with our eight-millimeter 608 bearing. We knew we weren't going to get the roller-skating industry to change its axle size, so we started making little metal adapter sleeves for the bearings that would

Above left: *Hobart "Hobie" Alter is shown shaping a balsa wood surfboard in the early 1950s. Before the end of the decade, he would join forces with Grubby Clark to pioneer the high-performance foam-and-fiberglass surfboard. By the early 1960s, Hobie was marketing the wildly popular Hobie skateboards and sponsoring a skate team.*

Above right: *Richard Novak, founder of NHS, skating in 1977.*

fit on the axle and make it work properly. We finally had the Road Rider urethane wheel with precision bearings, and everyone wanted them. Tony took the East Coast and Jay and I took the West Coast, and we just started selling the shit out of them.

At about the same time, Ron Bennett had developed the Bennett truck and G&S had the Fibreflex deck. We all ran into one another in Los Angeles in 1975 at the Hang Ten contest and said, "Okay, we have actual skateboard wheels and bearings. We have actual skateboard trucks. We have composite skateboard decks. The three main components are now all leading edge and designed specifically for skateboarding. We don't need to rely on the roller skate business for trucks or wheels. Now we have a real skateboarding industry." The group was made up of Bill Bahne, Jay Shuirman, Brian Logan, Dave McIntyre, Dave Dominy, Paul Sims, Ron Bennett, a couple of guys from *Skate-Boarder* magazine, and me. We were interested in setting the foundation of an actual skateboard industry—one that wasn't reliant on anyone but ourselves. We wanted to support pro riders, promotion, and advancement in technology. Before that, skateboarding was just a fad. After we set it all up, it was an actual industry.

We started exploding on the world. In England, Alpine Sports wanted to get into skateboarding and to sell our boards there. It was G&S skateboards, NHS, Sims, and Bennett. Jay and I knew

that if we got to England, it was only a matter of time before we went on to Europe and Japan.

We started working on margins. We needed the retail shops to make money. We needed the distributors to make money. We needed the skaters to make money. We needed money for marketing and advertising. We needed all of this money up and down the distribution chain for it to work. And we knew we'd need, at a minimum, 30 percent at the manufacturing level. I got all of this margin knowledge from Grubby Clark.

I think it was the first time that I saw success at the end of the rainbow. Building surfboards was a means to do something I liked. Building sailboats was the thing that got me access to sailing when I wanted. But I liked skateboarding. I thought it was really fun. It was dealing with kids—kids were exciting, kids were unpredictable. And kids were unbelievable athletes too. So, with NHS, it's been forty-nine years. Actually, it's been fifty-three years. We started the company in 1969, but we didn't have enough money to file for incorporation until 1973.

Open ball bearings in skateboard wheels tended to fall out and severely hamper the skater's ability to roll. The use of closed precision bearings in skateboard wheels, pioneered by NHS Inc. in 1974, changed skateboard wheels forever. This detail of a Road Rider 4 wheel dates from the earliest production days of NHS.

FROM BLACK HILL TO SIGNAL HILL

JANE ROGERS

The Black Hill in La Costa, California, is synonymous with the early, innovative days of skateboarding. Skaters took to the freshly paved thing of beauty every weekend to try out their new equipment. Tracker trucks were born here, as were innovations to skateboard design and construction, with an endless line of new products from Cadillac Wheels, Bahne, and Logan Earth Ski, to name a few. Superstars like Ellen Berryman, Kim Cespedes, Henry Hester, Gregg Weaver, and the Logans raced every Sunday, honing their skills, testing new product, and showing off for the crowd.

Di Dootson and Peggy Turner, the wife of SummerSki designer Bobby Turner, began the first grassroots publication in skateboarding. The *National Skateboard Review*, or *NSR* as it was known, was a four- to six-page monthly newsletter with photographs, race results, interviews with local talent, skateboarding tips, and safety lessons. Dootson invited skaters from across the country to send in skatepark news, legislation news, pro gossip—basically anything related to skate that was fit to print. Advertisers, which included some of the biggest names in skateboarding, would get one hundred copies to mail out with shipments to retailers, spreading the word of skateboarding across the country.

While all of this was happening at La Costa, just two hours up I-5 was another hill that was getting some skateboarding action. Signal Hill, just outside of Long Beach, California, was the site of a sort of precursor to the X Games, a 1975 competition to set the land speed record on a skateboard. Organized by Jim O'Mahoney, after being contacted by the ABC television series *Wide World of Entertainment* for a "David Frost Presents the Guinness Book of World Records" episode, and hosted by the United States Skateboard Association, this competition would be held on a thirty-degree-incline hill known as Signal Hill. O'Mahoney contacted local surfer Guy "Grundy" Spagnoli and asked if he wanted to give it a try. Knowing the steep hill, Grundy arrived on race day wearing a head-to-toe leather jumpsuit and a helmet. Most of the other competitors showed up in shorts and T-shirts. All of those brave but clever souls except one opted out. Garrison Hitchcock fell about a third of the way down the hill and dislocated his shoulder, leaving Spagnoli to finish the race and set the land speed record at 50.2 miles per hour.

The Vetter Streamliner skate car was designed and built within three months. The pilot would lie face down on the board, with arms forward to steer. Next, the top of the car would be lowered over the pilot and locked in place, and then gravity would do the rest.

The event was so successful that it was held annually for the next four years, and while the atmosphere was part keg party, part death-defying runs, the technological advancements to equipment and safety gear over these years were invaluable to the development of the sport. It saw the advent of the skate car, which proved more dangerous than the downhill boards due to the construction methodology, lack of steering, and, more importantly, lack of braking at very high speeds. The street luge was introduced and would become popular again in the late 1990s with its inclusion in the X Games.

After countless injuries, gnarly accidents, and near-death experiences, the Signal Hill Runs were stopped in 1979. Skateboarding was to see its second decline until it picked back up again in the early to mid-1980s with the new genre of vert. And while those early skaters sacrificed many Sundays on both hills to further the sport, they wouldn't have missed those rides for the world.

Top: *In this photo by Warren Bolster, a downhill racer skates at Black Hill in La Costa, California, ca. 1975. The low, bent-knee stance and outstretched arms increased speed and lowered wind resistance.*

Above: *This 1975 downhill skateboard, with Bennett trucks, Stoker wheels, and an unidentified deck, was used by local surfer Guy "Grundy" Spagnoli to set the first recorded Guinness Book land speed record on a skateboard, clocking in at 50.2 miles per hour. He wore this helmet on Signal Hill during the first downhill skateboard contest hosted by the United States Skateboard Association in 1975. Spagnoli was the only racer to show up with safety equipment, and all but one other contestant pulled out of the race after seeing how steep the hill was.*

MAGAZINES, CATALOGS, AND SKATEPARKS

BRYAN RIDGEWAY

One word epitomized the reach of skateboarding in the 1970s: magazines. There were three major publications, *SkateBoarder*, *Wild World of Skateboarding*, and *Skateboard World*. Nick's News Stand and Falcon, our local Huntington, West Virginia, skate shop, had all three, and we would buy them one at a time and share. We would then sit in the shop and read the magazines, and if we saw anybody buy one, that was it. "What are you up to? Come on over. Yeah, okay. And uhhh, bring that magazine too." It's probably how I got on the Falcon skate shop team. It was kind of a time-honored tradition to hang out in the local skate shop and learn what was going on.

It was all skatepark skating, equipment, and mail-order ads in those magazines. We were able to see the skateboard setups, how cool everything looked as a complete. Obviously, you could order anything you wanted, but you wanted to order the way it looked in the photos. The mail-order catalogs were another way we found the setups we wanted. Val Surf and Kanoa Surf were the main mail-order companies. It was like being in a candy store. People ordered different things from the catalogs, and when they showed up at the local skatepark, which was also called Falcon, their identity as a skater was defined by the brands and products they were riding. It was super cool.

I was a Hobie guy back then. Other people aligned themselves with Alva or Kryptonics. We all had the Kryptonics P-Tex and tried to use them as snowboards. Then Powell-Peralta came out. A skater (Jeff Cable) from Charleston, West Virginia, had a Powell-Peralta Brite-Lite or Beamer, which was the first time we'd seen a painted Day-Glo deck. Powell-Peralta hadn't started advertising much in the magazines yet, and magazines and catalogs were all we saw. I got a Brite-Lite and stayed on Powell-Peralta products for the next decade.

Next, I found out about Apple Skatepark in Columbus, Ohio, which was about three hours from my hometown. It was the best. The year was probably 1980. My dad took a small group of us up there, and after that, other parents in our group would take turns driving us once every three or four months. Then my friend Rick Summerfield got a car when we were in our senior year in high school. My mom didn't want me driving all the way to Columbus with him because he was only sixteen or seventeen, so I would buy a seven-dollar bus ticket to the next town, and he would pick me up there and we would drive together the rest of

In this 1981 photo, Bryan Ridgeway does a fakie foot plant at the homemade Crestmont skate ramp in Huntington, West Virginia.

the way. Falcon Skatepark eventually went out of business, but we would hop the fence and skate the abandoned park. We did whatever it took to skate until we could afford to go to Columbus again. Apple Skatepark also had some overnighters. You could skate all night long, there was music, and then you could sleep in sleeping bags in the pro shop and the main office.

One of the keys to progressing was seeing other people skate. We always wondered how people were doing the things we saw in the magazines. We could never figure tricks out from flat, static photographs: How did they get into that position? How was the speed generated? Apple Skatepark made the live version possible. We could immediately visualize how things could be done. And then we fed off and pushed one another and skated together, always trying new stuff.

Going to that park and knowing what the possibilities were and understanding how the flow happened—that was the beginning of our progressing. Then the next level was the local skaters. Those guys were on par with skaters in California; there were three or four who were supergood. Around 1983, Skateboard Hall of Fame pro Eddie Elguera declared, "Yeah, that's my favorite, smoothest park and has some rad skaters too!" California was the gold standard, and it was in our blood to try to get there, but when California skaters visited us, that was important too.

Back in 1982 and 1983, Steve "Cab" Caballero, Duane "M.O.D." Peters, Steve Olson, then Allen Losi, Freddie DeSota, and Dave Andrecht all came through, along with East Coast rippers Bobby Reeves and Jami Godfrey. We had them up on pedestals, and then they came and skated with us. Skateboarding has always been like that; we just didn't know it. They're like, "Yeah, we're pros, but let's go have some of those slushies and play video games in the pro shop." We were like, "With us? You want to hang with us? All right." Then we realized how skateboarding was. It was low-key and a unique family.

Everyone came to skate Apple. If you lived in Columbus, you could skate it all the time, but you had to pay, and that was tight for a lot of people. In California, you had to pay, but you could skate pretty much every day because of the great weather. It was natural for the California skaters to be better because they had more opportunities to skate. But Apple's indoor facility was helping Midwest and East Coast skaters progress more quickly because of the access now possible without worry of weather. The opportunity to skate 365 days a year in Columbus was leveling the playing field.

Falcon Skatepark in Huntington, West Virginia, was built in 1978 and was popular with skaters until its closing in 1980. Skaters seeking places to skate in the 1980s were often forced to "trespass," like Bryan Ridgeway did, seen here skating the abandoned, rundown Falcon in 1984.

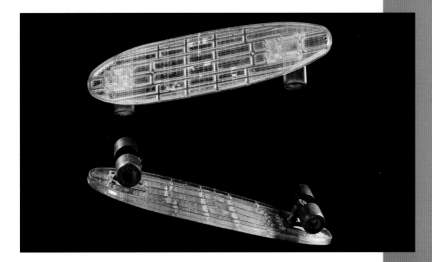

PUSHING ACROSS AMERICA

My first skateboard had steel wheels; my second had clay wheels. In the summer of 1974, I discovered Cadillac urethane wheels. My life changed. I competed at the Del Mar Nationals in 1975, where the Z-Boys had their coming-out party. I was a witness to skateboarding history. I just didn't know it at the time.

In 1976, I was nineteen years old and working at the local newspaper, skating every day, and hanging with my friends while trying to figure out what was next. Turns out "next" was pushing our skateboards across America. We sent a handwritten letter to Roller Sports that landed us an offer for all the gear we needed plus $500 each, but only if we made it.

Jeff French and Mike Filben were my teammates. Our route began in Lebanon, Oregon, and ended in Williamsburg, Virginia. Jeff's 1969 Pontiac Firebird was our support vehicle. Mike and I rode Lexan boards, Jeff's was fiberglass, and all were equipped with Chicago trucks and Stoker wheels. We came up with something we called the "leapfrog" relay system: Skater A would begin skating, the support car would drive three miles ahead and park, and then Skater B would begin skating. When Skater A arrived at the support vehicle, it would drive another three miles ahead and stop. Skater C would then begin skating. We were able to cover about one hundred miles per day, with each skater pushing thirty to forty miles.

We pushed across a desert, over the Rockies, and through the Great Plains. A ferry took us across Lake Michigan. The Appalachians seemed to never end. People would stop us on the road to ask what we were doing; some had never seen a skateboard before. Once in a while, people in cars yelled at us. Some called us hippies. Others invited us to stay in their homes.

Thirty-two days and three thousand miles later, we finished. Dana Hafke from Roller Sports handed us each $500. We had never seen that much money before; we thought we were rich. Years later, we would come to understand that we had become rich that summer not from our financial reward, which was soon gone, but from the experiences we shared during the first crossing of America by skateboard.

—*Jack Smith*

Top: Mike Filben, part of the 1976 skate across America team, does his leg in the "leapfrog" relay system somewhere in Ohio. (Middle) This Proline model skateboard, made by Roller Sports Inc. in 1976, was used by Jack Smith and his team. (Above) Team members (from left) Jeff French, Jack Smith, and Mike Filben paused for a group photo in Reed City, Michigan.

MY FIRST SKATEBOARD

TONY HAWK

My first skateboard did not seem like a monumental gift, but it eventually came to define me in almost every way. It was a hand-me-down from my older brother; he was a surfer and rode skateboards when the waves were flat. He taught me how to stand up on the board, push for speed, and make turns. By the time I got comfortable using it as transportation around my San Diego neighborhood, he was in college and rarely skating himself. Skateboarding had become a short-lived fad in the late 1970s, so some of my friends had also started skating.

Around the same time, I heard about a designated skating facility in my town called Oasis Skatepark. It sounded exciting and intimidating, and I had to check it out. On my first visit, I saw experienced skaters literally flying out of empty swimming pools, and I was inspired beyond words. I decided right then that I wanted to fly like them, and I would do whatever it took to get there. The first step: upgrading my gear.

My dad took me to a swap meet and bought me a generic deck that looked similar to a Dave Andrecht (a local pro) Sims model. It was way too big for my ten-year-old feet and heavier than most other skateboards at the time—and I loved it. I skated as much as possible, getting rides to the skatepark from my dad, mutual friends, and occasionally my brother who had introduced me to this obsession. Through broken teeth and a few concussions, I eventually learned to fly like those I had hoped to emulate.

Skateboarding became my identity. I loved the misfits who were drawn to it and the culture—music, fashion, style—that surrounded it. But mostly I loved the boundless creativity that it provided. Skateboarding is both an individual pursuit to be embraced in your own style and a community of people with a strong sense of camaraderie like nothing else I have experienced. We push one another to meet our private challenges and feed off one another's successes.

I have ridden hundreds—if not thousands—of skateboards over the past four decades and have lost, broken, or given away most of them. I lost others to theft and some to a housefire. Somehow this first board stayed with me, as if it knew of its importance more than I did. I never imagined that it would be considered an item of great value or significance, so I was shocked and honored when the Smithsonian offered to take it and put it on display. But I had to ask my brother first, as it was his to begin with. His reaction was immediate and astute: "That's where I always thought it belonged."

Tony (left) and Steve Hawk stand outside of the Smithsonian's National Museum of American History with Tony's skateboard after donating it to the Smithsonian collections. Notice the white gloves both are wearing to handle the now museum object.

Right: *Tony Hawk learned to skate on this 1977 Bahne skateboard, a hand-me-down from his brother, Steve.*

Below: *In 2013, Tony Hawk rode his 1977 Bahne skateboard for the last time on a mini ramp outside of the Smithsonian's National Museum of American History.*

CARVING A PATH IN SKATEBOARDING

JUDI OYAMA

I started skating when I was thirteen years old, but I bought my first skateboard in 1975 when I was fifteen. I went in on it with my brother for $21.95 at the O'Neill Surf Shop in Capitola, near Santa Cruz. It was a fiberglass Bahne skateboard with Cadillac wheels, which were still loose ball bearings, and Cadillac trucks. My brother used to threaten that he would sell his half if I didn't help do chores. I used to like surfer magazines and seeing people skateboarding and surfing. I knew my brother wanted skate, so I wanted to learn. Then I wanted to be better than he was, and that motivated me. In the mid-1970s, it was all guys in the magazines, but then I started to see more women, like Desiree Von Essen and Kim Cespedes. Seeing other girls skate inspired me to ride more and more.

My first contest was a slalom race down a hill in Capitola in 1975 when I wasn't sponsored yet. I crashed going down, and you can see scrapes and Band-Aids on me in the pictures that my dad took that day. I came in second to another woman, though there were only three women racing. I really enjoyed slalom racing, and that's when I was able to ride with some of the people who rode for Santa Cruz, such as John Hutson. I got more and more into slalom racing, which I still enjoy.

When I was sixteen, I was introduced to Richard Novak and Jay Shuirman of NHS, and I wanted to ride for their NHS skate team. They had a bank in back of the original NHS warehouse, so I had to skate in front of them on this bank, and then they sponsored me. Being sponsored at that point meant getting all the equipment you needed. When NHS first started producing Independent trucks with Fausto Vitello and Eric Swenson, I became one of the first women sponsored by Independent. There were only a handful of sponsored women at the time, like Terry Brown, Teri (now Terry) Lawrence, and Cara-Beth Burnside. Cindy Whitehead, a pro vert skater from Southern California, and I built a bond through skateboarding.

Most of the time, Southern California skaters would go in, skate, and all the photographers would take pictures. Then when it was the Northern California skaters' turn, all the photographers would leave and we would skate. The whole NorCal-SoCal divide was frustrating. From my perspective, all the magazines focused on Southern California skating. The photographers and a lot of the companies associated with the magazines were based in the south. Because of this, unless you lived in Southern California or were friends with the photographer, you never got in the magazines. So many people look at the magazines and say

Judi Oyama skates at the Capitola Classic, an annual Northern California downhill race, in 1980.

Right: In 1978, photographer John Krisik took this Judi Oyama publicity still for Santa Cruz Skateboards at Winchester Skatepark in San Jose, California. Oyama was one of the few girls sponsored by Santa Cruz at the time.

Below: Oyama was awarded this trophy at a skateboarding competition in Berkeley, California, in 1979. Although women had been competing in contests since the 1960s, the trophies did not account for female participation, as the male figure on the top of this trophy demonstrates.

Dogtown is where skateboarding started, but it really started all over the world. In the United States, there were skaters in Florida, Arizona, Oregon, Washington, and more, but they didn't get the coverage. Although the history is there in everyone's Polaroids and photo albums, from the viewpoint of the media, it looks like it was only Southern California.

By 1978, I thought I could make a living skateboarding. And I did for a little while in the Skateboard Mania tour. It was kind of like the Ice Follies of skateboarding. We had to wear costumes designed by the people behind *H.R. Pufnstuf,* a Saturday morning kids' television show with weird characters in over-the-top costumes. There were six women and thirteen men involved with the production. Tony Alva and Steve Olson auditioned for a part, but didn't get in as the production team was only interested in skaters they could control and who would listen to instructions.

Paramount Studios had a choreographer and $100,000 worth of plexiglass ramps. They would do Toyota commercials during the day, so we would start at five and practice until midnight. We skated with music and choreography to a story about earthlings and aliens. The pay was $300 a week plus food and lodging. Unfortunately, due to some unforeseen circumstances with the tour management, the tour never got off the ground, and the practicing was all a waste.

After that, it was hard for me as a woman to earn money in skating because there were no women's skateboarding events or races. I started working at a surf shop that Richard Novak owned. I managed it, did the window displays, and designed T-shirts and graphics. People would come in asking for skateboards for their sons or daughters, but they wouldn't want my help. They wanted to speak to one of the guys. Eventually that changed because they knew me from being in the business and designing products for NHS. I met Bob Hurley, who at the time ran Billabong clothing. This was before he even started Hurley. He liked my designs, and I flew down to Billabong with a whole proposal for skateboard ads and T-shirts. I got a one-year contract and walked out with a check to start my own business. I helped jump the one-year wait to get their ads in *Thrasher.* Work for Sessions clothing company followed. And so I established a design career in the action sports. In a roundabout way, I achieved my goal of working in skateboarding. But women like me always had to fight to be seen.

SO YOU WANT TO COLLECT A SKATEBOARD?

The number one question people ask me as a curator is, "How do you choose the objects that come into the collections?" One might think that the Smithsonian has endless resources and limitless space for collections, but it's not that simple. When the Smithsonian accepts an object for donation, it is kept in perpetuity, which involves creating a designated spot in our storage areas, determining conservation needs—especially when exhibiting or loaning the object—and allocating staff resources to catalog, conserve, rehouse, and interpret the item. And what all that means is that we collect quality versus quantity. The most important factor in deciding what objects to choose for the collections is that they tell a compelling story. As a curator of the sports collections with an emphasis on action sports, skateboarding is one of my areas of expertise.

So when William Conner Jr. offered his Chris Strople model Caster skateboard, I was intrigued. To date, the collections did not have any objects from pro skater Chris Strople or an example of a Caster board, and while the museum does not strive to collect something from every skater or every model board as a Hall of Fame might, we do like to have a wide array of brands to tell as complete a story of skateboarding as we can.

What sold me on the Caster board was the Conner family story surrounding it. When Conner Jr. began skating, his dad, William Sr., took an interest in the sport. William Sr. then built himself a skateboard and began skating at the age of fifty-three. After Conner Jr. turned pro at fourteen, skating for B&L Skateboard Shop in Norfolk, Virginia, he decided to buy his dad a "real" skateboard. On Father's Day in the mid-1970s, he presented his dad this Chris Strople pro model Caster skateboard with yellow G&S YoYo Pro wheels, Tracker trucks, and black griptape with a CASTER cutout on the top surface of the board. Conner Sr. rode the board for years. Fast-forward to the mid-2010s and Conner Jr.'s son, Jack, wanted to learn how to ride a skateboard, so the Caster board was fished out of the garage, and Jack learned to ride on his grandfather's skateboard.

The multigenerational appeal of skateboarding is fully encompassed in this one object. Objects like this are what we strive to collect. It not only tells the history of the Conner family's love of skateboarding but also manufacturing history, technological innovations, ageism, and the impact skateboarding has had on the American narrative.

—*Jane Rogers*

Top: *William Conner Jr., who rode for the B&L Skateboard Shop skate team, is seen here skating at Flo-Motion Skatepark in Richmond, Virginia, in the mid-1970s.*

Above: *William Conner Jr. and his son, Jack, stand outside of the Smithsonian's National Museum of American History before donating their family's Caster skateboard to the museum. Notice the No Skateboarding sign that adorns the grounds of all Smithsonian museums.*

This mid-1970s Chris Strople model Caster skateboard with Tracker Midtrack trucks and YoYo wheels, which William Conner Jr. gave to his dad, William Sr., for Father's Day, became the ultimate hand-me-down in the Conner family, demonstrating the strong generational appeal of skateboarding. After the Caster board was donated, the Conner family found the protective gear William Conner Sr. wore when he learned to skate while in his fifties. The helmet, gloves, and kneepads were added to the collection as another aspect of his skate story—evidence that he was safety-conscious. They also give us an idea of what a skater of that era would have worn, adding to our understanding of our material culture.

Within the blueprint image, the following labels are visible:

Skaters Center

Mogul Maze

Team Booths under
Cap 770

Free Style #1

Winners Circle

Free Style #2

N

SITE PLAN
CARLSBAD SKA
PALOMAR AIRPORT
CARLSBAD, CA.
Drawn by: Jack
Skatepark Const
1251 N Vulcan, Leu
714-753-9629

THE BEGINNINGS: CARLSBAD SKATEPARK

JOHN O'MALLEY

To get to the nitty-gritty on how Carlsbad Skatepark was made is to know my partner, Jack Graham. Jack was a mechanical genius, a visionary, an inventor. He was also my neighbor. Jack got it into his head that he could build a skatepark. At this phase of his life, he had turned himself into a grading contractor. He had the wherewithal to build a park already in hand, but he had no idea how it worked, so he asked around to find the best skateboarder in our area. He asked the guys who lived with me, and they all said the same thing, "Talk to John." So he comes walking up one day and goes, "John, they say you're the best skateboarder around." Blissfully unaware that I lived around the corner from Bruce Logan and Gregg Weaver, I'm like, "Yes, I'm the guy."

It's so funny how clueless you can be. This was still the early days, just after the Del Mar contest in the fall of 1975. Jack had seen something on TV about kids getting thrown out of a parking garage for skating. He thought that if there were a place for them to skate, they'd spend money to do it. I said, "They absolutely would. I know exactly what it should look like." We were off to the races.

Then it was all logistics. Jack had a dodgy piece of real estate that he had bought, and it looked like it would be perfect. But it had a big ravine going through it and was in a bad location.

Then we went to the Carlsbad Raceway, which already had a zoning variance for dangerous stuff, like a drag strip and moto-cross. The raceway people were happy to have the skatepark because it was quiet, and they didn't think it could be any more dangerous than a drag strip.

The blueprint we drew up was based on using the natural terrain to generate a natural design. It showed a long canyon reminiscent of a shallow, little California arroyo, meaning it was one hundred feet deep. We deliberately made it vague. We didn't really know what we were going to build there, so the blueprint was more like a site plan with a theoretical design. First we made the beginner's area, next we made a mogul area, and then the market turned and we stopped.

But we did get a lot of it done. At the top, there was a designated mogul area. Next came a dual slalom that looked like a U. A freestyle area was inside the curve of the U.

We had a strong tailwind, and the park was built quickly. In the beginner's area, we threw in some bank turns and followed

These are the original blueprints for California's first skatepark, located in Carlsbad. The success that John O'Malley and Jack Graham found from creating this park, which opened in 1976, led to the creation of many others in the few short years that skateparks were viable.

CARLSBAD SKATEPARK.

the terrain. After that, Jack's view of things held the designs down a bit. He had some conservative, dated ideas of what the banks should be. He wanted two feet, but I would have started at four or five feet. In the end, it did ride very well.

The primordial soup of it was that there were no skateparks, and then a couple days later, here was Carlsbad. There's a famous photo of myself, Lance Smith, and one of the workers riding it on the first day. Photographer Warren Bolster followed his gut and showed up just as we were about to ride. It was really kismet.

Top: *Photographer Warren Bolster was present at the inaugural skate at Carlsbad Skatepark in Carlsbad, California, where he caught (from left) Lance Smith, John O'Malley, and Kingfish in motion.*

Above: *This distinctive logo for Carlsbad Skatepark was created ca. 1975.*

I still have an original copy of the business card, which I always loved. It's old-fashioned, and the logo included a character aptly named ESPE, which is phonetic for SB, an abbreviation for skateboarding. John Breeden, an artist, developed the little animated skateboard character for us, and Jack wanted to use it throughout the park. It's unlike anything else as far as skateboarding goes, and it's a little bizarre.

We made great money. We had stiff demand, and people came from all over. Right away, Jack and I were hired as designers, and design fees were great. Then in 1979, things turned bad. The market crashed, and there were fewer skaters and less money. The recession continued to worsen, and then the skateparks lost their insurance. So that was the death knell of it. It's really heartbreaking to think that nobody has a memory of riding this park.

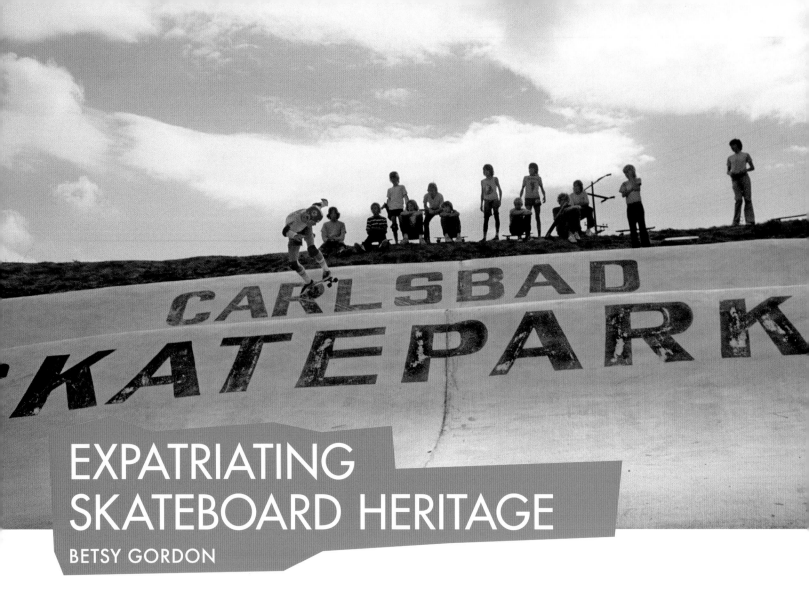

EXPATRIATING SKATEBOARD HERITAGE

BETSY GORDON

Skateboarding has always had its legendary spots, sites that have gained power and magic by being the place where the impossible trick was captured or where a legendary group of skaters congregated. They are known by skateboard shorthand: Brooklyn Banks, Pulaski, Southbank, Lyon 25. California's first skatepark, Carlsbad, was one of those spots. Opened in 1976, it closed by 1979, as the initial wave of skateparks started to decline along with the economy. Shortly after the park welcomed its last skater, the bowls were filled with dirt to flatten the topography. In the late 1980s, Bones Brigade skater Mike McGill briefly operated a wooden ramp on the site, but that also came to an end as street skating became dominant in the 1990s. For nearly two decades, the skatepark remained interred in California dust until land values in North County (a region of San Diego County) started to tick upward. In 2004, Dave Bergthold, owner of Blockhead Skateboards, heard that Carlsbad was sold for redevelopment and that the subterranean remains of the skatepark were going to be destroyed. He organized a "Save Carlsbad" campaign and enlisted the help of pro skaters and social media to rally the masses. Unfortunately, it was not enough to stall the dozers, and Carlsbad was demolished in early 2005.

Skaters flocked to the site to pick up any concrete remnants they could find. Mike Palm, guitarist for the band Agent Orange, mobilized to see what he could scavenge. He saved a small piece that was smooth on one edge, once part of the skateable surfaces that covered Carlsbad. Palm traveled across the country to personally deliver this relic to John O'Malley, one of the builders of the skatepark. O'Malley, in turn, donated it to the collections at the National Museum of American History, where it joined hundreds of other skateboard-affiliated artifacts. While O'Malley was donating his Carlsbad memorabilia to the Smithsonian, he also gave a number of smaller chunks to various friends and family, including me. It sat on my desk for many years, a combination good luck charm, paperweight, and shrine to skateboarding's history.

In 2019, I was part of a panel at the second Pushing Boarders conference in Malmö, Sweden. The topic was defining skateboard heritage through preservation efforts. Preserving skate sites is difficult. It is hard to convince local city councils that

Photographer Hugh Holland caught this group of spectators as they watched a skater at the Carlsbad Skatepark, in Carlsbad, California, in 1977.

Right: *This skate bowl is at Bryggeriets Gymnasium, a high school in Malmö, Sweden, that has skateboarding at the core of its curriculum.*

Below: *This seven-by-five-by-five-inch piece of concrete is from the Carlsbad Skatepark, which was built in 1976 and demolished in 2005.*

skateparks have historical significance, it's a challenge to wipe the stain of illegality off the minds of historic preservationists, and it is even more challenging to justify conserving land when real estate value escalates. A few skate heritage preservation campaigns have been successful, but many end up like Carlsbad.

Malmö, a coastal city in the south of Sweden, is known for its skateboard-centric view of education and city planning. Its public high school, Bryggeriets Gymnasium, uses skateboarding at the core of its curriculum. Malmö's city council employs a full-time skateboarding coordinator who facilitates the building of skateable spaces throughout the city. The city is full of skaters and skate spots that coexist without threat of demolition or arrest. I thought it would be fitting to take my little piece of Carlsbad to Sweden as a talisman and perhaps even mention it during my panel. Instead, it wound up in the possession of Gustav Eden, Malmö's skateboarding coordinator, as part of his plan for a new skate structure in Malmö.

Eden worked with a group of local Philly skaters to expatriate large portions of another sacred skate site, Philadelphia's LOVE Park, that, like Carlsbad, flickered for a brief moment before being extinguished by the forces of anti-skateboarding city planning. Eden awaits final approval from Malmö's government before incorporating tons of the site's infamous granite ledges in the Swedish version of LOVE Park, along with a little chunk of Carlsbad.

TRANS-WORLD

MAY/JUNE 1983
VOL. 1 NO. 1

$1.75

SKATEBOARDING

SKATE AND CrEATE

THE GREAT DESERT
☆ ★ RAMP BATTLE ☆ ★

DEL MAR
.... REVISITED

RUSTY HARRIS SERIES WRAP-UP 1982

COLLECTOR'S EDITION

TWO RAD CENTERFOLDS!

CHAPTER THREE

'80s

VERT, STREET, VHS, AND ZINES

The 1980s—how can you characterize a decade that gave us Krystle Carrington of *Dynasty* and Jello Biafra of the Dead Kennedys? When Ronald Reagan became president and Gordon Gekko proclaimed "Greed . . . is good" and John Lennon was murdered? The decade brought us the Rubik's Cube, Apple computers, MTV, AIDS, Prozac, the Chernobyl nuclear disaster, the fall of the Berlin Wall, and the first commercial dial-up ISP, known later as the Internet. CNN and MTV ushered in the twenty-four-hour news and entertainment cycle, while *USA Today* established an Anytown, USA, perspective for newspapers.

The decade began with high unemployment and inflation, setting off a deep economic recession. In 1987, the Dow Jones Industrial Average fell 508 points, losing 22.6 percent of its value, in a single day. The decade ended with another financial crisis, the savings and loan failures of 1989.

Skateboarding found a foothold among these societal contradictions and economic disasters and somehow managed to flourish, landing more on the Dead Kennedys side of the cultural spectrum than the *Dynasty*. It wasn't easy at first. In the early 1980s, most of America's skateparks disappeared, victims of untenable insurance premiums and diminishing attendance revenue. The closing of skateparks effectively erased the 1970s model for skaters to congregate, compete, and get paid. By

1982, all but two of the skateparks that hosted the Hester and Gold Cup Series closed. A couple of brave holdouts—Del Mar Skate Ranch and Pipeline in California—managed to stay open until the late 1980s before finally being bulldozed over for real estate development. As the new decade began, plenty of skaters wanted to continue skateboarding; they just didn't have the robust park and competition system that once nurtured them.

Many skaters, both amateur and professional, felt abandoned—orphaned even. As a result, the homemade wooden ramps still standing across America started to see increased usage and relevance. In addition, numerous skaters went back to their sidewalk roots and utilized the streets, curbs, walls, and other existing civic architecture to continue testing the limitations of four wheels on a plank of wood.

SkateBoarder magazine got thinner and thinner due to dwindling skate industry advertisers. Changing its name to *Action Now*, it added rollerblading, surfing, snowboarding, and BMX to pump up interest and ad revenue. Even with these additions, it struggled to maintain profitability and published its last issue in 1982. Rushing into the void left by the diminution of *SkateBoarder* magazine was *Thrasher* magazine, a new publication started by Independent trucks manufacturer Fausto Vitello. Based in San Francisco, *Thrasher* boasted being the first skateboard magazine with 100 percent skateboarder-produced content. Unlike the glossy full color of *SkateBoarder*, *Thrasher*'s humble debut was a mere thirty pages with black-and-white photos.

Opposite: Transworld Skateboarding *magazine debuted in 1983 with this May/June issue, with a photograph of skater Steve Caballero and the magazine's newly established motto, Skate and Create, on the cover.*

Following the format of *SkateBoarder*, *Thrasher*'s premiere issue featured contest results and a scattering of ads from skateboard distributors and manufacturers. In addition to the typical contest images, there were two photo essays extolling the virtues of non-skatepark terrain, proclaiming "skate architecture is everywhere—grind every edge," an unexpected edict that foreshadowed the decade's emergence of street skating.

The third issue introduced the "Wild Riders of Boards" (later Boardz). A precursor to the graphic novel, this essay featured cartoon-like drawings illustrating the story of two skaters, Eddy Boy and Blade, who were in a skate gang called the Zekes that liked to clash with their rival gang of skateboarders, El Vatos Bandidos De Vario X. This five-part monthly series promised "violence, sex, action galore" and helped establish *Thrasher*'s antiestablishment skater-as-outlaw aesthetic. Eight issues later, *Thrasher*'s cover said it all: "100% Aggression."

It might as well have also said "100% Male," as women began to disappear from the pages of *Thrasher*. Although the 1980s saw the first woman US Supreme Court justice, vice presidential candidate, and astronaut, women could not find significant skate-related representation in the pages of *Thrasher* unless they were provocatively selling a skate product. This not only reflected the general misogynistic and sexist attitudes prevalent toward women in the 1980s but also testified to the extreme lack of opportunities for women in the skateboard industry and community. As the skateparks closed, so did the contests they hosted. As the contests moved to backyard ramps, almost none of them included any women's divisions. As 1980s pro skater Cindy Whitehead summarized, "We were screwed!"

In response to *Thrasher*'s overt tones of anti-everything, Peggy Cozens, in partnership with Tracker Trucks cofounder Larry Balma, published *Transworld Skateboarding* magazine in 1983. In a direct rebuttal to *Thrasher*'s "Skate and Destroy" article in the December 1982 issue, Cozens writes "Skate and Create," an article questioning the destructive ethos being marketed in skateboarding. "The skate and destroy attitude makes you look un-rad and un-cool if you haven't vomited in a liquor store parking lot. That seems like a pretty limited form of self-expression."

Top: *This November 1981 cover of* Thrasher *promises "100% Aggression," announcing inside that aggression "is a bi-product" of the magazine. In this issue, readers also found tips on how to be a successful "pool mercenary," highlights from the "grueling, demanding, and intense races" at the Bellevue Open, and news of the Alabama skateboarding scene.*

Left: *After most of the skateparks closed in the late 1970s, skate competitions moved to homemade ramps. Although crude in construction, the Booney Ramp in Litchfield, Arizona, was the site of many epic competitions. Here, photographer J. Grant Brittain caught skater Neil Blender in a classic handplant at a 1984 Booney competition.*

Opposite: *In this 1986 photograph by J. Grant Brittain, Steve Caballero is seen doing a lien air over the channel at Chin Ramp in Oceanside, California. The enormous size of this skate ramp, built for Powell-Peralta for its video* The Search for Animal Chin, *required a cameraman in a helicopter to capture the skate footage.*

Hence, in the early 1980s, the 1960s template set by *Surf Guide* publisher and Makaha skateboard owner Larry Stevenson—make a product, sponsor a team, host competitions to showcase your team and products, and own the media that promoted your team, products, and contest results—was fundamentally what Vitello and Balma did with *Thrasher*/Independent Trucks and *Transworld Skateboarding*/Tracker Trucks.

In response to the closing of concrete skateparks, the 1980s saw the progression, standardization, and perfection of wooden skate ramps. The first ramps were completely improvised using the "let's just nail some plywood together and see if we can skate it" building system. They were typically half circles made of wood, in an effort to mimic the concrete drainage pipes skated in the 1970s. As skaters continued to experiment and make adjustments in the height, width, and curvature of their ramps, an archetype of the vert ramp emerged as well as the smaller mini ramp and the easily portable launch ramp. A proper vert ramp included a flat bottom between two curving walls, a top platform to allow skaters an area to stand, and metal coping on the edge of the platform to grind. In

1987, the apotheosis of the wooden vert ramp appeared in the Powell-Peralta skateboarding video *The Search for Animal Chin*.

Ramps were relatively inexpensive, portable, and easy to build, resulting in their proliferation throughout the United States. Whether in someone's backyard or driveway or on an abandoned plot of land, skaters began to organize an ad hoc system of ramp contests. Some contests offered prize money, while others offered beer, barbecue, and bragging rights. *Thrasher* gave the Texas Backyard Series a two-page spread in its May/June 1982 issue.

Along with the skate ramp replacing the skatepark in contest series came the ascent of vert skating. Vert skating on ramps distinguished itself from pool skating in concrete bowls: instead of skating a "line" from wall to wall in a skatepark bowl, the vert skater skates continuously back and forth between the two walls of the vert ramp while trying to perform as many tricks as possible. Similar to the 1970s, the 1980s saw an explosion of new vert tricks, with each trick acting as a building block to future tricks. And just as in the 1970s, the inventors of these

This Gary Scott Davis (GSD) model made by Tracker in 1985 was the first skate deck issued for a street skater. GSD, who is credited with creating the skate trick called the boneless and with publishing the longest-running skate zine, Skate Fate, *also wrote regularly for* Transworld Skateboarding.

tricks were teenagers testing the limits of their imagination and physical capabilities.

Skate-trick ingenuity and invention were not limited to the vert skaters. Similar to the explosion of trick progression from the bowl skaters of the 1970s, the early 1980s saw an explosion of creativity and technical brilliance coming from such freestylers as Rodney Mullen, Steve Rocco, and Per Welinder. Mullen took Gelfand's 1970s ollie and adapted it to flat surfaces, debuting it for all to see on the cover of *Thrasher* in October 1982. The article "Fear of Freestyle: Consider Yourself Warned" lavished twelve pages of photographs of freestyle skaters and declared, "The rapid sequences its practitioners are inventing are beyond the comprehension of all but the most involved."

After introducing the flat-ground ollie to the skate world, Mullen followed up with a trio of seminal skate tricks: the kickflip, the heel flip, and the impossible. These maneuvers freed the skateboard to rotate, or spin, airborne while underneath the skater's feet without the use of a ramp or bowl. Like the urethane wheel of the 1970s, Mullen's flat-ground ollie and kickflips revolutionized how and where people skated, enabling a new generation of skaters to skate over, up, and down things that were never conceived of being skateable. As 1980s skaters increasingly adapted freestyle tricks to the omnipresent asphalt, marble, and concrete pavement blanketing America, a new style of skating emerged: street skating.

Unlike the sidewalk surfers of the 1960s, the street skaters of the 1980s were not emulating surfing. They weren't even trying that hard to emulate ramp or bowl skaters. Repurposing the curbs, stairs, benches, railings, and other architectural elements found in public spaces across the country, they began to reimagine the urban landscape as an endless skatepark with unlimited skate-trick possibilities. As the street became the most accessible place to skateboard, requiring no entrance fee, ramp, or empty swimming pool, the skateboard industry gradually began to manufacture skateboards specifically marketed to street skaters.

While *Thrasher* and *Transworld Skateboarding* were the main suppliers of information to skaters around the country, two new content sources emerged during the 1980s: the skate video and the skate zine. From 1984 to 1989, Powell-Peralta produced six videos that featured its team of skaters, the Bones Brigade, as they skated and traveled around the country. Its timing was perfect. Americans everywhere were buying VHS video players and renting videotapes to watch in their homes, buoyed by outlets such as Blockbuster.

Unlike the static images seen in magazines, these videos captured skaters in real time hanging out, skating, and having a lot of fun. They introduced each team member as a distinct personality, with an individual style, ability, and sense of humor. Instead of seeing still photos of Steve Caballero in their magazines, hundreds of thousands of teenagers were able to see him actually skate: watching in slow motion, stopping on a certain movement, playing endless repeat, and analyzing every physical maneuver. The emulation and adulation stirred by these videos

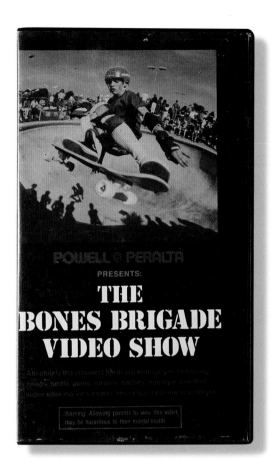

made the Bones Brigade instant celebrities. Like rock stars, they toured internationally, giving skate demonstrations to huge crowds all around the world. Other companies quickly followed the Powell-Peralta skate video paradigm, producing their own team videos and engendering their own squads of skateboard superstars. By the late 1980s, making videos rivaled contest results in maintaining a professional skate career. Skaters were known, judged, and elevated by what they produced on video-tape. Their role became less about winning contests and more about selling their sponsor's product by establishing a highly desirable persona for public consumption.

With increased skate celebrity came increased sales of skater-branded merchandise. As skateboard team members became celebrities, the individual graphics created for their signature skate decks became their individual "brand." The skateboard graphics produced in this era became deeply embedded, iconic images in the brains of teenagers everywhere. Like rock album covers, they created powerful personal identity connections between the brand and the consumer. Skate graphics trained an entire generation to the nuances of graphic

Top left: *In 1984, Powell-Peralta produced its first video,* The Bones Brigade Video Show, *to showcase its skate team. Directed by skateboarder Stacy Peralta, and with art direction by C. R. Stecyk, it ushered in the skate video genre.*

Above: *Made by Walker Skateboards, Mark Lake's 1985 Nightmare model, with its distinct nose and tail notches, is readily acknowledged as the most extreme example of a shaped 1980s skate deck. Lake insisted that these notches prevented his hands and feet from slipping off the deck when executing certain tricks.*

design. Whether they knew it or not, the skate graphic became a crash course in aesthetics and iconography for many who would never consider themselves connoisseurs of visual arts.

Young skaters not only wanted to skate like their idols but also wanted to skate on their hero's signature skate decks, imitate their hairstyles, and wear the same clothes. Scores of 1980s pro skaters became rich as the income from contest winnings was outpaced by the royalties from the sales of their skate decks. Becoming even richer were the skate companies, with Powell-Peralta, Vision, and Santa Cruz—the Big Three—dominating the industry. With the most popular skaters on their

This 2021 Pocket Pistols Treece pro model reissue deck came from Philadelphia skater Chuck Treece, who in 1984 became the first Black skater to be featured on the cover of Thrasher *magazine. Fellow skater-turned-artist Ken Sigafoos did the graphic for the board. Treece, who is also a musician, founded the 1980s skate punk band McRad and has performed on albums for Sting and Billy Joel, among many others.*

teams, they sold the most popular skate decks and controlled the skateboard market. However, by the end of the 1980s, many professional skaters began to leave these large companies to create their own brands and teams.

In contrast to the mass-marketed skate video of the 1980s was the homemade skate zine. Printed on a photocopier and distributed via local skate shops, word of mouth, and the US postal service, these publications were filled with hand-drawn artwork and a hyper-local editorial focus that often chronicled the backyard-ramp scene or the emerging street-skate sessions. *Skate Fate*, produced by street skater Garry Scott Davis (GSD), originated in Cincinnati, Ohio, and lasted an astonishing ten years. Other zines came and went, usually producing a few issues before disappearing entirely. Nonetheless, the skate zine was deeply influential for skaters, filling a void that *Thrasher*, *Transworld Skateboarding*, and skate videos could not fill. Most skaters were not professionals on a European tour or living in

California. Amateur skateboarders wanted something to connect them with their local community and their day-to-day skating reality. As GSD admitted in *The Best of Skate Fate*,

Above left: *Written by Steve Smith, "a story about a machine" is an homage to the history of skateboarding fanzines, or skatezines, especially the creation of Garry Scott Davis's* Skate Fate *and the search for the typewriter used to write it. Beginning in 1981 as the skateparks were disappearing and skateboarding was going back to the DIY crowd,* Skate Fate *was the first and longest-running skatezine delivering skate news through articles, interviews, cartoons, and photographs to skateboarders who still wanted to connect with one another even though their communities were dwindling.*

Above right: *The Skate Rags jacket seen here was worn by Stephanie Person, the first Black female professional skater. Person was sponsored by Skate Rags, a Southern California company that operated from the mid-1980s to the early 1990s. Created by skateboarders for skateboarders, it offered durable but cool clothing. Along with Person, company team riders included Mike McGill and Tom Groholski.*

"There was an underbelly of skateboarding that needed exposure, and homemade zines filled in that gap nicely with no nods at all to advertisers or parents or authority."

As skateboarding's third decade came to a close, the patterns repeated of boom and bust, reinvention and redefinition of how and where to skate, and the skate industry's control over skateboard media and content. What emerged in this decade was vert skating, the innovation to street skating, the power of the skateboard graphic, a new means to distribute content via VHS and the zine, and the marketing power of the skate video to provide another way to become a professional skater. Skateboarding became an even more profitable and influential force of youth culture, but emerging cracks in the foundations of the Big Three suggested that skateboarding's fourth decade would hold more changes and upheaval.

—Betsy Gordon and Jane Rogers

The 1980s

1980
- Rubik's cube debuts.
- At the 1980 Winter Olympics, the US hockey team defeats Russia, a victory dubbed the "Miracle on Ice."

- *SkateBoarder* magazine changes its name to *Action Now* to make room for other sports, such as BMX and surfing. It publishes its last issue just two years later.
- Brad Dorfman registers Vision Inc. in California. Vision forms a licensing agreement with Sims to produce Sims skateboards.

1981
- Fausto Vitello begins publishing *Thrasher*, the first magazine written and edited by skateboarders.
- Space shuttle *Columbia*, the first shuttle to reach space, is launched.
- The IBM personal computer is released.

- MTV, a twenty-four-hour cable television network for music videos, is launched.
- Sandra Day O'Connor becomes the first female Supreme Court justice.
- The US unemployment rate hits 10.4 percent, the highest since 1950.
- AIDS is recognized by the CDC.

1983
- *Transworld Skateboarding* magazine is founded by Larry Balma and Peggy Cozens.
- *Thrasher* magazine sponsors the first street contest in San Francisco's Golden Gate Park.

- Frank Hawk, Tony's father, creates the National Skateboard Association to help facilitate national skateboard competitions.
- Sally Ride becomes the first woman in space.
- The first commercial cell phone call is made.

1985
- Tracker produces the GSD skate deck, the first deck made specifically for street skating.
- In the film *Back to the Future*, Marty McFly creates the skateboard out of an orange-crate scooter (with the help of a DeLorean DMC-12 automobile/time machine powered by a flux capacitor) while running away from Biff Tannen.

1986
- Space shuttle *Challenger* explodes shortly after takeoff, killing all on board, including civilian social studies teacher Christa McAuliffe.
- The accident at the Chernobyl nuclear reactor in the USSR results in the largest uncontrolled radioactive release into the environment by a civilian entity.

1987
- Vision Street Wear issues the Suede Hi model, which incorporates both a rubber toe cap and an ollie patch for durability. The shoe gets incredible exposure through Ray Barbee's groundbreaking part in the Powell-Peralta video *Ban This*.
- Rodney Mullen leaves Powell-Peralta to form World Industries with fellow freestyle skater Steve Rocco.

1988
- George H. W. Bush is elected the forty-first president of the United States.
- Stephanie Person becomes the first Black female professional skateboarder.
- Tony Magnusson and Mike Ternasky form the skateboard company H-Street.

- Concerned by the lack of an organized contest series for his twelve-year-old son, Tony, Frank Hawk helps create the California Amateur Skateboard League (CASL). It strives to be the Little League of skateboarding.
- Rodney Mullen turns pro for Powell-Peralta at age thirteen, after beating Steve Rocco at the Oasis Skatepark in San Diego, CA.

- Ted Turner establishes CNN, the first twenty-four-hour cable news channel.
- Ronald Reagan is elected the fortieth president of the United States.
- The *Pac-Man* video game is released in the United States.
- John Lennon is murdered.

1982

- Rodney Mullen builds on Alan Gelfand's ollie to invent the flat-ground ollie.
- Powell-Peralta issues Tony Hawk's first pro skateboard.

- At the Eurocana skateboarding summer camp in Sweden, American skaters are introduced to the halfpipe, a skate structure that perfects the rudimentary backyard ramp.
- Michael Jackson releases his album *Thriller*, which goes on to sell 70 million copies worldwide.

1984

- Steve Jobs introduces the first Macintosh personal computer.
- Geraldine Ferraro becomes the first female candidate for vice president of the United States.
- The Summer Olympics are held in Los Angeles, CA.

- Chuck Treece becomes the first Black skater to be featured on the cover of *Thrasher* magazine.
- Powell-Peralta releases *The Bones Brigade Video Show*, a direct-to-consumer VHS video by Stacy Peralta and C. R. Stecyk. The skate video genre is born.
- Ronald Reagan is reelected president of the United States.

- SHUT Skates, the first East Coast skate brand, is born on a rooftop in Brooklyn, NY.
- Vision launches the Vision Street Wear clothing line, offering pants, shorts, T-shirts, berets, hip packs, backpacks, jackets, sweatshirts, and footwear. Street wear inspired by skateboarders enters mainstream fashion.

- Christian Hosoi designs his hammerhead-shaped deck, beginning the trend for oddly shaped decks.
- Airwalk opens in San Diego. By the end of the decade, the shoe company transforms the skateboarding footwear market with new designs that address skaters' changing performance requirements.

1989

- Nintendo releases the Game Boy, a handheld game console that goes on to dominate the market for a decade.
- The *Exxon Valdez* oil tanker runs aground in Alaska, contaminating hundreds of miles of coastline.
- Woodward Gymnastics Camp in State College, PA, adds skateboarding to its program. Gary Ream, the camp owner, becomes a central figure in the push to include skateboarding in the Olympics.

- Vans debuts the Steve Caballero signature shoe, and Etnies debuts the Natas Kaupas signature shoe, skateboarding's first two shoes to bear the name of a professional skater.
- The Berlin Wall falls.
- *The Simpsons* debuts, making Bart Simpson the most famous skateboarder in America.

POWELL-PERALTA DECK DONATION

As skateboarding evolved through the decades, there was an increasing nostalgia for the formative 1980s. During that time, skateboarding became something of an identity for outcast kids, and there were no rules to govern our growing fascination. In 2011, the All '80s All Day Vert Challenge was held. It was a "throwback" event of skateboard legends from that era skating on a smaller wooden halfpipe akin to what we would have been using in our youth. We—Christian Hosoi, Kevin Staab, Steve Caballero, and others—all wore nostalgic gear in keeping with the theme, and so I donated my old-school deck to the Smithsonian as soon as the event was over. It is a symbol of an important, evolutionary era in skateboarding and an ode to those who defied convention for the sake of progression.

—*Tony Hawk*

Above: *In 2011, Tony Hawk donated this 1986 Tony Hawk model skateboard, made by Powell-Peralta, to the Smithsonian, inspiring other skateboarders to offer their skate history to the museum.*

Opposite: *(top) While competing in the 2011 Quiksilver All '80s All Day Vert Challenge, Tony Hawk does a backside ollie on the skateboard he donated. (Left) At the ceremony to formally transfer his skateboard, Tony Hawk signs the official Smithsonian deed of gift, as Jane Rogers, curator of sports at the National Museum of American History, and Jeff Brodie, deputy director of the Smithsonian Lemelson Center, look on.*

THANKS FOR THE SKATEBOARD, TONY!

In 2011, the Tony Hawk Foundation reached out to the Smithsonian about donating one of Hawk's skateboards to the collections. There were a few caveats to this donation, including traveling to Florida to collect the board after Hawk rode it one last time. Hawk was skating in the Quiksilver All '80s All Day Vert Challenge, a 1980s-themed skateboard demonstration, with many of his 1980s counterparts, including Christian Hosoi, Kevin Staab, and Mike McGill. After the competition, Hawk was to sign the deed of gift to transfer ownership of the skateboard to the Smithsonian.

Having never been to a skateboarding contest, I was excited for the opportunity. Little did I know that this one collecting trip would begin my journey into the fascinating world of skateboarding. Two of my colleagues and I arrived in Florida and walked through the convention hall, visiting vendors of skate and surf equipment, clothing, and supplies. We eventually ended up at the halfpipe, where the competition was taking place, and were seated right next to where the skaters drop into the concave ramp.

It was an awesome experience to watch Tony Hawk soar high above the crowd. But when he flew right out of the halfpipe and into the hall below, I was a bit concerned that he was injured or that the board was damaged. But then he trotted around the corner, board in hand, and continued to skate. I was relieved that both he and the skateboard were safe. I soon realized that during these competitions skaters often stand at the top of the halfpipe and cheer on their fellow competitors by banging their skateboards along the metal edge of the structure. And that is exactly what Hawk did. I stared as bits and pieces of his skateboard flew through the air, hoping the board would be in one piece when I collected it.

After the competition, Hawk and I made our way to the middle of the halfpipe, where he handed me the board. It was still in one piece, albeit small chunks were missing from the sides. Wearing museum-quality, white cotton gloves, I held it tightly after he signed the deed of gift, making the handover official. That one donation snowballed into a wonderful relationship with the skate community, and the Smithsonian's skateboarding collecting initiative began, swelling the museum's forty skate objects into six hundred in just ten years.

—*Jane Rogers*

NO MORE SKATEPARKS
AND THE RISE OF THE ZINE

BRYAN RIDGEWAY

As a senior in high school, I applied only to universities near skateparks. I applied to Ohio State in Columbus, near Apple Skatepark, and to Rutgers in New Jersey, near Cherry Hill. I got accepted to both and then both Apple and Cherry Hill closed before I could even accept admission to either school. I decided to stay home, as I had a backup plan to attend my hometown school, Marshall University, in Huntington, West Virginia. I would study civil engineering and had a fellowship from the US Army Corps of Engineers that would fully fund my time there.

I was already sponsored, but the two years after Apple closed, I was skating only on backyard ramps. I would go to Falcon, the local skatepark, too, but it was hard to advance and to learn modern-day tricks. Everyone had stopped skating when Apple closed. Folks thought that it was all over. One friend of mine, John Wittpenn, stuck it out, and I convinced him that we should construct a ramp after I saw plans for building a halfpipe in *Thrasher* magazine. John and I needed a way to keep skating, and we knew we had to make it happen ourselves. We saved every penny we earned from the part-time jobs we had between our college classes and used the money to buy plywood one stack at a time, building the ramp one section at a time until it was done.

A year later, thanks to *Thrasher*, we found out about zines. We had seen a mention in *Thrasher* about the zine *Skate Fate*, which was put together by Garry Scott Davis in Cincinnati. That's when we started trying to create our own zine, *The Monthly Shredder*, and we soon realized that there were pockets of other skaters out there. I quickly saw how fast a month could go by and changed the name to *The Shredder*, so time didn't dictate when it was printed. I wanted to put it out only when I had enough material for an issue. I met Britt Parrott of Smyrna, Tennessee, near Nashville, through the zine, and we became pen pals. We were just seventeen or eighteen years old and were trying to figure out how to coordinate networks of people and create state and regional skateboarding events. We debated how to do this thing right. We became best friends—and later roommates, after we both moved to California—and that was the beginning of the Mid-Eastern Skateboard Series, or MESS, a kind of loosely affiliated skateboard league in four states, West Virginia, Kentucky, Ohio, and Tennessee.

Displayed here are all nine issues of The Shredder, *a zine started in 1982 by Bryan Ridgeway of Huntington, West Virginia, with the goal of creating a network of local skate scenes throughout the country.*

Above: The Shredder *was a group effort in the early 1980s and included (from left) Bryan Ridgeway, Rick Summerfield, Chris Carter, Tim Cline, and John Wittpenn, seen here in a more recent photo.*

Right: *According to Bryan Ridgeway, who pioneered the skate zine with* The Shredder *(first issue, June 1982), "The backyard DIY zine was indicative of the times and the individuals that had survived the total collapse of the skateboard industry and the skatepark era. More and more zines were created as word got out through* Thrasher *magazine.*

Skaters from thirteen states within our skate zine network helped to create this MESS contest series because skating was just no longer happening at an accessible level in the Midwest and on most of the East Coast north of Florida. To our surprise, people from seven states showed up at the little twelve-foot-wide and sixteen-foot-wide halfpipe contests we put together and judged ourselves. The West Coast skate companies noticed and began sponsoring some of the skaters in our series. We have to give it to the industry. We didn't know who was in charge out there in California, but we would write to companies and say, "Hey, we're trying to do this contest. Can you send us something?" They would send us stuff; we had prizes. It was totally legit. *Thrasher* was a major supporter along with, over time, the top companies in the industry. Our zines allowed skaters to keep in touch and enabled industry leaders to keep tabs on locals from spots they didn't have access to. We didn't know it, but we were motivating people around the country to form their own events and do their own zines—total underground DIY movement! Only the most hardcore skateboarders were able to survive closing of skateparks from that era.

After the zine thing happened, people signed up and subscribed. We wrote other zines, and together we created an active network through these publications. We had hubs for information and jobs for everyone. We had Indiana, Tennessee, Ohio, Michigan, West Virginia, Kentucky, and Wisconsin. We stayed on floors and in backyards of contest hosts.

That little zine, *The Shredder*, basically covered from 1982 through 1983. Several Midwest guys got sponsored and became internationally known pros because they received recognition from the contest series and the zine coverage. Among those who reached pro deck model level were Marty Jimenez (Vision), Rob Roskopp (Santa Cruz), Bill Danforth (Madrid and Alva), Ray Underhill (Powell-Peralta), Garry Scott Davis (Tracker), and Jeff Kendall (Santa Cruz). For me personally, *Transworld Skateboarding* used a story from *The Shredder* as a feature article in its very first issue. It also hired *Skate Fate*'s Garry Scott Davis and me as part of its first staff.

WE WERE SCREWED

CINDY WHITEHEAD

Women ran straight into the 1980s, firmly believing that we had it all. California was filled with skatepark options up and down the coast. Freestyle and slalom were moving aside for vert and bowl riding, which were now at their peak. At most of the major contests, the women even had their own divisions, complete with age ranges for amateurs and one division for pro. Most women were on teams and well accepted at the skatepark—if they charged hard and acted as if they belonged.

Skateboarding had exploded with new companies right and left, and teams were everywhere. Gone were the days when there were just a handful of companies and teams had only a couple of girls doing freestyle. The Gold Cup Series started things off in 1980. Select pro women were invited, and most of us traveled and skated at all five events. We wore racing-style bibs with an assigned number when competing, and there were bleachers set up around the pools for spectators—this was the big league! However, it was common during the 1980s for a female skater to travel to a contest and have to bunk in a hotel room with the boys. There just wasn't enough money (or so we thought) in skateboarding for girls to have their own accommodations, especially when each team had maybe one female member.

On numerous occasions, I shared rooms with my male teammates or pooled allowance money with my male friends to go out of town to a contest. Most times, since I was one of the youngest and smallest, I was dealt the floor. Perhaps in hindsight, my guy friends just knew it wasn't appropriate to share a bed with a female teammate they considered their sister.

But in many ways, we girls had it so wrong—there was money. We saw it at the contests we attended, where first place for pro women was $100 and for men was $3,000. We knew it when guys would have new cars and we'd be bumming rides. It wasn't even a secret. It was a financial discrepancy so wide it should have been hidden, but in that era, it was right out in the open for anyone to see. If you pick up a magazine from that time period and look at the contest results, you will see it in bold print. We women knew it, but we felt if we pushed too hard, we might be right back to no women's divisions, so we just kept doing what we loved—skateboarding. Male pros going to the same contests were paid additional fees by their team when they made podium or showed up in a magazine. Many were on a monthly salary. By the 1980s, the signature model pro boards that a few women had in the 1970s had disappeared. It was now male domination, financially speaking.

Photographer Brad Bowman captures Cindy Whitehead as she does a frontside grind in the upper keyhole at Marina del Rey Skatepark, ca. 1980.

Top: *In this 1979 photo, Cindy Whitehead is surrounded by boys as she waits to compete.*

Above: *This contest bib was worn by pro skater Cindy Whitehead at the Gold Cup Series contest in 1980.*

In between the contests, we tried to keep track of what the other girls were up to, trick-wise. Women were seldom featured in the magazines during this time, so we had to get creative to know what was happening. In 1980, there was no Internet or inexpensive cell phone plans, so Judi Oyama and I would write letters to each other in which we discussed rumors that we had heard about who was working on what. That way, we could gauge what we might be up against at the next contest. Obviously, a phone call would have been much faster and more effective, but in 1980, calling long distance from Southern California to Northern California wasn't something our parents wanted to see on the next phone bill. We were best friends who loved to skateboard but only saw each other at the Gold Cup Series stops.

By the mid-1980s, all that was about to change. It wouldn't matter much that we got paid less or what the other girls were doing to prepare for a contest because we were all about to lose the skateparks we called home. At one time, the United States was home to more than four hundred skateparks. Due to lawsuits and liability issues, these all started to close. It happened so fast. You'd go to bed at night and wake up in the morning to a friend telling you the Runway was no longer or Marina was closing. It bears noting that the oldest original skatepark still in

existence from that era is Kona Skatepark, which happens to be in Florida, not California.

After the skateparks closed, some of us girls stuck around and went back to our roots, skating backyard ramps, looking for those coveted ditches again, and searching endlessly for empty backyard swimming pools, which were a bit scarcer than they were during the 1970s drought years. The same was true in 2020. With the global pandemic, skateparks were closed and some were filled with sand or mulch to stop skaters from skating due to social-distancing requirements. Girls had learned to do exactly what we had to do in the 1980s: make their own ramps, find a ditch, or skate in an empty parking lot. But no matter what, we just keep skateboarding.

At the close of the 1980s, many of us went our separate ways, not to reunite again until the days of social media when we found one another online and continued with friendships right where we had left off so many years earlier. Skateboarding had that effect on all of us: we are still one big family. Like all "brothers and sisters," we sometimes have our differences, but at the end of the day, we will stand up for one another in the real world without hesitation—even forty years later.

Above left: *In this 1978 photo, Cindy Whitehead successfully skates a halfpipe while listening to music on a pair of Realistic headphones (above top right). "I wore big, clunky headphones when I skated, and [rocker] Joan [Jett] is who I listened to," recalled Whitehead in 2016.*

Bottom right: *As a pro skater, Whitehead was supplied with clothing and equipment by many different sponsors, like these 1979 Puma tennis shoes.*

MAIL-ORDER SKATEBOARDS AND THE OLLIE

BRIAN ANDERSON

I bought my skateboards at the Groton Schwinn Cyclery. The shop had a small corner with some Powell-Peralta, Schmitt Stix, Sure-Grip, and Santa Cruz boards. There was also an army-navy store in my hometown, and in the back was a small skate shop with four boards and some old 1980s wheels. No one would want those caveman wheels. Once a friend got a new board for his birthday, and I got his old board, but I had to promise to give it back if his new board broke.

I started looking at skate magazines and calling the mail-order places that advertised in the back. Like a kid looking at a Christmas catalog from Sears, Roebuck, I circled every board I liked. I'd hide the magazine in my schoolbooks and open it in study hall, dreaming, dreaming, dreaming. I saved my money from mowing lawns in the summer and shoveling driveways in the winter, plus my birthday and Christmas money. My mother would let me call, and I'd pass the phone to her. She would say, "This is Mrs. Anderson. Yes, we're allowed to do a COD delivery. I'm passing the phone back to my son." Then I would ask them if they had a certain board. If it wasn't in stock, I'd have ten backup boards ready. We'd pay cash on delivery, and that's how I got boards for a long time, through the mail.

At the local book fair, I got a book called *Skateboard Action*. It had glossy pages, mostly with guys skating vertical ramps, but there was a hand-drawn sequence of a guy doing an ollie. Looking at that drawn figure was how I learned to ollie. It had an explanation for each numbered step: put your front foot here after you hit the tail, slide it up, the back should come with you, and so on. I looked at that book a lot and studied all the vertical ramps.

My friend had a VHS machine and one of the Powell videos. It was probably *The Search for Animal Chin*. We would watch the video at his house, always rewinding to watch the skaters' feet. As our little group in our hometown of Groton, Connecticut, grew, another friend had a ramp and more underground videos, like *Gullwing Trucks' Inside Out*. Then eventually we got the H-Street videos, *Hokus Pokus* and *Shackle Me Not*. Those are the ones we really started rewinding and rewinding.

Because there wasn't a skatepark in Groton, the skate scene was small—ten to fifteen people. The videos started making skateboarding more popular. By the time we were in junior high school in 1988, I had a group of skateboarding friends, and that's what we did after school. We would watch whatever videos

Skateboard Action, a book published in 1987, came complete with collectable stickers and was sold to kids at school-held Scholastic Book Fairs in the late 1980s. It inspired an eleven-year-old Brian Anderson to learn to ollie.

someone had and then go to a little park or my dead-end street and skate our launch ramps. Some ramps would rot, and we'd build new ones. We kept changing the ramps. Sometimes we got injured. My mom would freak out, "You've got to stop the skateboarding!" I remember one time I hurt my ankle badly, and she hit one of the ramps with a hammer and punched holes in it. I was the youngest of fourteen kids. My mom is not violent or confrontational, but I think by her fourteenth child, she was fed up.

When I was eleven or twelve, I tried to ollie over a two-by-four. My sister Eileen, who is four years older, tried it, and she ollied before I did. I was proud of her but definitely a little jealous, and it motivated me. Eventually, I barely skimmed over the two-by-four. I probably just slid my front leg, and it pulled the back of the board. But in my mind, I bonked over the two-by-four and ollied, and that was it.

Every day I would try and bonk or fly and just lift over that two-by-four, and ultimately it turned into an ollie. Once my sister learned how to ollie, she was done with skateboarding, which was kind of cool. I thought, that's really punk rock. She's not a quitter, because she did the ollie and she was like, "I'm out."

Above left: *Released in 1987,* The Search for Animal Chin, *the third Bones Brigade skate video made by Powell-Peralta, featured Tony Hawk, Steve Caballero, Mike McGill, Lance Mountain, Tommy Guerrero, Rodney Mullen, and Mike Vallely. This was one of the first skate videos to have an actual plot, though it still included nonstop skating.*

Above right: *Ten-year-old Brian Anderson bought skateboards, decks, and equipment through ads like this one. They were prevalent in skateboarding magazines and allowed kids to place orders over the phone, but only if their parents gave the okay.*

I JUST WANT TO SKATE

SALMAN AGAH

I had been exposed to skateboarding in Washington, DC, when I was really young, but my dad thought it was too dangerous and wouldn't let me do it. So I forgot about it and starting riding BMX. But then in the sixth grade, I met Jeff Wendell and Steve Rafalo-vitch at school in San Jose, California. They were so cool. They wore Vans, and Steve had a bi-level haircut, with hair long on top and shaved on the side. They always had the coolest gear, and they both liked to skate, so I became friends with them. Every-one was skating at the time, and I thought, this is amazing.

I told my dad that I wanted a skateboard. A pro shop at the local roller-skating rink in San Jose sold skateboards, so that's where I got my first real skateboard. It was a black, white, and red checkerboard Vision Shredder 10 with Independent trucks and red Vision City Street wheels. I remember picking out all the stuff, and then it took the shop a week to put it together; I was so bummed. I bugged my dad that whole week to pick up my board.

At this point, which was the mid-1980s, skateboarding was pretty trendy. Leading up to the late 1980s, it became hugely popular. But none of that mattered to me. I just liked doing it and wanted to be good at it. Other kids started turning me on to videos. The first video I ever saw was *Terror in Tahoe*, which was a ramp contest at Lake Tahoe. Lance Mountain lit the tail of his board on fire. The whole thing looked amazing to me. There was

a vert ramp in the video, but we didn't have anything like that where I lived, so I just skated on the streets.

When I was in the eighth grade, I already knew that I wanted to be a pro skater. It wasn't even a decision. It was life or death. If I don't do this, I'm dead. I couldn't articulate that at the time, but that's how it felt, much to the dismay of my parents. My dad is from Iran, and he had no concept of this culture. It was really a subculture at the time, and with all of its edgy mystique, it was certainly not appealing to parents.

It was difficult to be a skateboarder in my household. There was a lot of clashing. My dad is the sweetest man, but at that time I thought his ideas were whack. None of this has anything to do with religion. It's just expression. But it was a war of ideas and ideals, and I was stubborn. I was going to skate no matter what, and we clashed on everything.

My friends could bleach or color their hair; I could never do that. I would, but then I would get in trouble. That's why I always had a shaved head. I would do something and then my dad would sit me down and cut off all my hair. It got to the point where my

Salman Agah does a slappy backside 5-0 grind in a parking lot outside of Almaden, California, 1986. The board he is riding, a Powell-Peralta Tony Hawk model with Tracker trucks and wheels, was put together with materials he found in the Go Skate shop dumpster.

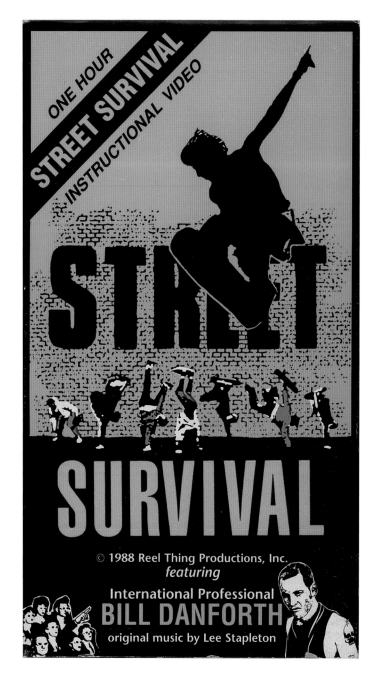

dad took my board away; I must have been a freshman in high school. But my friends Tom and Mike Miller's mom let us build a halfpipe in her backyard. A little crew of us were allowed to skate it, but I didn't have a board anymore. I dug in the dumpster at the skate shop and found a board that was basically destroyed. I found old hardware and bearings missing balls and put everything together, and that was my board.

It felt like I had to use that board for decades, but it was probably only six months. One of my dad's customers told him that he should let his son explore his passion. My dad gave me my board back after that conversation. I have photos of that day. I'm wearing a *Thrasher* shirt at Eric Goodwin's house. He lived behind my dad's business. He had a jump ramp, and I remember learning all these tricks that day. It's emotional. I got my life back.

Above left: *Written, produced, and directed by George Leichtweis and Michael Hays of Reel Thing Productions Inc., the 1988 video* Street Survival *helped skaters such as Salman Agah learn to skate. Instructional videos like this one revolutionized the way skaters learned tricks and increased the sport's popularity worldwide.*

Above right: *Salman Agah practicing his kickflips while his friends look on in Almaden, California, 1987. His dad had just returned his board to him.*

PUSHING ACROSS AMERICA, TAKE TWO

Two of my best friends, Gary Fluitt and Paul Dunn, were the impetus for my second push across America. In March 1984, the three of us pushed our skateboards along a closed sixty-three-mile section of California's Highway 1, between Big Sur and San Simeon. Over the years, Gary and Paul had heard the stories about my first ride across America in 1976, and as we pushed along the coast that day, we hatched a plan to make another cross-country push. We invited skater and friend Bob Denike, who was attending Cal Poly in San Luis Obispo, about forty miles south of San Simeon, to join the team.

This time around, we decided to raise money for a charity, and after a bit of research, we discovered that the Multiple Sclerosis Society spent most of the money it raised on actual research instead of fancy offices. We liked that and chose it to be the fundraising beneficiary of our push. A sponsorship package was put together and sent to possible sponsors. This was during a downtime for the skateboard industry, so we were surprised to receive sponsorship from Tracker, Madrid, Independent, Gullwing, Powell-Peralta, Kryptonics, and a couple of non-skateboarding companies, Chrysler-Dodge, which supplied a support van, and Spalding, which provided apparel.

We knew that with four skaters and improved gear—mainly those big, soft seventy-millimeter Kryptonics wheels—this push would be much faster than my first. We all rode Madrid longboards, with each of us choosing our trucks of choice. Tracker, Independent, and Gullwing supplied these. Beginning in Newport, Oregon, we followed the same route as my 1976 push.

In Wyoming, we were involved in a rescue of a young girl who had fallen into a river. We would not learn until 2011 that she survived. South Dakota, with its flat roads and sparse traffic, was a favorite. We skated across Illinois in a day and a half. In Ohio, Amish folks stared at us, not sure what to think. We struggled over the Appalachians, again. Gary got lost in Richmond; we still argue about who took the wrong turn. We finished in Williamsburg, Virginia, twenty-six days after we began and six days faster than my first crossing.

Growing older, the memories of so many summers run together, leaving me with a handful that I will never forget, the summer of 1984 being one of them.

—*Jack Smith*

Top: *Skateboarders (from left) Paul Dunn, Gary Fluitt, and Jack Smith make their way along Highway 1, just south of Big Sur, California, in March 1984.*

Above: *During a pause at Nye Beach in Newport, Oregon, at the beginning of the second skate across America, (from left) Bob Denike, Jack Smith, Gary Fluitt, and Paul Dunn pose alongside their Chrysler-Dodge support van.*

THE HISTORY OF SKATEBOARD GRAPHICS

MATT BASS

In 1999, I moved from New York City to Los Angeles to shoot and direct music videos. It was great, but I knew that I needed to do something bigger—that I needed a project that represented who I was. I had been skateboarding since elementary school and never really stopped. I was also collecting my old boards as time capsules, not knowing what was to come. After years of skateboarding, the DIY mindset became embedded into my creative process, and the older I got, the more relevant this became. *Disposable*, Sean Cliver's 2004 book about the history of skateboard graphics, rekindled many strong feelings and memories I had about skateboarding. As a filmmaker, I immediately wanted to watch a movie about the same subject. I couldn't believe there wasn't one about skateboard graphics. It was my aha moment. That's how I came up with the idea for *SK8FACE*, a documentary that presents a visual history of skateboard graphics by the graphic artists who made them.

I knew from reading *Disposable* that my film needed to start at the beginning of skateboard graphic history, so I started with Wes Humpston, the original Dogtown artist and whom many consider to be the godfather of skateboard graphics. One interview led to another, and fifteen years later, the film has more than sixty interviews. I started with Wes and the late 1970s because the 1960s didn't have the memorable graphics found in other decades. There wasn't any personal identity behind those early boards. They displayed simple corporate logo graphics in a generic font.

The 1970s was an interesting time for skateboarding. The whole Dogtown scene happened. It was a new attitude that said, "This is who we are. We've got our own style," and they didn't look like stick figures in gymnastics uniforms anymore. In the 1970s, skaters literally started flying out of bowls and over the coping. Skate photographers began capturing these new tricks for the magazines. That's when you first saw graphics on the bottom of the deck. Wes Humpston incorporated C. R. Stecyk's graffiti Dogtown Cross into a full graphic on the entire bottom of the board. When I asked him why, he said, "Why should I limit myself to this little area like a stamp? Let's just use this as if it were a canvas."

One of the most important things to come out of the decade in addition to the transition to full graphics on the board was the influence of punk rock. The music scene was rebelling against the hippie stuff of the 1960s and the groovy stuff of the early 1970s. Punk rock exploded on an underground level. It was aggressive and very expressive of the time, and it worked perfectly with skateboarding because skateboarding was also going

Vernon Courtlandt Johnson's Ripper graphic, created in 1983 for Powell-Peralta, became one of the most iconic skateboard graphics ever produced.

underground. By 1979, distributors and manufacturers had warehouses full of these skinny decks that nobody wanted. The boards got wider, new skaters came in—Steve Olson and Salba—and the attitude changed. Punk was a natural extension of the Dogtown attitude: "This is who we are. We don't care what you think of us." That insolence combined with punk rock completely changed the graphics on skateboards. Punk rock wasn't just a music-based movement. It was an aesthetically driven mindset that changed fashion, art, and music. Steve Olson began incorporating a checkerboard design on his deck and Duane Peters was using stripes, graphics inspired directly by the punk scene.

In the 1980s, skateboard companies began homing in on their brand image. Santa Cruz brings in Jim Phillips, Powell-Peralta brings in Vernon Courtlandt Johnson (VCJ), and Vision brings in artists like Bernie Tostenson and Andy Takakjian to create their distinct brand aesthetics.

Jim Phillips was an established graphic artist who had been designing rock and roll posters and surf stuff. He starts doing intricate skateboard graphics—full-color, intensely detailed drawings like his monster breaking out of a target series for Rob Roskopp, the Screaming Hand, and other seminal graphics that defined Santa Cruz. VCJ was conjuring up such ancient symbols as skulls, swords, and dragons. Vision was using punk-rock DIY-looking graphics, putting leopard-skin print on boards or a whole series of jagged patterns without including the skater's name.

During this time, companies would produce a graphic that sold for a couple of years. The only things that changed were the colorways. Hence, the graphic on the bottom of the board became synonymous with the skater who rode the board. Whether you saw them in magazines, mail-order catalogs, or skate shops, the skaters and their skate graphic became deeply imbedded in your psyche.

A big shift occurred in the 1980s when skateboarders started creating their own art. At the same time, people started putting out skate zines. Skaters began to realize that

Top: *Jim Phillips created his Screaming Hand graphic for Santa Cruz Skateboards in 1985. It has been reproduced on nearly everything, from skateboards to Band-Aids, and continues to be the most potent representation of Santa Cruz Skateboards.*

Middle: *Bernie Tostenson designed this Sims logo in 1976. Tostenson's career in skateboard graphic design stretched from the corporate logo 1970s to iconic graphics for Flip and Brand X in the 1990s.*

Right: *Rodney Mullen rode this 1980s signature Chessman skate deck, made by Powell-Peralta and with graphic design by Vernon Courtlandt Johnson. The condition of the deck shows how unconcerned Mullen and skateboarders in general were with preserving the artwork under their feet. The graphic is nearly obliterated by the placement of Rip Grip on the nose and middle of the deck.*

Far right: *Skater Christian Hosoi repurposed the Bernie Tostenson graphic from his Sims skateboard to form his own company, Hosoi Skateboards, in 1984. The distinct nose and tail shape of this 1984 Hosoi deck, known as the hammerhead, became a trademark of the company.*

skateboarding was a vehicle for creativity and self-expression. Neil Blender was the first pro skateboarder to put his own art on his skateboard. Chris Miller, Mark Gonzales, John Lucero, and others followed. Skaters began thinking, "Why do we need an art department when we can do it ourselves?"

Then, in the 1990s, a lot of the top pro skaters left these big corporations with their decks being branded by somebody else. Many went to World Industries, the company started by skateboarders Steve Rocco and John Lucero, who was later replaced by Rodney Mullen. World behaved like kids in a candy store. They didn't have Santa Cruz, Powell, or Vision saying, "Guys, you're

Above left: *By the mid-1980s, Sims was rapidly losing its skateboard industry dominance to Powell-Peralta, Santa Cruz, and Vision. On this early street-style model for Steve Rocco, it awkwardly attempted to match the eye-popping graphics its rivals by repeating its logo, using bright colors, and incorporating mismatched typography.*

Above right: *This ca. 1984 model for Vision skater Mark "Gator" Rogowski became one of the highest-selling skateboards of the 1980s. Greg Evans's swirl design was repeated over the years with a myriad of colorways, ranging from classic black-and-white to fluorescent greens, oranges, and pinks.*

taking it a little bit too far," so their board graphics reflected whatever crazy ideas they had in their heads. They ripped off images from Disney and received a lot of cease-and-desist letters from corporations. Their attitude was straight out of the Dogtown era of jumping fences and riding empty pools. It was, "Who's gonna stop us? If they stop us, we'll find another pool to ride—we'll go make another graphic." That attitude put World Industries on the map. That's when board graphics started turning over quickly, every few weeks or so.

It was interesting to see how the early rave scene in the 1990s was also influenced by skateboard art and culture. The rave locations were semisecret and usually shared by homemade flyers. The flyers were everything, pushing the limits of graphic illustration and, like World Industries, ripping off known corporate logos with spoof designs. Friends would wear a weird shirt that looked exactly like the Tide detergent graphic—same font, same colors—but it would say Rave.

World Industries soon becomes the dominant company in the skateboard industry. Just as before, many of the skaters who initially flocked to World to form their small, independent brands

started to resent being part of a large skateboard conglomeration. Many of the pros eventually left World to form their own brands. Overnight, World was riderless.

Rocco realized that without a team, he didn't need to pay his riders royalties on their deck sales, but he still needed something visual on his decks to sell product. Three Marc McKee cartoon characters, Devil Man, Flameboy, and Wet Willy, become the brand identity. Rocco took World's edgy and irreverent graphic legacy into a kid's cartoon that appealed to a new group of skateboarders. World started selling a lot of decks not to the core skateboarder but to little kids, the next generation of skaters.

Above left: *In 1988, Chris Miller created this artwork for his deck model, made by Schmitt Stix, following the example set by fellow skater Neil Blender. The deck's elongated upturned nose was a nod to the double-kick tail shape that came to dominate deck shapes in the 1990s.*

Above right: *This Unbreakable model, which features a photo by Horst Hamann, was produced by Zoo York in 2001. All proceeds from the sales of the deck went to help the survivors of 9/11. Cofounder Eli Morgan Gesner deleted the image of the World Trade Center towers from the skyline but kept their reflection in the puddle underneath the cars.*

The early 2000s saw a shift from graphics that looked cool to graphics that had meaning—that were beginning to have social relevance and power. They reflected the issues of the day that weren't being discussed widely in the mainstream media or in art museums.

As the decade progresses, every couple of months, there are more skateboard companies issuing even more graphics. In the 1970s, it was the Big Five, and in the 1980s, it was the Big Three. Now it's the Big Five Hundred. It also becomes a lot easier to print graphics on a skateboard: you go online, upload your graphic, order two hundred, and get them in the mail.

SK8FACE documents the visual history of skateboarding graphics over the decades. To me, these graphics are just as relevant as modern art—or even more important because modern art is focused on a handful of artists, whereas skateboard art has a myriad of people involved in its creation: the skaters, their teams, their companies, and so on. Skateboard graphics are the thing that we've all identified with and that have connected us to the skaters. That's what has kept us all interested. And, I think, underneath it all, that is what has always inspired us.

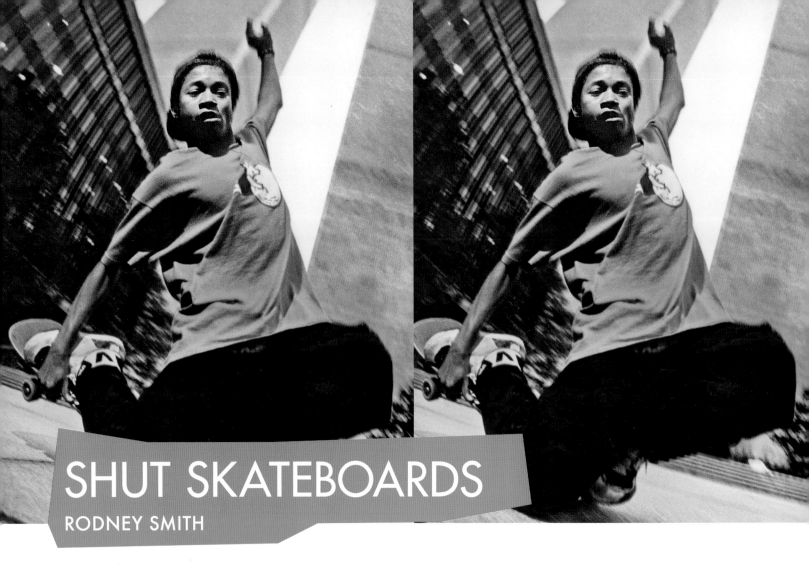

SHUT SKATEBOARDS

RODNEY SMITH

A skater could do no wrong if they were in New York City in 1985. Back then, skateboarding and skateboarders in New York City ushered in a fresh new perspective of what it was to be an outcast skater in the city. With the New York City police becoming more tolerant of skaters at places like the Brooklyn Banks, skaters becoming known in the club scene, MTV becoming mainstream, the release of the *Bones Brigade Video Show*, skaters in television commercials, the rise of skateboarding internationally, and the newfound acceptance of skaters by the NYC public, skateboarding in New York City became a sought-after concept, with even skaters in California looking at NYC as one of the greatest street skate cities of all time.

By 1986–87, Bruno Musso, Alyasha Moore, a host of other friends, and I decided to introduce our understanding/connection to street skateboarding. We started out by changing the current status quo in board shaping and design. Even prior to this board-reshaping venture, I was making board support riser pads (1986), called UT pads, in my parents' garage. The weak construction of the market boards of the time (made mostly for ramp skating and not really for street skating) was another reason we ventured into forming SHUT Skates. As most of us had sponsorships that we both respected and appreciated and that were popular skateboard companies of the time, we first chose to use the products we endorsed and had access to for

our redesign: decks from our sponsors. We cut new shapes out of the original decks we received from these sponsorships. Our first confused attempt at reshaping these boards (on Alyasha's mom's roof in Bedford-Stuyvesant in Brooklyn) proved to be a fleeting moment. The boards we redesigned and recut just became weaker, further eroding the strength properties needed to ride them aggressively. From there forward, we rapidly moved on to goal number two: figuring out how to properly make a finished deck.

Bruno Musso, being a thinker-doer type, decided to search for a way to get pre-pressed uncut boards for this next aspect of the venture. One hot summer day, Bruno let us in on his purchase of uncut blanks from an odd manufacturer who cut its own blanks into popular pro model shapes. We set off to Alyasha's mom's house and got to cutting the blanks. We soon figured out that there was a math quotient involved in shaping the blanks into finished decks that included proper length, width, weight, and wheel base. After cutting, drilling, and sanding, we had others who helped with making stencils for graphics and paint

This animated image of Chris "Dune" Pastras doing a G turn near the Twin Towers was taken by photographer Todd Laffler ca. 1989. Pastras skated for SHUT in his early teens but left for World Industries in 1990, a time when many other SHUT skaters were also being lured away. Pastras went on to create Stereo Skateboards with fellow skater Jason Lee in 1992.

work. Alyasha, Damani Beasley, and Wylie Singer provided their artistic skills and the spray paint. The name SHUT Skates was from Alyasha, Bruno, and Wylie making a suggestion that we title the decks based on my slang terms *UT IT* and *UT UP* as well as the phrase "Shut up and skate," which was used by some Texas skaters (company slogan of Zorlac Skateboards). To say the least, we had successfully gotten this project off the ground and running in a more functional way than previously. With fall and winter of 1987 coming fast, we temporarily moved manufacturing of the decks into my parents' garage. Working out of this space served its purpose for the moment. We then moved operations to Manhattan (262 Mott Street in Little Italy), and things got really interesting from there.

We were well on our journey of making skateboard decks for our personal use and our product-endorsing amateur team, which at the time included Bruno and me, Beasley, Felix Arguelles, Ritchy Garcia, Barker Barrett, Mike Kelly, Jeff Pang, Harold Hunter, Chris "Dune" Pastras, Angel "Coco" Santiago, Rick Ibaseta, Mike Kepper, Billy Waldman, Brian Blake, Qulon Douglas, Jamal Simmons, and many others. Known pros for SHUT were Jeremy Henderson, Jim Murphy, and eventually Barker Barrett, who turned pro in 1989. With the business growing and expanding rapidly, SHUT's clientele was expanding as well, spurred on by our touring skateboard team, which was making a substantial mark domestically like no other small-time, ragtag, unknown company in the skateboard industry.

One faith-filled day arrived when a friend named Mike Agnew (Intensity Skates, a retail and mail-order skateboard operation) decided to hook us up. He was selling more SHUT product at that time (for a few months) than he was product from most companies on the West Coast. Mike Agnew ran three-page advertisements in *Thrasher* magazine, and he thought it would be a great idea to place SHUT decks in the deck section of his ads. He gracefully never told us, so it came as a big surprise. We couldn't believe our eyes when we saw our product next to the products of the prominent companies of our time. His idea propelled SHUT forward (like ten years ahead), up there with the fifteen- to twenty-year-old brands of the day. Up until this point (1987–88), we hadn't advertised in endemic skateboard magazines, and yet we kept becoming more and more popular. The issue hit the subscribers and skate shops everywhere. When the West Coast establishment got wind of this advertisement, they scrambled to find out how this could've happened without them knowing about it. *Thrasher* magazine had multiple chances to see it, yet it slipped through the cracks, and history was made right under the noses of the industry leaders. Not long after this happened, we received a call from one of the top skate industry brands (Vision), who wanted to buy SHUT Skates for a fairly large sum of money. We refused two offers (due to our love of what we had started and the offer not feeling sincere). We also had grace on our side when Stacy Peralta and George Powell cosponsored our team in our first go-around. But our sponsorship needs really happened when

Top: *In this 1986 photo, Bruno Musso (left) and Rodney Smith (right), founders of New York City's SHUT Skates, sport jackets with the company crest.*

Above: *These ca. 1985 skateboard stickers are just two of the many stickers SHUT Skates created until it closed its doors in the early 1990s.*

two founding members (Fausto Vitello and Eric Swenson) of the skate industry brand-manufacturer Ermico and High Speed Productions (*Thrasher*, Thunder Trucks, Independent Trucks, Venture Trucks, Spitfire Wheels, etc.) covered all of our product sponsor needs. In so many words, they "took us under their wings." This was due to our dedication to endorsing their products prior to growing SHUT into an internationally known brand. The key to this came to us through "third wheel man" at Ermico, Keith Cochran, who is responsible for the creation of some Ermico products (Venture, Spitfire, Deluxe Distribution, Think Skateboards).

SHUT experienced some insincere partnerships in late 1991. A deal with a distributor went bad that resulted in a legal challenge of who SHUT's rightful owners were. Although there were no questions about that on paper, as we were legally bound by a trademark established in 1987, we were served with a cease-and-desist order by a potential business partner. Needless to

say, we came through it all as the victor, though the business suffered a bit for a year. We made a comeback, but the year away from manufacturing and distribution out of New York put a strain on the entire operation.

Team riders were stolen by other companies and popularity waned for the whole establishment. From this point, SHUT would go down in history as New York City's first-ever skateboard company, a sincere claim to the world that was in itself an honor.

Left to right: *This 1986 hand-cut deck by SHUT Skates was made specifically for the SHUT skate team and was not sold to the public. The design for the SHUT logo used on decks and stickers was supplied by sixteen-year-old Eli Morgan Gesner, a New York City graffiti artist. This 1989 Shark model by SHUT was among the first production models of the company that were factory made and sold to the public in 1988 and 1989. Before the Zoo York skate brand debuted in 1993, the name Zoo York was associated with the legendary New York City skate and graffiti crew known as the Soul Artists of Zoo York. This 1987 Zoo York model by SHUT Skates dates from that period.*

THE BONES BRIGADE ON THE ROAD

I began working at Powell-Peralta Skateboards in 1987, ostensibly to work with Stacy Peralta on his Bones Brigade video productions. Within a short while, I became the promotions manager directing every aspect of the company's twenty-plus professional and fifty-plus amateur skateboarders. Video productions, photography assignments, contest appearances, domestic and international touring schedules, product development, marketing, and advertising—all were my responsibility.

Skateboarders around the world were transfixed by the Bones Brigade, arguably the most popular and well-known group of skateboarders of any time. Rodney Mullen, Kevin Harris, Per Welinder, and Cameron Martin excelled in freestyle skateboarding. Tony Hawk, Mike McGill, Steve Caballero, Lance Mountain, Chris Borst, Ray Underhill, and Mike Frazier skated vert ramps with style and with such daring maneuvers as the McTwist (540), the half cab, the 360, the 720, and later the 900. Street skaters included Tommy Guerrero, Ray Barbee, Steve Saiz, Mike Vallely, Frankie Hill, and many others who excelled at ollieing over and onto such street elements as benches, ledges, stairways, and handrails.

Featured in dozens of video productions and appearing in hundreds of magazine advertisements, members of the Bones Brigade were known to skateboarders around the world. In the 1980s and into the 1990s, the popularity of the group did much to spread the impact of skateboarding in communities throughout the United States. As part of the 1988 World Tour, the Bones Brigade performed in the parking lot of the Social Security Administration outside Baltimore, Maryland. The crowd was estimated at five thousand enthusiastic skateboarders. Later that year, a parade was organized in Lausanne, Switzerland, where thousands of spectators applauded as Bones Brigade skateboarders waved from a Ford Mustang convertible. In El Paso, Texas, thousands of skateboarders joined Terry McChesney in one-hundred-degree-plus heat to see the Bones Brigade grind, slide, and ollie on the elements built in the parking lot of Terry's skateboard shop.

In 1989, I traveled in Europe on the Bones Brigade World Tour with Mike McGill, Tommy Guerrero, Steve Caballero, and Mark Saito. Twenty-five years earlier, in 1964, I had traveled to Europe with twelve clay-wheeled Makaha skateboards. I had skateboarded through sixteen European countries—everywhere I could find smooth pavement. While skateboarding in London, I had drawn the attention of dozens of people in Piccadilly Circus; in Paris under the Eiffel Tower, an even larger number of onlookers had clapped in astonishment.

With the Bones Brigade, I discovered the expansion of skateboarding's reach. In 1964, four or five folks in Biarritz paid attention to what I was doing on my skateboard. In 1989, thirty-five hundred screaming and yelling fans were in the Biarritz audience when Mike McGill pulled a McTwist on the vert ramp. Bedlam!

— *Jim Fitzpatrick*

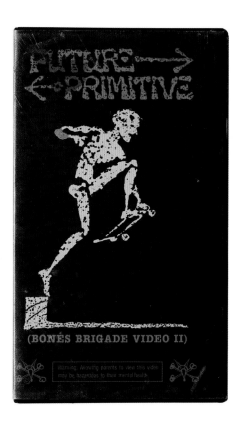

Top: *This 1986 portrait of the Powell-Peralta Bones Brigade skateboard team, with everyone sporting a team jacket, was taken by photographer J. Grant Brittain at Del Mar Skate Ranch.*

Above: *The video* Future Primitive, *released by Powell-Peralta in 1986, was the second of three videos about the company's Bones Brigade skate team.*

NHS: SURVIVING SKATEBOARDING IN THE LATE 1980s

BOB DENIKE

I **began my career** with NHS in 1987 as team manager for the rock stars of skateboarding, which sounds glamorous, but it was not an easy job. I was a coach, father figure, brother, uncle, therapist, money handler, equipment manager, and tour guide. It really helped me cut my teeth on people management and people psychology, in good times and bad times. I've worked at NHS for thirty-five years. I've known Richard Novak, one of the original founders of NHS, for forty-five years. The first time I met him, I was fourteen years old, and he gave me a set of wheels to test. I wrote him a letter with a not-so-glowing review of the wheels, and he said he always remembered that. I came into NHS in 1987, when we were at our peak in sales. We did about $50 million that year. But by 1992, we were down to about $4 million. We went from 160 employees down to 18. The industry crashed.

During this period of downward spiral, a lot of the management at NHS weren't really doing anything to fix or turn around the business. I went into Richard's office one day and said, "I want to work in skateboarding. It's my passion. I want to run this company someday. What do we need to do to survive?" He responded, "Write me a business plan." I was in my late twenties and had never written a business plan. I took a commonsense approach and put together maybe a ten-page document. It basically said here are the things that aren't doing us any good, let's get rid of them, and then we're going to focus on the things that are doing well. He read it over the weekend and the following Monday he told me, "You are now vice president. Go for it." At the time, I wasn't exactly sure what that meant. Unfortunately, I found it meant laying off a lot of people, which was very difficult, but we stopped the bleeding and reorganized the company. That was the first of about four times skateboarding would boom and bust over the next three decades.

The 1980s crash was caused by a mix of things. Demographically, we were going into a different period in which there weren't young men at the prime target age for skateboarding. Skateboarding had gotten too big too fast, and when things get too big too fast, they become uncool. There was also some economic uncertainty in the country around that time, and all those things just collapsed in on themselves.

The businessmen of the 1980s kind of got lucky. A lot of it was being in the right place at the right time. Some of them

confused their luck with their business acumen. Richard Novak had the sense to understand the business went in cycles. He survived the 1970s boom and bust, and he began to pull things back and say to others in the industry, "Hey guys, this thing is not going to last. Let's regroup." They didn't listen. They thought it would go on forever. Vision Skateboards collapsed. George Powell had a lot of problems with Powell-Peralta. Tracker Trucks had setbacks. A lot of companies went bankrupt. The magazines became unstable because they also thought the success was never going to end. Richard always said, "When the tide goes out, all the garbage is on the beach." And when the business declined, the beach was a real mess.

We navigated it by the skin of our teeth and barely made it through. There were days when I had to choose which bill to pay: the utilities company, rent, or someone else I owed money.

I made so many mistakes that I wish I could fix now, but I also made a lot of good decisions just to survive. It came down to sheer survival, keeping the doors open, keeping a group of people that we could continue to employ, and just hanging in there. I remember telling Richard that I didn't think the skate industry was ever coming back. He looked at me and said, "Yeah, yeah, yeah, it's going to come back. These things go in cycles. Let's hold it together." He'd already seen the 1960s boom and decline and the late 1970s boom and decline. Every high in the business is higher than the last one, and every bottom is lower than the last. He knew enough, and had enough faith, to hang in there for the next boom, and he was right. And here we are today, almost fifty years in the skateboard business.

Opposite: *Bob Denike, seen here doing a frontside double grab at Summit Ramp in Los Gatos, California, in 1981, started his career as a team rider for Santa Cruz Skateboards. He is now CEO of NHS Inc.*

Above right: *Founded in 1973 in Santa Cruz, California, by surfers Richard Novak, Doug Haut, and Jay Shuirman under the moniker NHS Inc., Santa Cruz is the oldest, continuously operated skateboard company in the world.*

CHAPTER FOUR

'90s

NOT JUST GUYS AND NOT JUST CALIFORNIA

The 1990s decade introduced many of the issues we still grapple with today: economic turbulence, deadly weather events, military intervention in the Middle East, acts of terrorism against Americans at home and abroad, gun violence in schools, police brutality against people of color, sexual harassment in the workplace, and political infighting that caused the US government to shut down. It was also the decade in which we saw the ascent of the World Wide Web, dial-up Internet connectivity, email, and instant messaging.

The decade opened with an eight-month-long economic recession that was soon followed by a series of deadly natural disasters: hurricanes Andrew and Iniki in 1992, severe flooding in Mississippi and massive snowstorms along the Eastern Seaboard in 1993, a 1995 heatwave in Chicago that killed 739, and a 1999 record-breaking 318 miles per hour tornado in Oklahoma that killed 50 people—events whose recovery costs totaled in the billions of dollars.

This was also the decade in which Al-Qaeda, Osama bin Laden, jihad, fatwa, and sleeper cell become part of our daily vocabulary. The Gulf War, which began in 1990, started a thirty-year series of military interventions in the Middle East. Terrorism started to be used to describe acts of violence against US citizens at home and abroad, with bombs being the weapon of choice: the 1992 World Trade Center bombing, the Oklahoma City

bombing in 1995, the bombing at the 1996 Atlanta Summer Olympics, the 1996 Khobar Towers bombing targeting US military personnel in Saudi Arabia, and the 1998 bomb attacks on two US embassies in Africa. Throughout these years, gun violence in classrooms continues an upward trend, with the 1999 mass shooting at Columbine High School in Colorado capping the decade.

Televised legal hearings captivated Americans during this decade. The 1991 Senate hearings for Supreme Court nominee Clarence Thomas featured the testimony of attorney Anita Hill, whose claims of sexual harassment sparked a public debate about workplace conduct. The 1992 acquittal of four Los Angeles police officers on trial for the brutal beating of Rodney King ignited a five-day protest against police brutality in Los Angeles. Other high-profile hearings of the decade included the 1995 trial of O. J. Simpson, acquitted of the murders of Ron Goldman and Nicole Brown Simpson, and the 1998 impeachment trial of President Bill Clinton, acquitted of lying under oath and obstruction of justice.

Despite electing a Democratic president twice during this decade, the Senate and the House of Representatives were controlled by the Republicans. This set up a series of power impasses between the presidency and Congress that resulted in a government shutdown in 1995 and again in 1996.

The decade ended with a global anxiety attack fueled by forecasts of computer systems failing the moment the clock ticked beyond midnight on December 31, 1999. This crisis, known as Y2K, became synonymous with global bank failures, disruption

Opposite: *Safiya Martinez skates near the Rookie Skateboards office in New York on July 6, 1996, in this photograph taken by Lizabeth Ronk.*

of food and water supplies, failure of the power grid, and a myriad of other doomsday predictions. Luckily, nothing much happened, and the world woke up to a January 1, 2000, looking exactly as it did the day before.

Like they did in the previous three decades, skateboarders in the 1990s found a way to continue skateboarding through the decade's economic turmoil, climate crises, global terrorism, social upheavals, political gridlock, and predictions of a computer apocalypse. It wasn't easy. The continuance of the pro skater career archetype of the 1980s—contests, demos, videos, and hefty royalty checks from deck sales—rapidly disappeared with the onset of the economic recession of 1990. The skateboard industry was hit hard, with many companies laying off staff, reducing their skate teams, or declaring bankruptcy. First on the chopping block were the vert skaters. The fickle teenage taste of what was "cool" in skating quickly shifted from vert to street skating, which left skaters such as Tony Hawk and Christian Hosoi with dwindling skate deck sales. Hawk saw his deck royalties shrink from $20,000 to $2,000 a month.

In addition to the reality of unemployment and dwindling revenue, the teenage superstars of the 1980s were in their twenties. Like many young adults, they wanted to separate from the parental figures represented by the George Powells and Brad Dorfmans of the skateboard industry. As they began to question the rules, regulations, and payment structures enacted by their companies, an industry-wide wave of defections

occurred from the Big Three (Powell-Peralta, Vision, and Santa Cruz). Skaters formed their own skateboard companies, taking with them the best established and/or up-and-coming skaters. As these breakout companies began to amass affiliated brands under their distribution hubs and sponsor other companies, a complicated web of skate brands and subdivisions formed. Making things even more convoluted were the skaters who jumped from company to company. For example, in 1989, Mike Vallely left Powell-Peralta to form World Industries, left World in 1991 to join the New Deal team, left New Deal to start TV Skateboards in 1992, rejoined Powell after TV went under in 1993, and joined Black Label Skateboards in 1998. Although most skaters were not as peripatetic as Vallely, the number of new companies forming in the 1990s provided many skaters alliance opportunities that didn't exist in the previous decades.

The size, shape, and graphic attitude of Mike Vallely's pro deck for World Industries, released in 1989, set the tone for

Above left: *The double-kick design of this 1998 Santa Cruz skateboard ridden by Tim Brauch typifies the shape and size of skateboards during the 1990s, when street skating dominated the industry.*

Above right: *Ron Chatman drew the graphic and Barret "Chicken" Deck did the layout for this Milk Skateboard Goods (MSG) reissue (right) of Chatman's pro model deck from 1991 (left). This is the first board MSG made for its relaunch under Scream Distribution in 2021. Chatman rode for World Industries in 1989 and starred in the World video* Rubbish Heap *alongside Chris Pastras, Steve Rocco, and Mike Vallely.*

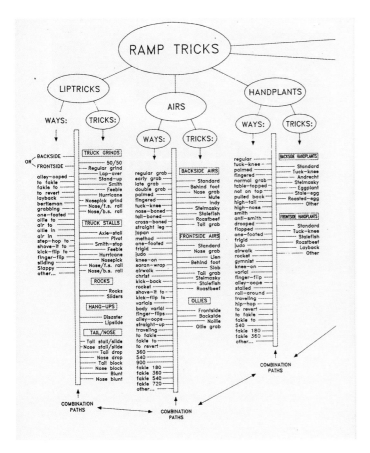

most of the 1990s. Skate decks became lighter, thinner, and had a double-kick profile to accommodate the needs of street skateboarders performing kickflips and boardslides. Some argued that this resulted in a more easily breakable skate deck, requiring the skate consumer to purchase more decks and benefiting the profits of the skateboard brands. Most deck graphics moved past the apocalyptic imagery of skulls, screaming hands, and dragons of the 1980s and began to include super models, rockstars, cartoon characters, graphic representations of both male and female anatomy, liquor bottles, drug paraphernalia, and just about anything else.

Skate videos matched the number of new companies debuting in the 1990s. The skateboard team video pioneered in the mid-1980s became the most important way to gain visibility and relevance to the skateboard consumer. Since the majority

Above: *This manuever chart was published in* Poweredge *magazine. The page, which was part of a spread, breaks down skateboard tricks into different categories, which is more accurate to the actual connectivity between maneuvers.*

Top right: *This set of master keys dates to the first year of the Skatepark of Tampa (SPoT), which started in 1993 as a DIY warehouse hangout space for a few local die-hard vert skaters. SPoT has grown to host two of the most globally important skate competitions, Tampa Am and Tampa Pro.*

Lower right: *Zoo York cofounder Eli Morgan Gesner used his signature graffiti tag to create the company logo, shown here on a ca. 1993 Zoo York sticker.*

of skate videos from this era featured street skating on city landscapes, the location of each skater's part became fetishized by skaters around the world. Many traveled to sites just to skate the same terrain as their favorite skater in their favorite video. Emulation of skateboarders by their fans widened not only to include clothes, shoes, and equipment but also to embrace a series of iconic sites known by insider nicknames, such as the Gonz Gap, Pulaski, and LOVE Park.

Equally important as the footage seen in these videos was the soundtrack that accompanied each skater's part. For many viewers, this was the first time they heard punk, hip-hop, and other genres of music not often played on radio stations. *411 Video Magazine*, which was started in 1993 by Josh Friedberg and Steve Douglas, was a video series, first on VHS tapes and later on DVDs, released four times each year. It was known not only for the sheer amount of skateboard footage presented to the consumer but also for its music curation. While most skate videos featured a single skate brand's team and took at least a year to produce, *411* came out every three months. This gave the skateboard consumer unprecedented access to both pro and amateur skaters and a glimpse into skateboarding around the world.

Preceding *411* were the print magazines *SLAP* and *Big Brother*, both of which debuted in 1992. World Industries founder Steve Rocco was behind *Big Brother*, while *SLAP* was devoid of any obvious skate industry connection. Even though in the 1990s skateboard print media was no longer dominated by *Thrasher*

and *Transworld Skateboarding*, skateboard brand owners were still influencing what was seen in skateboard magazines.

While most of the proliferation of new skateboard brands was located in California, a number of New York City brands emerged in the 1990s, including SHUT (1989), Zoo York (1993), Supreme (1994), 5Boro (1995), and Rookie (1996). These brands were unapologetically East Coast and offered no excuses for featuring the gloom and grime of New York City instead of the palm trees and sunshine of California.

Rookie, the first skateboard company to be founded by women, featured a diverse team of both men and women, a rarity for 1990s skateboarding as women were still nearly invisible in the industry. In the last decade of the twentieth century, there were two women on the United States Supreme Court but only one woman on the cover of *Thrasher* (Jaime Reyes, 1994), one woman in a skate video (Elissa Steamer's 1996 part in *Welcome to Hell*), and a single women's pro signature skate shoe (Cara-Beth Burnside's 1997 shoe for Vans).

In 1995, cable television network ESPN produced the Extreme Games (changed to the X Games in 1996) in Rhode Island. Events included bungee jumping, rollerblading, mountain biking, sky surfing, and skateboarding. Although some skateboarders derided this event as corporate and inauthentic, the mass exposure given to skateboarding by ESPN had a positive effect on skateboarding's popularity within the general American public. It also gave a much-needed visibility bump to vert skaters, who had been almost entirely absent from skate videos and magazines. At the 1995 games, Tony Hawk won a gold medal in vert, while Chris Senn won gold in street. No women skateboarders were included in this inaugural competition. In fact, it took another eight years for women to gain entrance to the X Games.

At the 1999 X Games, after ten failed attempts and well after the regulated time given for his run had expired, Tony Hawk completed the first 900 landed in a skateboard competition. The 900, a vert trick accomplished by riding the skateboard for two and a half rotations, was the holy grail of tricks, something that many people thought could not be done. The year 1999 was a very good one for Hawk. His video game, *Tony Hawk's Pro Skater*, debuted on PlayStation and generated millions of dollars in sales worldwide.

The end of the 1990s saw skateparks become legal again and not restricted by punitive liability laws. In 1997, the California State Legislature passed AB 1296, which effectively protected skatepark owners and operators against litigation for accidents or injuries. Nike made its first attempt to enter the skate shoe market. Vans opened the largest indoor skatepark in the world, Rocco and Mullen sold their vastly successful World Industries for an estimated $20 million, and Hollywood began to show interest in an article in *Spin* magazine titled "The Lords of Dogtown." At the end of its fourth decade, skateboarding was popular and profitable again, with new corporations and media conglomerates taking notice. As it approached the new millennium, skateboarding was tested again by economic instability, global societal conflicts, the fickle pronouncements of what is cool, core, and authentic, and the influence of the unforeseen monster known as the Internet.

—Betsy Gordon and Jane Rogers

The 1990s

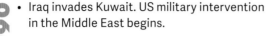

- Iraq invades Kuwait. US military intervention in the Middle East begins.
- The largest art theft in US history occurs in Boston, MA, when two thieves posing as policemen steal more than a dozen works of art, among them three Rembrandts, a Vermeer, and a Manet, from the Isabella Stewart Gardner Museum.

- Paul Schmitt closes Schmitt Stix and launches New Deal Skateboards with Steve Douglas and Andy Howell. Harnessing the marketing power provided by skate videos, New Deal distributes a team skate video before it makes its product available.
- Skateboarder Jason Lee appears in Sonic Youth's music video directed by Spike Jonze.

- Spike Jonze shoots *Video Days*, the first skate video for Blind.
- Mike Ternasky, Danny Way, and Colin McKay found Plan B Skateboards. Ternasky is instrumental in convincing Rodney Mullen to adapt his unique style of freestyle to street skating.

- Stacy Peralta leaves Powell-Peralta to focus on his filmmaking career.
- Tony Hawk and Per Welinder leave Powell-Peralta to form Birdhouse Skateboards.
- Bill Clinton is elected the forty-second president of the United States.

- New York City's World Trade Center is bombed by terrorists. Six people are killed and over one thousand are injured.
- A fifty-one-day standoff begins in Waco, TX, when a government agency attempts to arrest Branch Davidian leader David Koresh on federal arms violations. Four agents and cult members are killed in the raid.

- Copying its format after Andy Warhol's *Interview*, *Juice* magazine debuts with the subtitle *Sound, Surf & Skate*.
- Jake Phelps moves out of the distribution warehouse to become editor in chief of *Thrasher*.
- Intel ships the first Pentium chips, revolutionizing computer processing.

- Nicole Brown Simpson and Ronald Goldman are found murdered outside her home in Los Angeles, CA, on June 12. Five days later, her husband, football star O. J. Simpson, is arrested for the crime but is acquitted sixteen months later. The trial revealed a culture of racism in the Los Angeles Police Department.

- With the release by Etnies of the Sal 23, Sal Barbier becomes the first African American to have a signature skate shoe.

- *The Simpsons* becomes the longest-running primetime cartoon series.
- Lobbying on behalf of IASC, Jim Fitzpatrick gets AB 1296 passed through the California legislature. This protects skatepark owners and managers from legal claims of injury at their facilities.
- Cara-Beth Burnside and Vans launch the first women's pro signature skateboard shoe.

- John Glenn becomes the oldest astronaut in space.
- President Bill Clinton denies his relationship with former White House intern Monica Lewinsky in a televised interview and in a subsequent grand jury hearing. Clinton's denials are proven false and lead to an unsuccessful impeachment of the president.

- Neil Blender, Chris Carter, and Mike Hill open Alien Workshop.
- Mark Hubbard and Mark Scott begin to build a skatepark under the Burnside Bridge in Portland, OR, without the city's permission. It flourishes as a perpetual work in progress as skaters continue to add and remake concrete skate features to this day.

1991
- The World Wide Web, commonly abbreviated as "www," becomes available as an Internet service.
- Powell-Peralta skater Tommy Guerrero and SMA's Jim Thiebaud start REAL Skateboards under the umbrella of Fausto Vitello's Deluxe Distribution.

1993
- Jim Fitzpatrick founds the International Association of Skateboard Companies (IASC) and becomes its executive director.
- Mark Gonzales leaves Blind to ride for REAL.

- Rick Howard, Megan Baltimore, Mike Carroll, and Spike Jonze found Girl Skateboards. In later years, Jonze becomes a prolific filmmaker, director, screenwriter, and actor, winning an Academy Award, two Directors Guild of America awards, a Golden Globe, a Grammy, and a Writers Guild of America award.

- Plan B's second video, *Virtual Reality*, shows several team riders skating in Adidas Campuses and Superstars and Puma Clydes. This sparks a multiyear trend of skaters hunting down vintage Adidas and Puma basketball shoes.

1994
- Republicans gain control of both houses of the US Congress for the first time in forty years.
- DC Shoes launches under the mantle of footwear innovation with an all-signature product offering that includes models by Danny Way and Colin McKay.

1995
- ESPN debuts the Extreme Games in Newport and Providence, RI.
- Timothy McVeigh and Terry Nichols explode a bomb outside the Murrah Federal Building in Oklahoma City, killing 168 people in a domestic terrorism attack.

1996
- Vans sponsors the inaugural Triple Crown of Skateboarding.
- Toy Machine releases *Welcome to Hell*, introducing the skateboarding world to Elissa Steamer.
- Bill Clinton is reelected president.

1999
- A mass shooting at the Columbine High School in Littleton, CO, kills thirteen and wounds more than twenty others before the two teen gunmen commit suicide. A national debate on gun control follows but yields little new federal gun regulation.

- PlayStation debuts the *Tony Hawk's Pro Skater* video game.
- At the X Games, Tony Hawk successfully lands the first 900 (two and a half rotations in the air).

THE TRUTH LIES BETWEEN STYLE AND SUBSTANCE

TED BARROW

Skateboarding is a trick-driven sport whose material culture is determined by the urges of twelve-year-olds to emulate their cool eighteen-year-old heroes. It is to be expected that things shift as rapidly as the random tastes of a teenager, and when one decade ends and another begins, things get weird. As the 1980s transitioned into the 1990s, this was typified by the McSqueeb, an asymmetrical haircut involving a hair flap on top and at least one buzzed side. Poised firmly between punk and new wave, this uneven coiffure spoke of mixed alliances and, of course, awkward adolescence. As skateboarding entered the 1990s, this teenage struggle between style and technique would birth skateboarding as we know it today.

Between 1988 and 1992, the plywood assuredness of the 1980s Big Three, Powell-Peralta, Vision, and Santa Cruz, got as soggy and splintered as a neglected vert ramp behind an abandoned asbestos-walled warehouse skatepark. Street skating was more accessible to legions of twelve-year-olds, so street shapes soon replaced the baroque flairs of the Big Three. By 1992, some experimental gambits of the late 1980s, such as making Popsicle stick–shaped, nearly symmetrical decks that can be ridden switch (leading with the opposite foot of your normal stance), became the industry standard, while others, such as Boneite decks, fell to posterity's document shredder.

The decks of the late 1980s and early 1990s tell this story in intense, multicolored layers—plies even. The Alva Bill Danforth model, for example, stands as the consummate late-1980s skateboard, along with the Mark Lake model by the eponymous brand. Both neon color–screened decks boast absurdly grotesque and bombastically macabre graphics girded by plastic rails, state-of-the-art trucks resting on the plinth of a riser pad (both would be gone by 1992), large, squarish wheels (Alva Speed Skins and Bullet 56s by Santa Cruz), high kicktails, and short, flat noses.

Alva Skateboards, started by former Z-Boy Tony Alva in 1978, promoted a miscreant image of leather jackets and punk aesthetics through the 1980s. Danforth's Circle of Skulls graphic, conceived of in 1986, draws deeply from the punk roots of the brand. As Danforth describes in *Thrasher* magazine, the graphic was first conceived of on a napkin, then redrawn for a small batch of 250 boards by fellow Alva pro Jef Hartsel, finally to be redrawn a third time by Mad Marc Rude, a San Diego–based punk promoter and artist. Rude's conception, which was wildly popular, incorporated a circle, a reference to the Los

In this mid-1980s photograph by J. Grant Brittain, Tony Hawk models the then-popular McSqueeb hair style at Del Mar Skate Ranch.

Angeles–based band the Germs, and skulls (always a plus). Today a napkin, tomorrow the world. The neon colors and gruesome imagery were the period's aesthetic regime, while the smooth contours and relatively versatile shape of the deck made it a huge seller. The custom griptape job on the top constitutes an ornate and loud example of the craft and creativity of late-1980s skateboard art. The 1980s were skateboarding's medieval period, with powerful guilds representing the big brands, an emphasis on craftsmanship and stylized imagery, and the skull a moribund reminder of both glam and glum.

The 1980s skateboard was both a vehicle and a fashion accessory, a proclamation of one's values. "That's why I wanted the skulls and the Germs circle on my board," Danforth explained in *Thrasher*. "Those were things that meant something to me." Danforth's graphic embodies how 1980s graphics became heraldic emblems for the rider, and this proved marketable. The G&S trucks, constructed of a composite plastic and hollow alloy axle, sit on custom plastic risers also linked to Danforth and

The shape, wheels, riser pads, rails, and graphics of these decks—ca. 1988 Mark Lake model (left) from Lake Skates and ca. 1986 Bill Danforth model (right) from Alva Skates, with a graphic by Mad Marc Rude—typify the late 1980s.

Alva, with the Speed Skins branded by Alva bearing the same claw slash marks. Loyalty to a skater and a brand was forged through consonant pieces (sold separately, of course). True Danforth fans didn't simply buy the deck. They bought the whole setup. Danforth's model was pivotal as the end of one tradition— that of the skull-patched graphic whose iconology could be linked to the rider's own punk roots and whose shape was linked to an aggressively retrograde street skateboarding style of acid drops and launch ramps but little in the way of the technical board maneuvers of the next generation.

Why then, a mere two years later, did Danforth's skull-encrusted punk aesthetic seem ossified and clunky to 1990s youth? Two words: *video days*. The increased ubiquity of VHS cassettes (replacing contests and demos) among younger skateboarders meant that the next generation spent more time studying skateboarding in a controlled environment, rewinding and reviewing tricks that they themselves performed repeatedly before their appearance on tape. The late-1980s generation was raised on street skating studied in videos, practiced in driveways, and then shared with others downtown. While skateparks and backyard jams were an extension of the punk rock venues of the 1980s—consider Devo playing at Del Mar Skate Ranch as the iconic fusion of these two worlds—parking lots, sidewalks, and

By the mid-1990s, skateboards had changed drastically from the 1980s. Shapes became standardized, and graphics moved away from the ubiquitous skulls and animals to politics, history, and societal issues, as this 1995 Julien Stranger model by REAL Skateboards illustrates as it acknowledges the millions killed in the Holocaust.

urban plazas soon became the backdrop to skate videos. Video cameras invited everyone to the stage.

Inversely, while the boards themselves shed their plastic accoutrements, the street tricks got more technical. The soundtrack of these new videos was thoughtful and sensitive, and there seemed to be a sonic link between the emotional tenor of the songs and the isolation of the skaters in the parking lot. This was skateboarding outside of the spotlight, often illicit and on private property, with technical triumphs on the skateboard broadcast to connoisseurs of the current. Nobody understood. Waah. After the celebratory, brash, loud tone of skateboard imagery in the early 1980s, an increasingly somber mood descended on the sonic and graphic landscape of street pioneers. Things morphed from macabre to melancholy in a matter of months.

By 1990, smaller, younger companies catering to street skating embraced a DIY aesthetic that matched their fledgling nature. The pared-down industry, such as it was, was built on collaboration, engendering a synergy of risky gambits and bold experiments. This is the background of Jim Thiebaud's pro deck on REAL Skateboards. Unlike the skully punk rhetoric of the year before, the *Hanging Klansman* made no bones about its politics. Thiebaud, who skated as an amateur for Powell-Peralta throughout the late 1980s, was supposed to go pro for them, but when he saw his proposed graphic ("this terrible snake thing that I just wasn't into at all"), he decided to join his friend Natas Kaupas over at Santa Monica Airlines, turning pro for them in 1989. Countermanding the totalitarian aesthetic of spirit animals and iconic skulls that determined Powell's graphic direction in that period, Thiebaud and Kaupas envisioned something melancholic for his first board. According to Thiebaud, Natas sketched a "morose superhero sitting on a gravestone with this evil character looking down on him." They took this sketch to Jim Phillips at the in-house studio at NHS, Santa Monica Airlines' distributor, and that sketch was transformed into something less nuanced, less self-deprecating. Within a year, Thiebaud would reunite with former Powell colleague Tommy Guerrero and Jeff Klindt to start REAL Skateboards.

By 1993, deck shapes had standardized, and graphics themselves could be outrageous or meaningless, hand drawn or subversively ripped off from larger brands. The punk upstarts of the 1980s had become the new establishment of the 1990s, yet certain graphics still shocked. Take, for example, Julien Stranger's 1995 pro model graphic for REAL Skateboards: in bold red and black paint bleeding against an institutional gray backdrop, blocky, stencil-like text reads "NEVER FORGET 6,000,000 DEAD." Below the front truck is a black, rectilinear swastika, while at the same position beneath the back truck, on the tail, is a Star of David. A clear reference to the Holocaust, the graphic was as jarring then as now, and singular in the history of skateboard graphics. According to a phone call with Stranger in 2019:

I had seen *Schindler's List* the night before and was deeply affected. I went into Deluxe [distribution] the next day and talked about the graphic. . . . None of us saw a problem with the use of a swastika at the time since the context seemed so clear to us. It was actually my mom who saw it and told me how wrong it was to show that symbol anywhere near a Star of David. All I can say is that I was young and it was a mistake. Obviously, it looks a lot different in these times of unbridled bigotry from sick backward segments of America. Also, not that it matters, but I'm Jewish.

This graphic remains searing, digging into a raw nerve of global history that remains bloody and tender. While it may be unthinkable to reproduce or reconsider this graphic for release in the twenty-first century, it stands testament to the political and historical imperatives at the core of some brands.

In 2017, the Columbia, South Carolina skate shop Blue Tile reused the Thiebaud *Hanging Klansman* graphic to protest racism in the South, with Thiebaud's full support. In what other sport, subculture, or art movement could a trademarked image be reappropriated with permission and still remain relevant? What better image, loaded with its legacy of skate lore, than Thiebaud's graphic from 1990? That Natas's original graphic could draw from urban graffiti styles, Shel Silverstein, Public Enemy, Minor Threat, and politics and personality proves that the template for modern skateboarding has always been diverse. In the 1990s, skateboarding left its plastic shell and found its identity.

Skater and artist Natas Kaupas adapted his original ca. 1989 Hanging Klansman *artwork for this 1991 Jim Thiebaud model deck (above right) made by REAL Skateboards.*

ROOKIE
SKATEBOARDS
CATHARINE LYONS

The 1990s were a time of transition for both skateboarding and New York City. Skateboarding's popularity was on the rise again after a big drop from its 1980s peak, when California and vert reigned supreme. The expansion and evolving dominance of street skating combined with the free and democratic availability of pavement (especially in New York City) was a ticket off the sidelines for many. City skaters, without access to ramps, skateparks, or empty swimming pools, rolled from spot to spot to do tricks on ledges, jersey barriers, stairwells, bumps in the sidewalk, garbage cans, and any other piece of urban architecture they could get at.

During this time, the eternally changing New York City was in the middle of an evolutionary leap. The blight and bankruptcy of the 1970s had given way to a boom and then a crash in the 1980s, altering New York's neighborhoods in a multitude of ways. Areas of the city whose buildings had been filled with manufacturers began to lose their industrial and sweatshop tenants, leaving commercial loft spaces vacant. This moment of opportunity, before a new wave of rezoning and development swept through the city, allowed three young women to rent a big, vacated Chinatown sweatshop space and start a small, arty skateboard company.

Elska Sandor and I met while working retail at neighboring stores, the skate shop Swish and the street-wear shop XLarge,

on Tompkins Square Park in the far East Village. One serendipitous night in 1995, we both attended an art show opening held in the Brooklyn Bridge Anchorage. An artist had installed a halfpipe and invited skaters to come ride it as a sculpture-in-motion.

The plywood ramp was overflowing with exuberant young men shuffling to claim and hold an inch at the coping and get a chance to drop in, slapping their boards in solidarity after someone landed a good trick. Only the most assertive could get a turn to skate, and not one female skater was on that ramp.

This raucous event epitomized what is so compelling about skateboarding. It is more than the act of skating itself or landing the tricks. It's a camaraderie and a belonging, a creative expression, a bond across demographics and personalities, and indeed it is an art form. For both Elska and me, this event also put a spotlight on the truth that, for whatever the reasons, female skaters were not included. That night in the Anchorage propelled us to commit to an idea we had: to start a skateboard company together.

In early 1996, we teamed up with our friend Jung Kwak (who left the company in the early years) to found Rookie Skateboards, the first women-owned and -operated skateboard company. At

In this 1998 photo, Elska Sandor captures Rookie team skaters (left to right) Jessie Van Roechoudt, Jaime Reyes, and Lauren Mollica and Zoo York pro Harold Hunter hanging out at Supreme on Lafayette Street in Manhattan.

Above left: *A woman pioneer of 1990s street skating, Jaime Reyes grew up in Hawaii, turned pro in 1993, and joined Rookie Skateboards in the mid-1990s. The company introduced this Jaime Reyes deck model ca. 1997.*

Above right: *This Rookie Skateboards Empire deck dates from 1996, the first year of the company. When describing her brand, Rookie cofounder Catharine Lyons stated, "New York City was our celebrity partner."*

the time, the most tangible female presence in the skateboarding industry was overtly sexualized: non-skating images found in graphics and advertising. We saw a glaring absence of female riders in any skate media, very little support for female skaters, and a conspicuous lack of product with female skaters in mind. With Rookie, however, we did not aspire to create a separate parallel industry for female skaters. We simply strove to expand the existing industry and to sow a more inclusive path for all. Fundamentally, anyone bitten by the bug of skateboarding and out riding a deck is a skater. Female skaters don't need the prefix *girl* if they don't want it. Through the makeup of our team, Rookie recast the idea of who a skater (and a company owner) could be.

From the start, Rookie Skateboards quickly snowballed into a busy if chaotic little company selling decks and gear throughout North America and, before long, the world. Our early-1900s Canal Street factory loft was part office design studio, part distribution warehouse, part home, and part clubhouse. Friends and members of our team were often there to help load in heavy boxes of product up the three long flights of stairs and then would stay to hang out for the day or dinner or late into the night. Fellow New York City skate companies, including Zoo

York, Brooklyn Boards, 5Boro, and Supreme, embraced Rookie and our vision. These companies helped us by sharing manufacturers and warehousing as well as vital friendship and encouragement. Perhaps due to the common bond of striving to make a skateboard company in New York City, the camaraderie of the city's skaters, as it turned out, extended to the business of skateboarding too.

Weaving into the mainstream California-based skateboarding world proved harder and happened more slowly. Being the combination of women owned and from New York, Rookie was literally the definition of outsiders to the conventional skate industry. In some ways, this status was liberating. It freed us to do things our own way, and so we did, whether intentionally or because we just didn't know any better. While we were creating an entrée for female skaters, we were also offering an alternative to a large and growing population of male skaters who were also looking for something different.

Above left: *This felt-letter, zip-up hoodie was produced by Rookie Skateboards in 1997. Rookie created classic skate apparel in sizes and cuts to fit the female skater.*

Above right: *This SLAP magazine ad from 1998 features Rookie Skateboards team members Lauren Mollica and Jaime Reyes.*

The Rookie aesthetic and graphics were subtle, artist based, and urban. Manufacturing small runs only in the United States, we supplied decks and clothing to an uncommon and shrewd customer. We believed that the kid in the skate shop was not just buying a deck to ride but also buying a piece of art. Partnering at times with many different artists, such as ESPO, Dalek, Beci Orpin, and Andre Razo, Rookie appealed to the budding skater–art collector.

Rookie's roster of skaters included Jaime Reyes, Lauren Mollica, Tino Razo, Jessie Van Roechoudt, Sean Kelling, Jon Klein, Lisa Whitaker, Kyla Duffy, Shane Medanich, and Amy Caron, among others. Hawaiian skaters Jaime and Sean named our Rookie crew Ohana, the Hawaiian word for "family," embodying the spirit of the company—the loyalty, love, dedication, and the dysfunction.

Rookie, perhaps, was only a seed planted, but its influence on the sport and particularly its relationship with female skate-boarders helped to forever shift the American skate scene. Today, female skaters in skate spots of New York City and beyond can be seen claiming their inch at the coping and taking their turn.

This 1996 photo by Christina Mack shows the combined display booth of fledgling New York skate brands Rookie Skateboards and Brooklyn Boards at the Action Sports Retail trade show in San Diego, California. Deciding to collaborate rather than compete against each other in the hyper-competitive trade-show atmosphere, they cohosted a steady stream of buyers, visitors, and well-wishers to their shared space. (From left) Brooklyn Boards founder Dan Zimmer sits beside Rookie cofounders Elska Sandor, Jung Kwak, and Catharine Lyons.

FLORIDA GIRL IN A CALIFORNIA WORLD

ELISSA STEAMER

I grew up in Florida and didn't start skating until 1985 or 1986, when I was ten or eleven. I was into BMX before I got into skateboarding. At fourteen, I was the only girl skating for miles and miles around. During the summer, the Florida Amateur Skating League held contests every other week all over the state. They had divisions based on age and status: 1-A, 2-A, 3-A for the amateurs, then divisions for sponsored and pro skaters. When I entered 1-A, there was only one other girl.

After I turned seventeen and graduated from high school, I worked at a bookstore. I used to dress nicely for work; I wore skirts and hose because I was supposed to be presentable. When it was time to skate, I would go to the back room and change into a purple New Deal shirt, baggy pants, and a pair of big, old Airwalks and then go to the contests. I was supposed to work, but all these demos would come through, and I couldn't miss them. One day, I called my boss to tell him I wasn't going to make it to work, and he said, "Oh, well, you're going to have to quit." But I'm glad I didn't go back to work because I got so many free boards that summer. That started me on this path.

Everybody who came to town gave me a board because I guess they had never seen a girl skate rat of my caliber. Barker Barrett gave me my first free board, a Creature. Guy Mariano gave me a Keenan Milton board, and Chad Muska gave me a Toy Machine board. My friend Matt Milligan got sponsored in high school and rode for New Deal. He got boxes of boards from them for free and would sell them to me for twenty-five dollars apiece. He went to California after graduation, and when I tried to go with him, he told me there was no room in the car.

I was left behind in Florida, but I wasn't there for long. One of my California friends told me to call Lance Mountain, a former Bones Brigade skater. I called Lance, and he told me to come on out to skate in California. At this point, I was twenty-one and wanted to be a pro skater, but I didn't know what it would look like because I had never left Florida. My friend Lovey and I decided we'd drive a Volkswagen bus from Fort Myers, Florida, to Seattle, Washington, because my sister had moved to Seattle. I knew bigger and better things awaited us.

Above left: *These Gnarhunters Elissa Steamer model Nike skate shoes date to 2020. Before creating the Gnarhunters brand, Elissa Steamer was one of the few girls to keep up with the boys of skate, winning four X Games gold medals in street from 2004 through 2008.*

Above right: *This vest worn by pro skater Leo Baker in 2020 features a Gnarhunters patch. The name Gnarhunters comes from the slang "shred the gnar," which is used in surfing and skating to mean go big or never give up. Steamer's Gnarhunters brand combines the laid-back style of surfing with an edgier skate style.*

Elissa Steamer was the only girl to be included in the thirty-minute video Welcome to Hell, *made by Toy Machine in 1996. Featuring many of the best street skaters of the day, including Mike Maldonado and a young Brian Anderson, the video was instrumental in launching Steamer's career.*

After the bus broke down a few times, and we had spent all of our money trying to fix it, we got as far as Los Angeles. I called up Lance and he told me to come over. We skated most of the night with Lance, and he shot a photo of me. We shot a "Check Out" that day, which is this special section in *Transworld Skateboarding* magazine for sponsored amateurs and flow skaters. Flow is a level of skateboarding sponsorship that includes skaters who get products from a specific brand or other enterprise but no money, as opposed to amateurs who get paid but don't receive a pro model of their own. But after a few weeks, I ran out of money and went back to Florida.

Then three years later, in 1995, Toy Machine came knocking on my door. I said I was ready to leave Florida again for California and make this happen. That was in December, and the pro contest was in January or February. Jamie Thomas came to the pro contest, and we filmed our *Welcome to Hell* material during that week. Right after *Welcome to Hell* came out, we went on a long tour. I knew I had made it when I was walking through the Warped Tour and somebody grabbed me and said, "I just saw you in a magazine."

Still trying to make money at this skateboarding thing, I rode for Etnies, and then another shoe company asked me to ride with them. After that, I was regularly switching among three different companies, and then Etnies said they'd give me my own shoe. I didn't have an agent or "people," so I had to figure out everything myself.

Although I didn't know it at the time, I was experiencing pay inequality in the skate business. Gender discrimination was also there, but the guys I skated with looked out for me. I was special to them. They protected me, almost like a little sister. I had my crew, and if some guy came in and said something stupid or lame, he got ousted. I was lucky. It wasn't as easy for some women in the industry, but it is better now than it was.

Skate has come a long way. I have my own brand, Gnarhunters, and I'm so proud because all of it came from my brain. I've had tons of help along the way, but what I make is synonymous with me. You're not going to see Gnarhunters and not think of me. If I'm giving something that's the most inclusive of every aspect of me that I can give, that makes me happy.

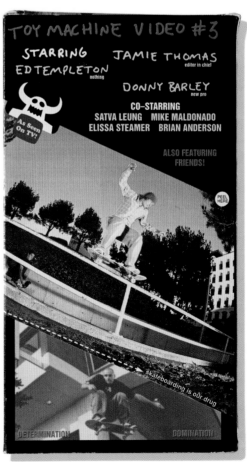

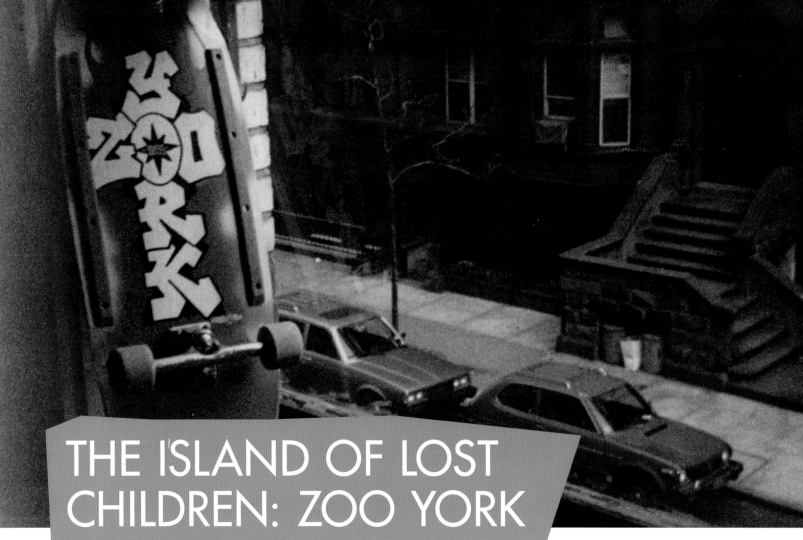

THE ISLAND OF LOST CHILDREN: ZOO YORK

ELI MORGAN GESNER

As this book attests, skateboarding is not only uniquely American but decidedly Californian. And yet, on a steel and concrete collection of urbanized islands, a secluded, bastardized, and important skateboarding evolution also occurred thousands of miles away.

In the spring of 1965, *Life* magazine published a photo story by Bill Eppridge showing New York City kids skateboarding through the streets of Manhattan. By this time, *Gidget* and Southern California surf culture had swept across America. But even in these early pictures of kids skating through the urban landscape, it was clear that the magnitude of New York City had already begun to alter the DNA of Southern California skateboarding.

Gone were the sunny beaches, palm trees, and bikinis. In their place was a more cosmopolitan style—a skater dressed for a night out in Soho, complete with dress shoes and button-down collar rather than barefoot and tan. But perhaps the most notable thing in these pictures is the diversity. White, Black, and Latino skaters, both male and female, ventured out together on this new vehicle through the towering urban metropolis. It was a marked departure from the endless landscape of California beach kids.

By the mid-1970s, New York City locals began to take ownership of this new skateboard identity. Led by Andy Kessler,

the best skater in New York City at the time, and taking their inspiration from their friends, the legendary Z-Boys of Los Angeles, they explored the decaying outskirts of the city in search of empty pools to skate. Keeping with what was already a long tradition for New York City kids, they left their mark by covering the streets in graffiti tags as they went. In Riverside Park, they cobbled together a ramp out of stolen wood, dubbed it the Outlaw Ramp, and the best skaters in the city would meet there.

In a coincidence that would forever affect the outcome of my life, the Outlaw Ramp was built next to the playground where my mother took me to play as a small child. Some of my earliest memories are of watching in awe as these kids skated a rickety quarter pipe covered in graffiti tags, their actions forever burned into my five-year-old brain.

A tight-knit crew that could only dream of California's 1970s concrete skateparks formed at the Outlaw Ramp. But this skateboard crew needed a name. The term *Zoo York* is credited to the seminal graffiti writer Marc André "ALI" Edmonds, president of the Soul Artists graffiti crew. But in 1976, Andy Kessler and the New York City skateboarders, inspired by the iconic

This 1984 photo of a skateboard owned by legendary New York skateboarder Andy Kessler includes Eric Haze's hand-painted Zoo York logo rendered in the style of the Dogtown Cross.

Dogtown logo designed by C. R. Stecyk, began emulating their West Coast brothers by writing "Zoo York" in a cross on their ramps and decks.

In 1979, in an inspired act to unite the skateboarders and graffiti writers of the city, ALI called a meeting at the Cathedral Church of St. John the Divine. Dramatically, he presented everyone with a new magazine that he had just made—*The Soul Artists of Zoo York*—which was to be more than just a magazine. ALI had a vision that everything these NYC kids were doing was more than just trivial vandalism. It was art—all of it, from graffiti to skateboarding—an idea decades ahead of its time.

By the 1980s, just like the beloved concrete skateparks they yearned to skate, the original Zoo York skateboard crew began to fade away. So potent was the California pool skater fantasy, that without that dream to pursue, what was left? Skateboarding in NYC died and, in its place, the other half of the Soul Artists of Zoo York triumphed—graffiti.

Above left: *In the mid-1970s, skaters built an unauthorized wood ramp in New York City's Riverside Park, appropriately naming it the Outlaw Ramp. This 1975 photo shows Eric Haze skating it.*

Above right: *This New York City brick wall, captured by photographer Matt Webb in 1985, displays artist ALI's Soul Artists of Zoo York tag, which he protected with a 1979 "copyright."*

Like so many kids in New York City, I started writing graffiti. But at ten years old, I created most of my art in my bedroom, hunched over sketchbooks, trying to emulate my older graffiti heroes. I got good at it, or at least good enough to impress the older graffiti writers in my hood. I snuck out of my house one night to go bombing with them, and to my amazement, they all rolled up on skateboards. There it was: my rickety, old, graffiti-covered skateboard dream that had been burned into my five-year-old brain. Somehow it was still alive in the dark, forgotten corners of the city streets.

I got my first skateboard in 1982, when I was twelve. It was a Vision Gator. I hooked up with the small pack of die-hard skater kids who were still skating in New York City, and we began to hang out downtown in Washington Square Park. There were no more mystical concrete skateparks left to dream about in a far-off magical land called California. Now, for us, there was only New York City, so we targeted our skateboards on that.

Every single day, we hunted the endless city streets in search of something that no one had skated before: curbs, stairs, ledges, banks. And even though none of us knew it at the time, together we were inventing a new type of skateboarding—street skating. And as was the tradition in New York City, most of us carried a graffiti marker to write our tags on the walls as we went.

All I did in school was draw. I was a terrible student. In 1985, the best skater in the city was Ian Frahm, and he also wrote graffiti under the tag "THOR IBM." One day, I drew a graffiti piece of Ian skating. Later that same day, at our local skate shop, Soho Skates, I ran into Ian. He liked the drawing so much that I tore it out of my loose-leaf binder and gave it to him. Two weeks later, without my knowledge, Soho Skates had turned my drawing into an exclusive T-shirt graphic for sale in its store. It was my first piece of professional artwork, and I was given two free T-shirts as payment. I was fifteen.

By 1986, it was becoming upsettingly clear to all the New York City skaters that the boards we were buying from California were built for backyard ramps and not for exploring the unforgiving streets of the big city. And no one knew this better than two of the city's most veteran skaters, Bruno Musso and Rodney Smith.

Together, Bruno and Rodney started New York City's first skateboard company, SHUT Skates, which was also the world's first street-skating-only skateboard company. Bruno and Rodney organized the tragically ignored East Coast skateboarding talent pool into one of the most formidable skate teams ever. And for SHUT's graphics, they looked to New York City's graffiti heritage.

Mistakenly assuming that I knew what I was doing because I drew the Soho Skates T-shirt, Bruno and Rodney hit me up to design their logo for SHUT when I was only sixteen. I drew for

Top: *Photographer Henry Chalfant became enamored of the evolving graffiti art he saw on the New York City subway cars in the early 1980s. He began documenting it and eventually produced more than 150 images of these ephemeral moving murals. This 1981 image shows the work of Marc André "ALI" Edmonds proudly declaring his love for Zoo York.*

Above: *In 1979, Marc André "ALI" Edmonds made a magazine for the crew of skateboarders and graffiti artists known as the Souls Artists of Zoo York. One of the three remaining copies of the magazine was given to Eli Morgan Gesner by the graffiti artist, ZEPHYR, in 1995.*

them the SHUT barbed-wire-block logo and the legendary SHUT crest—both still in use today by the very same SHUT Skates. The combination of the raw, urban graphics and the power of SHUT's multiethnic skateboarding gang quickly resonated back to California. SHUT had put New York City on the global skateboard map.

To this day, the original 1980s SHUT Skates Posse is the stuff of skateboarding legend, but unable to fend off both skaters being lured away by big California skate companies and predatory business partners, SHUT was forced to close (it was relaunched in 2006). And as the 1980s came to an end, another giant hole was left in New York City skateboard culture.

During this time, most of the kids I grew up skating with quit or, if they were good enough, moved to California to pursue a career in the industry. Defiantly, a few skate shops, like Skate N.Y.C. and O.D.'s, fought to stay open and support the dwindling skate survivors. But these ventures were doomed from the start. Skating died, and I ended up taking a young graffiti writer, OJ, under my wing. He and I skated, virtually alone, every day for years.

But through all this, Rodney Smith never lost faith and learned from his mistakes. He committed himself to, once again, creating a world-class New York City skateboard company. This time the company would overtly focus on the fact that it was not from California. Indeed, it would beat people over the head with the fact that it was born and raised on the streets of New York City.

In 1993, with the help of the graffiti writers FUTURA 2000 and STASH, Rodney got in touch with ALI and received his blessing to use the name Zoo York. Next, Rodney partnered with Adam Schatz and myself, and together we put what little money and resources we had into making Zoo York into a skateboard company.

To honor the legacy of the original Zoo York skateboard and graffiti crew, I created the infamous Zoo York tag graphic. Almost overnight, the combination of Zoo York's stark NYC imagery, graffiti iconography, and new roster of untapped East Coast skateboard talent put Zoo York on the skate-industry map.

Not wanting to be subjected to the controls of the California-based skate industry, Rodney set up a wood mill (with Gregg Chapman, who would later found Chapman Skateboards) in Long Island to make our boards exclusively on the East Coast. But despite our best efforts, we could not manage to screen print a full deck graphic from tip to tail. Not surprisingly, no one in the California skate industry would divulge this secret method to us. But necessity breeds invention, so with no other options, I looked to my New York City graffiti roots and, using spray paint, developed a spray fade technique to create unique color-fade effects. This technique ended up making Zoo York decks highly coveted.

The biggest thing in skateboarding at the time was *411 Video Magazine*. Curious about what we were doing way out in NYC all by ourselves, *411* asked us to make an "industry section" video. Knowing that it would be seen by everyone in the skate industry, I set out to make something as Zoo York as possible—dark, urban, decaying, and decidedly dangerous. We won Best Industry section that year and could feel the world's eyes turning toward the East Coast.

Seeing the success that we were having at Zoo York, the graffiti writer ZEPHYR, an original member of the Zoo York skateboard crew, gifted us with one of the few remaining copies

of *The Soul Artists of Zoo York* magazine in a show of support. We have kept it safe for the past few decades, only now donating it to the Smithsonian's National Museum of American History.

Then in 1994, James Jebbia opened a much-needed skate shop. Beginning with the concept of making a physical location that looked like a Soho art gallery, and creating a logo inspired by the fine artist Barbara Kruger, James named his skate shop Supreme. At first, Supreme was simply our cool, new local skate shop, albeit slicker and more sophisticated than the average skate shops of the day. But since then, over the past three decades, Supreme has evolved into a cult-like fashion mega brand. In 2021, Supreme had a valuation of $1 billion, making it one of the most successful fashion brands in the world.

Our mission statement at Zoo York was to represent New York City street culture, not just skateboarding. For years, I had quietly been visiting my friends DJ Stretch Armstrong and Bobbito "The Barber" Garcia at their late-night underground hip-hop radio show on WKCR. I had amassed an impressive collection of never-before-seen video footage of some of the most popular and influential rappers of the time. This, we decided, was to be the soundtrack to our first skateboard video. And so, the *Zoo York Mixtape* was born. Even though rap and graffiti had made appearances in skateboarding before, this single video is now recognized as the definitive inflection point between skateboard and hip-hop culture.

The 1990s were a seismic shift for New York City skateboarding. With Zoo York, Supreme, and the surprise hit movie *Kids*, it was as if the entire focus of the skateboard world shifted to New York City. Not only did other city-based companies begin to grow, like 5Boro and the tragically short-lived Rookie (the first female-owned skateboard company), but even California-based companies scrambled to make out-of-left-field skateboard companies with that New York City vibe. Some of the industry's most beloved pro skaters, such as Jason Dill and Mark Gonzales, moved to New York City. No longer were we a novelty item for the Bones Brigade to parade through on their way to skateboard glory. New York City had become a focal point of the skateboard world.

Today, the dues that we local New York City skaters collectively paid over the past half century have cemented our city as one of the international capitals of skateboarding. Tyshawn Jones, a native New Yorker, was made *Thrasher's* Skater of the Year in 2018. It is now impossible to imagine a time when New York City wasn't synonymous with skateboarding, but that's not how it always was. New York City was the island of lost children, outcasts to our California brothers and sisters and ostracized by our fellow New Yorkers. It took relentless sacrifice by the toughest of souls through decades of neglect to make New York skateboarding what it is now.

When Andy Kessler and the original Zoo York crew built the Outlaw Ramp back in the 1970s, they were dreaming about skating the perfect concrete bowls in far-off California. But the loveless streets of New York City were all they had, so they made them work however they could and by any means necessary. Now, just a short push away from the exact location of that original ramshackle ramp, the ramp where I first saw people skateboard, stands the Andy Kessler memorial concrete skatepark in Riverside Park. The park that Andy grew up skateboarding in—and the dream that Andy devoted his life to—has come true for the next generation of New York skaters.

Above left: *Combining a hip-hop soundtrack with the aggressive New York City street skating scene made Zoo York's 1997 Mixtape skate video one of the most iconic representations of 1990s skating.*

Opposite top and top middle: *When Zoo York first started to produce decks, they didn't know how to screen print graphics on the curved surface of a skate deck, and no one in the business would show them how. Instead, cofounder Eli Morgan Gesner would spray paint the brand name, as shown on the 1994 Zoo York Graffiti model and the 1994 Oyola Puerto Rican Flag deck. Although the spray fade technique was created out of a lack of screen-printing knowledge, the Zoo York decks were unlike anything being produced by other skateboard brands and sold out immediately.*

Opposite bottom middle: *After receiving a cease-and-desist letter from New York's Metropolitan Transit Authority (MTA) over the use of its subway line graphic on a 1996 MTA Train Z deck, Zoo York negotiated the first product licensing agreement the MTA had ever done. Today, product licensing for the MTA brings in close to a billion dollars a year.*

Opposite bottom: *Zoo York issued this Tiger Bomb model for team rider Jefferson Pang in 1997. The name is a play on the popular Tiger Balm ointment.*

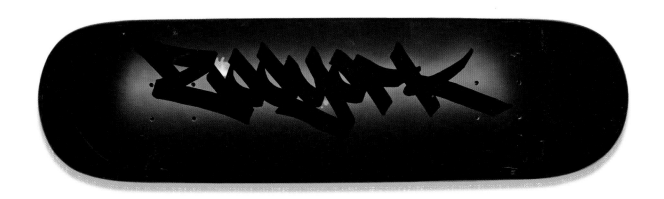

Ricky Oyola
-1994-
Zoo York

241 St
Bronx

Flatbush Ave.
Brooklyn

Z

NYC 212-718-

TIGER BOMB
SKATEBOARD
JEFFERSON PANG (ZOO YORK)

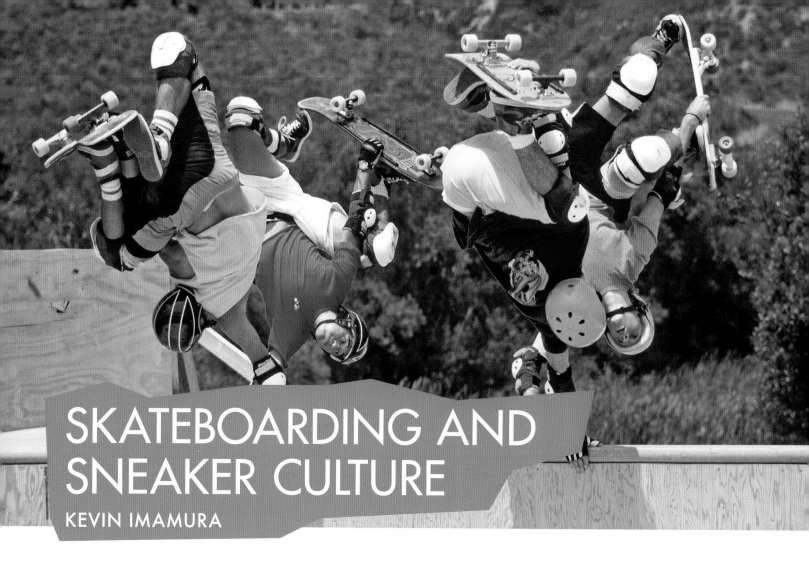

SKATEBOARDING AND SNEAKER CULTURE

KEVIN IMAMURA

At skateboarding's inception as the stepchild of surfing some seventy years ago, it was *sans* footwear. But with the game-changing introduction of urethane wheels and griptape in the 1970s, shoes literally became an extension of a skateboarder's equipment: urethane gripped the concrete and griptape stuck to shoes like Velcro. While footwear may not have started out as a requirement, it certainly helped skaters push the boundaries of what was once thought possible. The true potential of the ollie—the trick that propelled skaters skyward without the use of hands, straps, hooks, or any other wizardry—became fully realized through the union of footwear and griptape. Just about everything else in contemporary skateboarding is an aftershock of that initial explosion.

On first inspection, skateboarding and modern-day sneaker culture appear to be odd bedfellows. Skateboarding, because of its physically harsh nature, relegates every aspect of its components as disposable. And specifically because griptape destroys skaters' shoes in a matter of days, it is incredibly difficult to be precious with them. But here we are, more than a half century in, and the "hobby" of collecting skateboarding artifacts of all types (skate shoes included) is stronger than ever. Following roughly the same timeframe, sneaker-culture aficionados have been collecting and appreciating the beauty of athletic shoes since

they were given the option of more than one gym shoe brand or color to choose from, the holy grails being the new or unused "dead stock" sneakers that get heralded as museum pieces. And as those gym shoes morphed into street wear and later into wardrobe staples and high-fashion statements, sneaker culture became popular culture.

The main reason why skateboarding and sneaker culture dovetail so nicely is because the footwear shares the same DNA: the ultra-grippy, vulcanized rubber court shoe. By using that as a starting point, it is easy to see where the journeys of skateboarding and sneaker collecting to the present overlap and intersect not just with each other but with multiple genres of music and street wear fashion. The real historical sparks happened due to the free-form, individualistic, and often contrarian nature of skateboarding. Until the early 2000s, the average skateboarder would never admit to collecting shoes or even consider themselves aware of sneaker culture because they saw themselves living an outsider lifestyle devoid of traditional fashion trappings. The connection point between sneaker collectors and

Three of the four Bones Brigade team members are wearing Nike Air Jordan 1s in this 1986 J. Grant Brittain photo of their iconic quadruple handplant on the Animal Chin ramp in Oceanside, California.

skateboarders is that they spend most of their time staring down at their shoes: collectors due to obsession and skaters because they are setting up for tricks. For many skaters, the outsider lifestyle remains, but the fashion element has most definitely evolved.

Skateboarding as an activity—unlike basketball, tennis, or any traditional sport—has no uniforms and no rules to define it. In its purest, noncompetitive form, there is no "winning," only movement. The skateboard, as a vehicle of freedom and expression, encourages its users to adapt to whatever is in front of them. Similarly, when it comes to skateboarding footwear, skateboarders have made it up almost every step of the way: appropriating when it suited them and adapting as necessary. With a few notable exceptions (Vans #95 and Slip-On specifically), most skateboarding shoes took their stylistic and performance cues from basketball shoes: toe caps, overlays, padded ankles, and, most importantly, the vulcanized rubber outsole popularized by Marquis Converse at the beginning of the twentieth century. For brief periods of time in every decade since griptape was introduced, basketball shoes *were* skate shoes.

During the 1970s, skateboarding was creating its own new world complete with equipment brands, clothing companies, and several shoe companies. Founded the prior decade as a casual lifestyle brand, Vans quickly gained popularity with skaters and, by the mid-1970s, was making models exclusively for them that checked all the right boxes: looks, performance, elite rider endorsements, and the "Off the Wall" tagline that would help them become the world's premier skate-shoe brand. But for everyone else who either couldn't get Vans (because they did not live in California or couldn't get them via mail order) or wanted something else, most simple basketball shoes of the day not only fit the bill but also set the template that many skaters still adhere to today (the Nike Blazer and the Converse Chuck Taylor). In the mid-1980s, skateboarders were blasting tricks higher and further than ever before, so their performance needs warranted footwear improvements. Leather cupsole basketball shoes led the sea change that would shape the look of modern skate footwear. It is what skaters did with shoes, however, that changed the way that people and shoe companies started to view them.

Skateboarders' ability to shape their sport has always been a mix of internal and external forces and influences: music, art, fashion, popular culture, and other sports. Choosing not to wear shoes officially "made for skateboarding," either out of economic necessity or simply for the panache, has always been done and continues to this day. But the true gift that skateboarding gave to sneaker culture—basically a "missing link" moment—is when influential pro skaters started customizing their leather basketball shoes en masse (the Nike Air Jordan 1—AJ1—specifically) with paint pens, permanent markers, and spray paint. Skaters had been dyeing and drawing on their canvas sneakers as early as the late 1970s. Brand-manufactured shoe customization was established by this point as well. Vans offered custom colors and

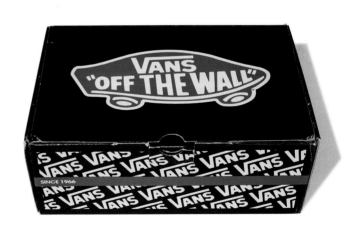

Top: *Vans pushed the stylistic envelope with its now iconic checkerboard pattern on the Old Skool, also known as #36, from the late 1970s.*

Above: *As Vans's shoes became synonymous with skateboarding, the company adopted its "Off the Wall" logo to describe the airborne tricks skaters pioneered in the mid-1970s.*

patterns early in the company's history, and Adidas released its adicolor capsule in 1983. However, these acts of artistic customization—on one of the most important sneakers of all time—just hit differently in the late 1980s, occurring as skateboarding was experiencing its own massive boom in popularity. When the heroes of 1987—Lance Mountain, Tommy Guerrero, Chris Miller, and Mark Gonzalez—started appearing in *Transworld Skateboarding* and *Thrasher* with painted up AJ1s, skaters could feel that this style was new and real: customization and art done on shoes by some of the most influential skaters of that generation.

Just as the abundance of brands, materials, and colors gave basketball players a means to stand out in the early 1970s, do-it-yourself shoe customization became yet another way for skateboarders to express their individual style. The notion that a leather basketball shoe could be used as a "blank canvas" and a vehicle for storytelling would become the inflection point for sneaker culture and skateboarders in the decades to come. Whether skaters colored the entire shoe with their own palette or painted only parts of it to amplify elements of the AJ1's design not originally intended by the shoemaker, it was truly an unlock for shoes that was 100 percent skateboarding.

But as influential and popular as the Air Jordan 1 was with skaters, the second the shoe was no longer available, several new homegrown skate shoe companies began filling the void and stretching their wings. With Nike and Adidas almost entirely ignoring skateboarding until the second half of the 1990s, these new brands created a booming industry that began to have its own sway on popular culture. As mainstream athletic footwear brands pushed their own boundaries of innovation and aesthetics in that era, so too did skate shoe brands such as Airwalk, Etnies, DC, and the handful of new companies that seemed to pop up monthly. The functionality of skate footwear was well established by this point, so the performance needs simply required refinement, allowing a greater emphasis on design flair and hitting skaters over the head with pseudo-technical advancements. But as those elements became more and more exaggerated and turned into bloated caricatures of what a skate shoe needed to be, the pendulum started to swing in the other direction.

Above: *Nike Air Jordan 1s (1985 model pictured here) were a favorite of skateboarders because of their performance attributes, but also because the shoe's leather upper allowed for easy customization with paint pens, permanent markers, and spray paint.*

Opposite: *Photographer J. Grant Brittain catches Neil Blender mid-eggplant in Sacramento, California, in 1986. A close look at Blender's mismatched Air Jordan 1s reveals a host of modifications, including unique colors and custom art.*

Having long ceased production in favor of new designs, by the mid-1990s, the only way to get coveted classic basketball sneakers was to hunt for them in thrift stores, closets, or by traveling to Japan, where the vintage basketball sneaker had been elevated to exalted status. By the end of the decade, the rise of the Internet and online auction sites enabled a new generation of sneaker enthusiasts and collectors to find each other. Most of them grew up on punk, hip-hop, and club music and one other common denominator: many of them skated. The oldest sneakerheads grew up with pictures on their walls of Tony Alva wearing Vans or Nike Blazers. And the younger ones grew up admiring J. Grant Brittain's famous *Animal Chin* invert photo, where three of the four skaters are wearing Air Jordan 1s. But within that crew, there is also a collective appreciation for old-school hip-hop and the shoes that went with it: Puma Clyde and Adidas Campus and Shell Toe. These new collectors lived in New York, London, Tokyo, and Los Angeles and were building their own brands. Or they were running magazines or record labels or skate shops, all while quietly building up their shoe collections and singing the praises of classic shoes, further launching both subcultures into worldwide notoriety.

At the end of the twentieth century, the global explosion of hip-hop culture and sneaker enthusiasm showed no signs of slowing down, and all the major shoe brands had found a way to scratch the growing itch everyone was feeling toward old shoes with the "reissue." By the time Y2K was upon us, if an old shoe hadn't already been brought back, someone at the company was plotting it. Even the Nike Dunk—a slightly less favored shoe, essentially the baby brother of the AJ1—got reissued, both in its original form and in unique colors and materials. Some of the earliest and most exciting examples of this came from Nike's CO.JP collection (a set of store-exclusive makeups for Japanese retailers that included Air Jordan 1s, Dunks, and Air Force 1s) and had special names, colors, and stories attached to them. Another key element was that they were only available in a select few shops around the world. Those tremors set off alarm bells with people in the know, and the shoes were snapped up

Above left: *The Converse Chuck Taylor All Star (ca. 1980s) made its debut in 1917 and has been an integral part of skateboarding footwear since skateboarding's genesis.*

Above right: *With the 1994 release by Etnies of the Sal 23, an early sample of which is shown here, Sal Barbier became the first African American to have a signature skate shoe. This iconic shoe also took inspiration from basketball shoes and applied it to a shoe specifically made for skateboarding.*

Opposite: *Skater Chris Miller at a Witts store demo in Oceanside, California, in 1987.*

quickly. The skaters among the underground collecting network instantly "got it" because it was more than a bit reminiscent of what they had done to shoes in the 1980s. This "official" version of customization and storytelling was to become standard operating procedure. Nike Skateboarding quietly launched in 2002 and used all these mechanisms as the template for its success with the Dunk Low Pro SB.

The chain reaction started by the Nike SB Dunk caused people to view not only skate shoes differently but also sneakers in general. For skaters, it didn't hurt that this one-time basketball shoe looked like it was designed for skateboarding since the performance attributes were already built in. Many skaters recognized the shoe's utility and historical reference—and skated in them. But many more people also viewed these Dunks as both a means of self-expression and as pieces of art—to be collected, traded, and sold. Certainly, other brands

had customized shoes before and told stories with them. But never had a singular shoe that used those tools been so obsessed over and coveted.

In a short time—and with the help of the digital revolution—the crossover of sneaker culture and skateboarding became the bedfellows that we know today, in a cultural moment where hip-hop superstars are asked to color up a skate shoe and when other collaborations on that same shoe are mentioned on a company's quarterly earnings calls. Whether most people realize it or not, the genesis of the current sneaker revolution came about because skateboarders did basketball shoes their way.

In this 1986 photo by J. Grant Brittain, Tommy Guerrero skates The Dish at San Francisco's Hilltop Park in a pair of highly customized Air Jordan 1s.

THE SKATEBOARD THAT CHANGED AMERICA

In 1988, I had a conversation with Fausto Vitello, cofounder and publisher of *Thrasher* magazine. We were at the Action Sports Retailer (ASR) trade expo in Long Beach, and I was exclaiming at the lack of skateparks in the United States. There were only two at the time! He said directly, as was his style, "Look, you've got to do this. You're the only one who can pull it off. You've got to do it! Make public skateparks possible!"

I sought out the counsel of Jack O'Connell, my local state representative in Santa Barbara, California. His nephew was in the Montessori school I ran, and I'd talked to him a few times, though never about skateboarding. I asked Jack how I could get public skateparks in California, and his immediate response was that it would never happen—we'd need tort reform, and trial attorneys would never go for it. It was impossible.

It took me four years of daily work. It involved thousands of phone calls, thousands of faxes, dozens of treks to and from the state capitol in Sacramento, and as many as 150,000 letters from skateboarders, police chiefs, mayors, council members, parks and recreation staff, and moms, dads, and grandparents. In 1993, I founded a 501c3 nonprofit, the International Association of Skateboard Companies (IASC), and immediately launched IASC's letter-writing campaign: Do You Want Public Skateparks?

Paul Schmitt, founder of PS Stix, Schmitt Stix, and other skate-affiliated brands, helped IASC create stickers, flyers, and even skateboard decks to ensure skateboarders would understand what we were attempting to accomplish. Skaters were initially slow to respond, but eventually most everyone seemed to realize the importance and benefit of public skateparks.

After years of meetings and lobbying, I arrived before the California State Senate's Judiciary Committee in 1997 carrying five thousand letters in US mail bags as a sample of the type of support we had created. In my bag, I also had my Roller Derby #10 skateboard. Fortunately, the Honorable Bill Lockyer was on the committee, and once he saw the board, he declared that he had the same one as a kid.

It was that personal connection, one small, steel-wheeled Roller Derby skateboard, that proved O'Connell wrong. That group of California state senators voted to change the state's liability laws, which allowed cities and towns to develop and build public skateparks in California without the threat of liability for injuries. With California setting an example, states from coast to coast adapted their own approach to eliminating liability for skateboarding injuries in public parks. Today, twenty-five years later, there are more than thirty-two hundred public skateparks in the United States, with more being designed and constructed each month.

—*Jim Fitzpatrick*

Top: *In 1997, the International Association of Skateboard Companies produced these skate decks, labeled with stickers from PS Stix, to lobby for the passage of SB994. When it eventually became law, it allowed skateparks to be added to the California Hazardous Recreational Activities (HRA) list. The HRA list protects California cities and communities from liability when people engage in certain sports, including tree climbing, basketball, spelunking, and surfing.*

Above: *The #10 model skateboard by Roller Derby was one of the most ubiquitous skateboards of the 1960s. The ca. 1964 #10 pictured here was owned by Jim Fitzpatrick and traveled with him when he lobbied to change the liability laws in California that prohibited the building of skateparks.*

FROM SKATEBOARDER TO SNOWBOARDER AND BACK AGAIN

CARA-BETH BURNSIDE

When I was twelve, I was skating against seventeen- and eighteen-year-olds. For me, it was like skating with the grown-ups. I have so many trophies from going to contests. I was at that age where I just wanted to win trophies. I was skating in pool contests, but then the skateparks closed.

Street skating evolved from that, and then I would skate here and there. Later, after high school, I would see people skating ramps. They would build them in their backyards or just pull out a quarter pipe and put it on the road. I started skating those and getting good, and then I was doing contests with the guys. I ended up going pro, but nobody cared. I was just a girl skater to them.

I could compete at a pro level and place in the top ten or fifteen out of sixty guys. But none of the companies would give girls a pro model. I didn't care what they said. I loved skateboarding and just wanted to skate.

It took stepping away from skateboarding and learning how to snowboard for me to learn how to succeed in skating. People would tell me that snowboarding was geared toward women—that women could win prize money. Snowboarding wasn't as easy as I thought it would be, and I knew that I needed to

practice. I went to Mount Hood, which has a year-round snowboarding season, and realized if I went there every summer, I could do both, snowboard and skate. I was in more magazine photos than in the past, and I was doing snowboarding videos. That video coverage led to filmmakers also shooting me skateboarding. It helped to be out there, but I was still not really getting anywhere.

Dealing with snowboarding and Burton's marketing scheme for the company's women's signature boot led me to try and convince Vans that people would buy a women's skater pro model shoe. Vans was doing signature shoes at the time, and I thought why not do my own shoe—a CB shoe?

I got a meeting with the president of Vans and his son, and I gave them the idea of doing my own girl shoe. I don't think the president even knew who I was or that I skated, but he liked the idea, and he immediately brought a couple of people into the meeting, Jay Wilson from marketing and Saudi, a woman

Cara-Beth Burnside was a member of the inaugural snowboarding team at the 1998 Nagano Winter Olympic Games (pictured first from left in the middle row). She came in fourth, just missing the podium behind teammate Shannon Dunn.

designer. The designer was very open to my design ideas and was glad to see a woman skater designing a woman's skate shoe. I photocopied my initials and said I wanted the CB inside a sun design on the heel. The design would be simple because girls were not going to buy an expensive skate shoe. It was going to be more of a lifestyle shoe. We could be at a price point where it would sell because you want numbers. You don't want not to be able to sell the shoe. We started with an existing gum bottom sole because soles are the expensive part of a shoe. After a few meetings with the designers, some of the design aspects were cut, but the flames of the sun surrounding my initials stayed.

Vans made several models of the shoe. When the first ones came out, they had a lot of pop, which really helped people

Above left: *In 1999, Cara-Beth Burnside created the design for her Vans pro model shoe. An existing gumshoe sole was used to keep costs down and she designed the sunburst with her initials inside, which was placed on the heel of the shoe. It went on to become one of the most popular style Vans for that year, luring consumers who were not skateboarders.*

Above right: *With the release of the August 1989 issue, Cara-Beth Burnside became the first woman skater to be featured on the cover of Thrasher magazine.*

notice them. It was a cute shoe for anyone to wear, and I could wear it skating. It was affordable—a pair cost maybe fifty bucks—and it came in different colors. Some girls bought the light blue, but I didn't like the light blue. I liked the black. I had to think like that—in terms of this being a business. You want to make something that appeals to everybody, and I understood that from when I was snowboarding and working with Burton. Burton was very receptive to working with women snowboarders, so Burton guided me while designing by own model snowboard boot. This helped immensely when working with Vans designing my own shoe. I kind of knew what to expect and what might be popular with our target audience of young girls.

My mom always told me, "No one's going to do anything for you. You have to toot your own horn." That's what I started doing, and it worked out with that shoe because I think women like to see other women doing things, then they buy into the story. The shoe did really well, and all of a sudden, skateboarding had its first women's pro model shoe.

PROUD TO BE A SKATER

I was at my dad's, and out the window, I saw two kids skate-boarding under the light. That's the first time I remember seeing someone skate, at least in person. I was obsessed; I kept asking for a skateboard, even though I didn't know anything about skateboards. I didn't even know a brand. I remember I took the first skateboarding magazine I got—*Big Brother*—to my fifth-grade class, and it was confiscated. I got it back and still have that magazine with the green cover.

Going into the skate shop, I just picked the graphic I liked. The clerk offered me stickers, and I asked myself, is that what skaters do? I always felt excited to be in a skate shop. Once I was skating better, I was there to show off. People didn't think that girls could skate, so I was going to skate. I never felt scared, which is probably why I was able to get better. I can see how skating can be intimidating.

I see little kids, especially girls, who don't know how it works at the skatepark. There will be a girl sitting on the side, scared to take her turn. All I can think is, every time some guy gets five turns and a girl is too scared to go, the guy is getting five times as much practice.

I don't think my mom has ever seen me skate in person. When I skated in the garage, I would lock the door and put up a sign saying no one was allowed to come in. I was always scouting out the empty parking lot that was smooth enough and lit well enough but where no one could see me skate.

It was different around skaters. I was shy around nonskaters because I felt like they didn't really get what they were looking at. To this day, I have friends who say, "I passed skaters and thought of you, but they weren't good." They could very well have been good. People don't understand that 50 percent of the things you try, you end up falling on the ground. Usually, you fall a lot. I didn't like people watching me who didn't understand that.

I didn't want anyone to feel sorry for me if I fell. When you see a person walking on the street and that person falls down, everyone is immediately worried. That reaction comes from a good place. Falling isn't a normal thing, so people are concerned when they see it happen. In skateboarding, falling is normal. Everyone is bad when they start skating. Skateboarders are, in general, really good about seeing someone battle and work for a trick, even if it's the simplest trick, and recognizing doing it is an accomplishment for them. Skateboarders are genuinely cheering when they see that. There may be some negative aspects of skateboarding, but that camaraderie is one thing I've always been proud of as a skateboarder.

— *Alexis Sablone*

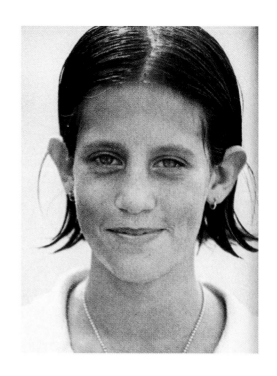

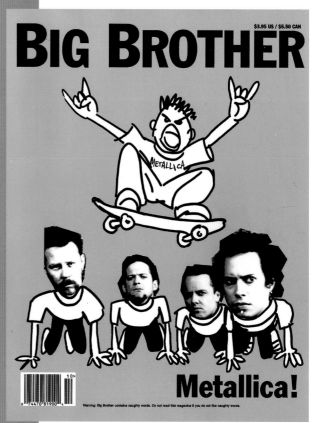

Top: *Alexis Sablone competed in her first skateboard contest—an all-girls competition—when she was just twelve years old, a year before this photo of her was taken.*

Above: *Alexis Sablone's fifth-grade teacher confiscated this copy of Big Brother magazine (issue 24, 1997) from her when she was in elementary school. She eventually retrieved it and still has it today.*

GEORGE ORTON AND THE RISE OF THE X GAMES

JANE ROGERS

Beginning in 1979, ESPN was the first all-sports cable network. In those early years, in order to fill twenty-four hours, it featured some little-recognized sports, like men's professional slow pitch softball. Eventually, it landed the big four, the NBA, NFL, MLB, and NHL, and with the creation of the NCAA's March Madness, ESPN was on its way. In 1993, ESPN2 was created to air more "alternative" sports, such as poker, and more extreme sports, including skateboarding, motocross, and surfing.

These alternative sports seemed to interest the elusive younger viewing audience, so in 1995, ESPN created a made-for-television "sports festival" known as the Extreme Games. While skateboarding was included, so were the more bizarre sports of bungee jumping, sky surfing, and street luge. The latter entailed a rider lying face up on a metal "luge" that was actually a jacked-up skateboard and riding it on a downhill S-shaped course very, very, fast.

Enter George Orton, a legendary 1970s skateboarder who is one of a few credited with inventing the frontside air, a skateboard move that allows a skater to fly up a vertical wall, gaining height up and over the edge of the pool or ramp. Orton had retired from skateboarding in 1982, started a career, and began raising a family. But not one to stay idle, he tried his hand

at motocross and was ranked second in the United States in amateur waterskiing. After being asked back to the skateboarding world by some of his old friends, he began skating for Santa Cruz in 1992.

Orton had always been a bit reckless, or at least that's how some would characterize breaking the land speed record of 61.87 miles per hour while standing up on a skateboard headed straight downhill! His ADHD kept him in constant motion, as a kid and as an adult, so when he heard about a street luge competition at the 1997 X Games, the recently renamed Extreme Games, he decided to give it a try. Orton raced his way into fourth place in the super mass downhill, six street lugers racing down two lanes on Rancho del Oro Drive in Oceanside, California.

Early on, athletes saw an opportunity to further their careers by displaying death-defying feats and introducing new tricks at the annual games. Tony Hawk performed his first 900 at the 1999 games. The event has grown into a legitimate sports

Above left: *This race bib was worn by George Orton at the X Games in San Diego in 1997.*

Above right: *George Orton, who was one of the best vert skaters of the late 1970s, won this second place medal in street luge dual at the Summer X Games in 2000.*

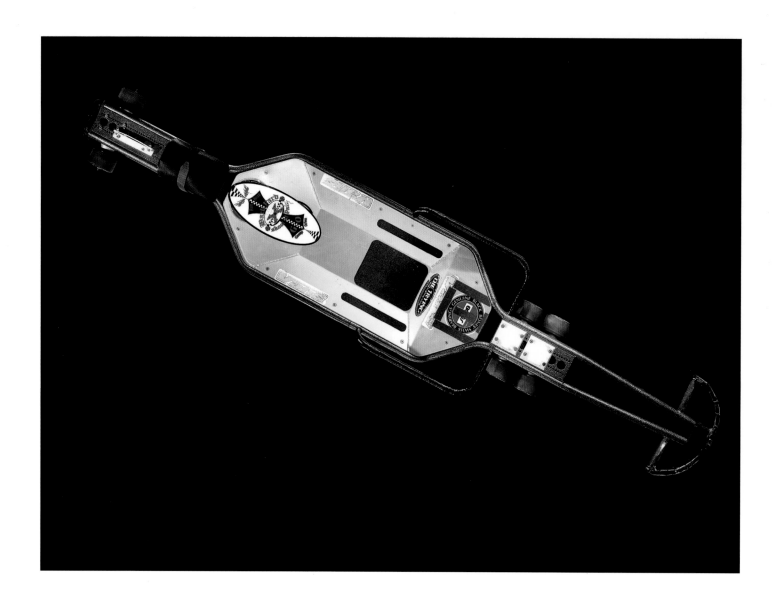

competition, launching the careers of many extreme athletes and bringing some of those extreme sports into the mainstream.

The original plan was to hold the games once every few years, but the huge following prompted ESPN to launch an annual competition, adding the first Winter X Games to the schedule in 1997. Athletes competed for medals along with prize money, although for the first few years, the competition was ridiculed by the media. One *USA Today* columnist called the X Games the "Look Ma, No Hands Olympics." But it was the media, high-profile sponsors, and top-notch athletes that would ultimately propel the X Games and the participating athletes into the sports lexicon. The introduction of skateboarding and surfing into the 2020 Tokyo Summer Olympics further legitimized these extreme action sports, providing a new level of credibility to the X Games.

Above: *This custom-made street luge was ridden by luge and downhill skater George Orton in the 1990s. He would lie face up on the luge and steer the board with his feet, reaching speeds of up to sixty miles per hour.*

Opposite: *Hand painted by Van Houten to resemble a shark's head with the teeth surrounding the darkened visor, this fiberglass skateboard luge helmet was worn by George Orton during his street luge career.*

TURNING PRO

BRIAN ANDERSON

I thought about becoming a professional skateboarder, but I was working in restaurants and was interested in having a life, money, and a career, so I decided to go to culinary school to become a chef. But then I went to California a few times, where some of my friends had gotten even further into the skate industry and become professional.

I sent my video with the stuff I had done in San Francisco and Sacramento to Toy Machine in San Diego. My friend Donny Barley was already on Toy Machine, and I had skated with Toy's founder, Ed Templeton. The folks at Toy Machine said they would fly me to San Diego to skate with them for a month or two, and if it went well enough, they would put me in a video. And I thought to myself, Wow! This is so incredible. These guys think I'm that good and will give me a shot. Actually, it was these guys and a gal, because that's where I met Elissa Steamer, the only woman skating for Toy at the time

I slept on the floor in different houses all around San Diego and recorded some great tricks on video. We went through the video parts they had already stockpiled and edited mine quickly. Ed Templeton and Jamie Thomas said they definitely wanted me to be on Toy Machine.

This was a different turn in my life. Within a year, Ed and Jamie said I should be pro. I didn't want to step on the toes of

other guys on the team, Satva Leung and Mike Maldonado, but both of them said, "No, Bri. We think you're ready." It was cool to have their blessing.

The starting rate for a pro skater was $750 per month. Before that, as an amateur, I made $250 per month and was given five skateboards a month. Even though I broke a lot of the boards, I would still try and sell them. A board was worth twenty-five dollars, so that was an extra fifty bucks a month if I managed to sell a couple of them. I ate ramen and vegetables and drank that orange stuff, Tampico, cut with water. That was how you lived.

Once I was professional and earned more money and received lots of free things, I started saving equipment and would look for the kid with the most beat-up board or wheels at demos. I'd have four partially used wheels on a shoelace and just walk up and give them to the kid. It was great. You're recycling. You're making some kid's life for the summer.

So in the beginning I was getting $750 per month and whatever for free—jeans, hooded sweatshirts, baseball caps—plus sometimes people would give me cases of beer. It all worked out. I had enough stuff to feel comfortable and happy

Detail of Brian Anderson's Toy Machine deck with double-headed eagle graphic by Ed Templeton, 2000.

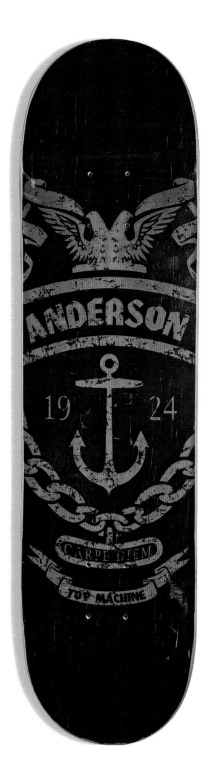

and to survive and pay some cheap rent. That was kind of all you want at nineteen—at least that was all I wanted. Once you have proven yourself over the first year of being professional, you might end up getting a small paycheck to be with a shoe company and then maybe you'd pick up a wheel sponsor and get another $200 a month.

If you started at $750 and kept showing that you're reliable and did a good demo and were good to the kids and weren't a pain on the road, people wanted you to be in the van. They wanted you in their magazine. They wanted you in their video. Then you started getting paid more and more, and then you felt you were getting what you deserved—at least I did.

Toy Machine produced this Brian Anderson pro model skate deck in 2000, a few years after he began riding for the company. A year prior, in 1999, Thrasher magazine named him Skateboarder of the Year.

SKATE STOPPERS

The velocipede was the skateboard of the early nineteenth century, a newfangled fad pursued by young men who wanted to see how fast they could go down a road *sans* horse. Popular in England, the velocipede quickly spread to the eastern coast of the United States. By 1819, many American newspapers were reporting on the popularity of this predecessor to the bicycle, stating that it was all "the go" in London. That very same article warned that "the crowded state of the metropolis does not admit of this novel mode of exercise, and has been put down by the magistrates of police." And sure enough, less than two months after lauding its popularity, the newspaper printed a story about a "melancholy accident" involving a young boy who was run over by a hit-and-run driver of a velocipede, fracturing the boy's leg.

A novel mode of transportation becomes wildly popular with young men, causes accidents, and is then banned—when else has this happened? Sounds a lot like the early 1960s boom-to-bust cycle of skateboarding. Newspapers of the time declared sidewalk surfing the "nation's newest fad," followed by these same newspapers warning about its inherent perils, alarming insurance companies and medical doctors.

Unlike the velocipede, the skateboard did not entirely disappear and, in fact, roared back in the 1970s to become an international industry and youth pastime. No matter how many bans, city ordinances, fines, and No Skateboarding signs appear, skateboarders kept finding ways to skate in the street.

Fueled by decades of public annoyance over young people on wheels, in 1998, brothers Chris and Michael Loarie patent the Walkway Abuse Deterrent System, soon to be known the world over as the Skatestopper. As described by the Loaries in their original patent application, "This invention relates generally to inhibiting defacement of curbs, rails, benches, and other walkway features and, more particularly, to inhibiting, for example, a wheeled, personal mobility unit, such as a skateboard or in-line skate, from sliding or grinding over such walkway features and the like surfaces." Their desire for a solution came about in part because Michael Loarie, a sergeant in the Escondido Police Department, had grown tired of trying to stop skateboarders from grinding (sliding) along the edges of curbs, benches, handrails, and other public property. As of 2020, the Loarie brothers still own and operate Skatestoppers. They estimate that there are over one million units in use in more than ten thousand locations worldwide. Visitors to the Smithsonian grounds will see these skate deterrents in liberal use.

—**Betsy Gordon**

Top: *Metal devices similar to these, commonly known as skate stoppers, are used extensively by the Smithsonian to discourage skateboarders from utilizing its public architecture.*

Above: *Here, skate stoppers have been installed on a concrete ledge to ward off potential skateboarders.*

Top: *The velocipede, also known as a pedestrian curricle, gentleman's hobby horse, or swift walker, became popular in England around 1818 and gained a following among wealthy young men. In the United States, a fad for the device in the 1820s inspired constant innovation and helped lay the groundwork for the modern bicycle industry. The model shown here dates from ca. 1866.*

Above: *This 2019 prototype for a No Skateboarding sign was created for use at the National Museum of the American Indian but never used.*

CHAPTER FIVE

'00s

SKATEBOARDING LOOKS BACK

When the clock ticked to 12:01 a.m. on January 1, 2000, the doomsday predictions of Y2K failed to emerge. Nothing happened to create massive bank failures or infrastructure paralysis among the food, water, and power supply. America breathed a giant sigh of relief. But it wasn't long before every crisis and tragedy first seen in the 1990s seemed to get increasingly worse as the new century emerged: climate disasters grew in size and scope, terrorist bombings became more frequent, wars in the Middle East continued for years without any real sign of victory, economic instability included sharper highs and lower lows, the US government became more polarized, gun violence in schools took more innocent victims, and the Internet began to insidiously affect every aspect of our lives.

In the first decade of the new century, the skateboarding community almost unanimously adopted the street as the terrain of choice. Although some vert ramps and bowls still existed for the skaters who wanted to pursue that form of skating, it was hard to compete with the omnipresence of the American concrete landscape outside many front doors. Skate-trick progression, previously fueled by innovations in materials science (urethane wheels), skateboard-specific design (trucks, closed-bearing wheels), and skateboard shape and composition (kicktail, maple ply, double kick), was now

Opposite: *San Francisco Bay area photographer Rick Chapman took this 2002 portrait of Tony Hawk in Carlsbad, California, a year after Hawk's first autobiography was published.*

motivated by the skater's reaction to terrain, architecture, and space. An infinite variety of tricks could be performed by stringing together variations in going up, down, onto, off of, and across curbs, stairs, ledges, handrails, benches, fire hydrants, poles, and countless other elements in the urban landscape. A notable exception to the ubiquity of street skating was the invention of the mega ramp, a hyper-large version of the 1990s vert ramp. Fostered by skater Danny Way's drive to push skateboarding to height extremes, a typical mega ramp was more than sixty feet tall and three hundred feet long. In 2005, Way successfully jumped over the Great Wall of China using a mega ramp.

As the United States became mired in an increasingly fraught present, the skateboarding community looked to its past. In 2001, Stacy Peralta directed *Dogtown and Z-Boys*, a documentary about his 1970s Zephyr skateboard team. Peralta's film went beyond the niche viewership of his skate videos and introduced skateboarding to a mass global audience. It won two awards at the Sundance Film Festival, made $1.2 million in its first year, and began a wave of skateboard nostalgia within the skateboard industry. Other films that explored skateboarding soon followed, including the biographical documentaries *Rising Son: The Legend of Skateboarder Christian Hosoi* (2006) and *The Man Who Souled the World* (2007) about World Industries' Steve Rocco.

As nostalgia for skateboarding's past seeped into the zeitgeist of this decade, skaters, skateboard artists, and skate

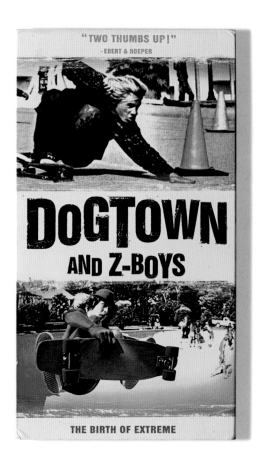

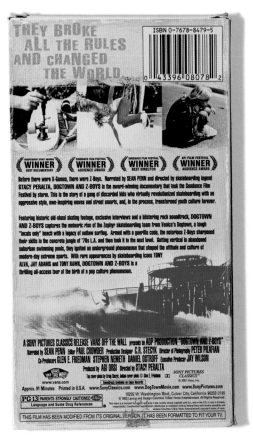

companies began to think about their legacies. They published books such as Tony Hawk's *Hawk: Occupation: Skateboarder* (2001), Sean Cliver's *Disposable: A History of Skateboard Art* (2004), and Independent Trucks' *Built to Grind: 25 Years of Hardcore Skateboarding* (2004). Skate competitions included a new category of competitor: the forty-something legend skateboarder. In 2008, Stacy Peralta joined George Powell to reestablish Powell-Peralta. It consciously sold nostalgia as it reissued eleven different Bones Brigade skate decks with their original graphics. The "reissue" deck soon became a part of the skateboard industry, with brands like Santa Cruz and Vision releasing a series of their most iconic 1980s decks. People were buying skate decks not to skate but to hang on their walls as an homage to their heroes and mementos of their youth. For many skateboarders of the previous decades, this emerging appreciation shown to the past allowed them to delay or even deny growing up, growing old, and growing irrelevant within this culture defined by youth.

In 2009, driven by a desire "to honor the passion and dedication to skateboarding—and contributions to its history and industry—by pro skateboarders and industry," the first annual Skateboarding Hall of Fame ceremony memorialized forty years of skateboarding by inducting Bruce Logan, Tony Alva, Tony Hawk, and Danny Way. Induction ceremonies are held every year. To date, there have been over 130 inductees from all eras of skateboarding's history.

Suddenly, skateboarding was an art, and its memorabilia collectible, worthy of competitive auction prices and museum displays. eBay fostered a healthy market for older skate decks, trucks, wheels, stickers, and clothing. In 2004, the traveling museum exhibition, *Beautiful Losers: Contemporary Art and Street Culture*, opened in Cincinnati at the Contemporary Arts Center. It firmly established skateboarding's influence in the art world by including a long list of photographers, graphic artists, filmmakers, and other artists who proudly claimed roots in skateboarding.

The 1990s model of small, independent, skater-owned brands was augmented by corporate buyouts. In 2001, Marc Ecko Enterprises acquired Zoo York, and Billabong bought Element. VF Corporation purchased Vans for $396 million in 2004. These acquisitions by non-skate-centered corporations often provided much needed cash and stability to companies that were struggling after the economic turbulence of the 1990s. Other brands found their skate relevance diluted as they were bought and sold numerous times. Vision, once a dominant brand in the 1980s, was sold to Collective Brands (now Payless

Left: *Directed by former Z-Boy Stacy Peralta and written by C. R. Stecyk, the 2002 documentary* Dogtown and Z-Boys *revived an interest in 1970s skateboarding.*

Opposite: *This shot from the 2004 Beautiful Losers installation at the Contemporary Arts Center in Cincinnati, Ohio, shows a mix of street-inspired photography, graffiti, film, skateboard graphics, and other media, in a groundbreaking moment for nontraditional artists.*

Holdings) in 2004, then sold again in 2009 to Finish Line, then sold again in 2017 to Authentic Brands Group, an international conglomerate that owned more than fifty consumer brands. Despite the turmoil in the American economy, skateboarding continued to be seen by many corporations as a source of lucrative shareholder profits.

In this era, skate brand team videos no longer dominated as the primary method to introduce new skaters and establish brand awareness. As cameras (especially those on a smartphone), editing software, and other filmmaking tools became more easily accessible and affordable to the layperson, a plethora of free skateboarding content was made available online. In addition to a never-ending supply of new skate footage, many brands reissued their archive of skate videos and premiered new videos on the Web for free.

Skateboarders were among the first to start using YouTube to bypass the traditional conduits for distributing and consuming skateboard content. Skaters used the online platform to launch such influential YouTube channels as Braille Skateboarding, Nka Vids Skateboarding, VLSkate, and Andrew Schrock (ReVive Skateboards). They uploaded skateboard tutorials and video part from young and unknown skaters from around the world.

These popular channels generated enormous viewership figures—followers in the upper six figures, hundreds of millions of views—and it was all free. As a result, a new genre of skateboarder was born: the YouTube skater. This type of skater gained prominence in the world of skateboarding not by competing in contests, being featured on the cover of *Thrasher*, or going pro for a popular skate brand. These YouTube personalities even began assembling their own skate teams and selling product, all enabled by the millions of clicks they received on their online content.

Shoe brands such as Nike, Adidas, and Converse seeking to launch into the skateboarding market created their own YouTube channels. The numbers of potential viewers, and future customers, were just too large to ignore. Their targeted consumer did not have to wait years to see a skater in a team or brand video. They could get weekly, even daily fresh skate content on a brand's YouTube channel.

By the end of the decade, there was a glut of skateboard footage—old, new, pro, sponsored, grom—available to watch every minute of every day. Because of this, demand diminished for paid access to skate footage. In 2005, *411 Video Magazine* issued its last edition. Skateboard print media giants *Thrasher*

US skater Danny Way used a mega ramp to make the first skateboard jump over the Great Wall of China, as seen in this July 9, 2005, photo. Way broke a world record by becoming the first person to successfully jump the wall without motorized assistance.

and *Transworld Skateboarding* kept their monthly print magazines going but wisely established digital websites and YouTube channels for their readers.

Believing strongly in the power of skateboarding to bolster self-esteem, teach discipline and perseverance, and provide healthy physical activity, many skateboarders used their skateboarding skills and mainstream fame to start nonprofit foundations. In 2002, Tony Hawk founded the Tony Hawk Foundation (renamed The Skatepark Project in 2020) to help underserved communities build skateparks. Since then, the foundation has awarded over $10 million to more than six hundred public skatepark projects in all fifty states. Australian skateboarder Oliver Percovich established Skateistan in Kabul, Afghanistan, in 2009 to empower children and youth through skateboarding and education. Today, Skateistan offers programs in South Africa, Cambodia, and Jordan, and nearly 50 percent of the participants are female. In 2010, former Alva skate pro Jim Murphy joined Oglala Lakota activist Walt Pourier to form the Stronghold Society to address the high rate of suicide among the youth on the Pine Ridge reservation. To date, they have built two skateparks on the reservation and have two more planned.

Skateboarding matured enough in the first decade of the twenty-first century to look back nostalgically at previous generations. It was an early adopter of Internet-based media and established an entirely new way to document and distribute skate content. While focusing almost entirely on street terrain, it invented a new form of skateboarding using a supersized version of a vert ramp. It became a collectible, an art form displayed in galleries, and the inspiration behind nonprofits and NGOs across the globe. As it moved into its sixth decade, skateboarding would continue to redefine itself as a luxury consumer good, an Olympic sport, and a voice of social justice.

—Betsy Gordon and Jane Rogers

Top: *The graphic for this 2009 sticker, which shows a skater destroying an automatic weapon with a skateboard, was created for Skateistan's first NGO in Afghanistan.*

Above: *In 2020, the Tony Hawk Foundation released this sticker with its straightforward message. Formed in 2002 to help communities build skateparks, it changed its name to The Skatepark Project in 2020.*

Opposite: *This 2009 poster was designed by Walt Pourier (Oglala Lakota) for the Stronghold Society. The society, which was founded by Pourier and Jim Murphy, uses skateboarding as a way to address depression and suicide on the Pine Ridge reservation in Pine Ridge, South Dakota.*

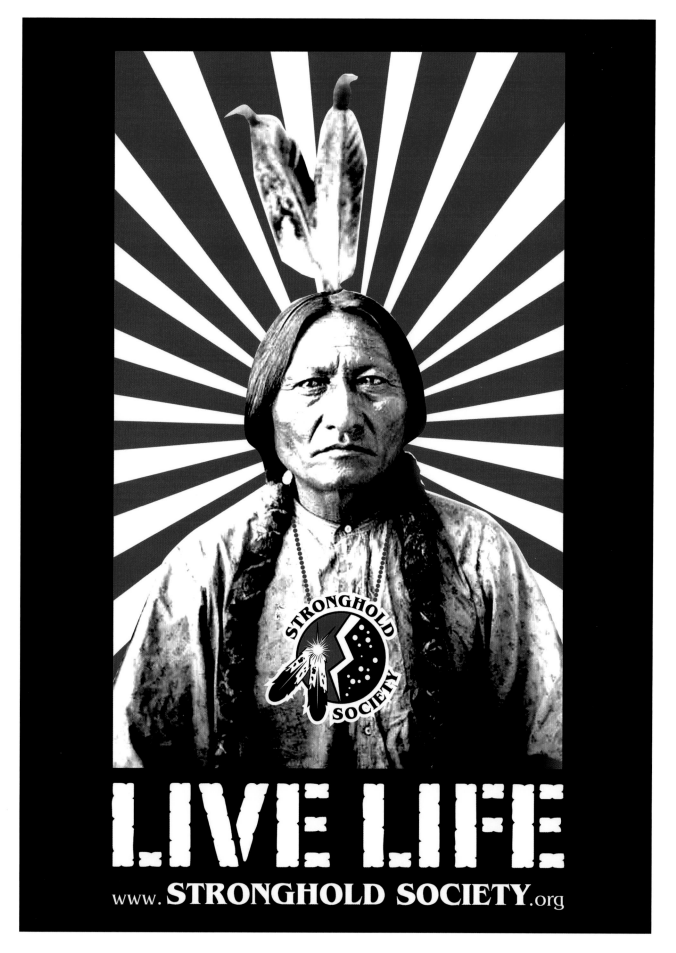

The 2000s

2000
- The October issue of *Transworld Skateboarding* estimates that there are 180 concrete skateparks in the United States.
- Vladimir Putin is elected president of Russia.

2001
- George W. Bush is inaugurated as the forty-third president of the United States.
- On September 11, two hijacked jetliners ram the Twin Towers of NYC's World Trade Center, a third hijacked plane flies into the Pentagon, and a fourth crashes in rural Pennsylvania. They are the deadliest terrorist attacks on American soil in US history.

2002
- Toy Machine founder Ed Templeton has a solo art exhibition at the Palais de Tokyo in Paris.
- After a failed attempt five years prior, Nike Skateboarding reenters the skate market with a single shoe, the Dunk Low Pro SB.

- In his first State of the Union address, President Bush labels Iran, Iraq, and North Korea the "axis of evil."

- MTV broadcasts *Viva La Bam*, a series about skateboarder Bam Margera.
- Boost Mobile Pro Contest in Las Vegas, NV, offers the largest cash prize ever ($40,000) to first place winners in street and vert.
- Women's skateboarding is included at the X Games for the first time.

2004
- George W. Bush is reelected president.
- Go Skateboarding Day is launched by the International Association of Skateboarding Companies to highlight skateboarding globally.
- Facebook is launched and quickly surpasses MySpace as the most popular social network.

2006
- Twitter, a new micro-blogging and communication app, is launched.

2007
- Democrat Nancy Pelosi of California becomes the first woman Speaker of the House of Representatives.
- Apple announces its one billionth downloaded song and launches the iPhone.
- The United States experiences its worst economic downturn since the Great Depression.

2008
- Barack Obama becomes the first African American elected president of the United States.
- Brothers Joe and Gavin Maloof inaugurate the Maloof Money Cup skateboarding competition, offering the largest money prize ($160,000) to first place winners to date.

- Independent Trucks celebrates its twenty-fifth anniversary.
- Skateboarders Steve Berra and Eric Koston open a private warehouse skatepark called The Berrics. Based on the basketball game HORSE, they host the Battle of the Berrics, a flat-ground skate competition using the letters SKATE to eliminate competitors.

- After the 9/11 attacks, the United States begins its war in Afghanistan. It becomes the most protracted war in US history—longer than World War I, World War II, and the Vietnam War combined.

- Wikipedia is launched.

- Letters containing anthrax spores are received by several news media and two US senators. In the span of a few weeks, five people are killed and seventeen others are sickened. Despite the FBI's extensive investigation, no organization or person is arrested for these attacks. A prime suspect commits suicide before charges can be filed.

2003

- Pop singer Avril Lavigne's "Sk8er Boi" receives a Grammy nomination for Best Female Rock Vocal Performance and sells over 1.8 million copies worldwide.

- Lisa Whitaker founds the Girls Skate Network, a website that features content for female skateboarders.

- The United States leads a military invasion of Iraq on the assumption that Saddam Hussein is manufacturing and stockpiling weapons of mass destruction. This assumption later proves false.

- Space shuttle *Columbia* explodes upon reentry into Earth's atmosphere, killing all seven astronauts on board.

2005

- Hurricane Katrina causes catastrophic damage to Mississippi and Louisiana.

- Skateboarder Rob Dyrdek opens his first skate plaza, to mimic the urban terrain elements—ledges, benches, rails, stairs—found in public squares and streets around the world.

- YouTube, a free online video-sharing app, is launched.

- Paul Schmitt's skateboard factory, PS Stix, produces four thousand skate decks a day.

- Aaron Kyro posts a how-to skateboarding video on YouTube and goes on to form Braille Skateboarding, an online skateboard tutorial site with over 5 million subscribers.

- Netflix adds an online streaming service to its mail-order movie rental business.

- Amazon releases the Kindle, a handheld device for e-books and other digital media that enables content to be downloaded directly from Amazon without a computer or monthly fee.

- Electronic Arts releases *Skate*, a video game for the newer gaming platforms, Xbox 360 and PlayStation 3. Most users find it superior to *Tony Hawk's Pro Skater* games.

- MTV airs *Life of Ryan*, a reality television series that documents the life of eighteen-year-old skateboarder Ryan Scheckler.

- Cara-Beth Burnside and Mimi Knoop establish hoopla skateboards to "encourage girls' participation and progression in skateboarding."

2009

- After a fifteen-year hiatus, Converse reenters the skateboarding market with a new rendition of the Chuck Taylor built specifically for skateboarding.

- Pop star Michael Jackson dies at age fifty.

- The US Senate approves the nomination of Sonia Sotomayor to the Supreme Court. She becomes the first Latina justice and the third woman to serve.

SKATEBOARDING IN THE NEW MILLENNIUM

TED BARROW

It is hard to imagine a time when television commercials didn't include skateboarding, skateparks weren't found in most small towns, and skateboarders were not celebrities and social media stars. That time was not too long ago, and the path that brought us to the mainstream was pretty smooth. The generation that started at the turn of the millennium grew up with an activity that was mainstream not niche, accepted not rebellious, and if it didn't look so similar to what "classic" skateboarding resembled, it would be unrecognizable. Around the turn of the millennium, the teeth of those gears can still be seen.

"You made those shoes to hurt people, didn't you?" probed Mike Burnett of Geoff Rowley in an April 2001 interview for *Thrasher* magazine. Rowley's pro shoe was stripped down compared with other specimens. Vulcanized and almost Spartan in its simplicity, Rowley's shoe harkened back to the increasingly legendary roots of skateboarding: beach culture, boardwalks, and canvas boat shoes.

Over the previous year, Rowley, originally from Liverpool, England, had been doing mind-blowingly gnarly tricks (360-flip lipslide sequence from *Thrasher*) wearing a pared-down uniform of Dickies 874 work pants, a white shirt, and canvas Vans Old Skools. The "uniform" has been a standard of skateboarders

from the mid-1990s onward: basically, the cheapest wardrobe you could afford; it quickly became a classic.

Rowley's case is noteworthy for the following reasons. First, he was one of a new wave of non-American skaters who had grown up watching early skate videos produced in America. Their idea of the level of American skateboarding was formed through seeing American pros perform at the highest level (not knowing how many tries these feats must have taken them) and then incubated through a combination of indoor skateparks in the wet months (of which there are many in the United Kingdom) and rugged, brutalist postwar architecture in the Liverpudlian industrial rustbelt (also in high supply in Britain).

Second, his retro Vans shoe shows the nostalgic turn that skateboarding was taking at the turn of the millennium. In a sport where few of the professionals had lived for three decades, the Rowley Vans model was emblazoned with a 66/99

Above: *This 1988 Steve Caballero model was Vans' first signature pro model for a skateboarder.*

Opposite: *When skaters discovered that the waffle-like pattern on the soles of Vans shoes gave them extra grip on their skateboards, they instantly adopted them as the preferred skateboard shoe. This 1976 pair of well-used #95 Vans is evidence of that popularity.*

code, commemorating the year of the founding of Vans with the year of Rowley's endorsement of them.

Vans boasted board feel and grip; its "waffle" sole mold proved to have a second life at the end of the decade that saw skateboarding blow up. Similar to the stripped-down simplicity that street skating offered a plastic-accessory and pad-weary culture at the end of the 1980s, by the turn of the millennium, skateboarders started to mine their own history for new ideas. Every culture has a classical period, and in the early aughts, the 1990s became that for us.

The progression of skate shoes is seen first in the blue-and-red canvas shoe designed for Tony Alva in 1978, an immediate classic whose descendant was seen on Rowley's feet in 1999. An even more substantial shoe for modern skateboarding was released in 1989. Called the Vans Cab, short for Caballero, it was one of the first signature pro model shoes. Rather than drawing on leisure footwear of the 1970s, the Cab appropriated the supportive straps of leather and high tops of basketball shoes from the 1980s to offer a more advanced shoe. At the same time, the Cab's sole was virtually indistinguishable from Vans's twenty-year-old prototype, as some skaters still preferred board grip and "feel" to padding under their feet. Although over the

next decade the Cab itself would be adjusted to accommodate more movement, first by skaters simply cutting them down and later by Vans producing the Half Cab, skate shoes would begin to take more and more cues from athletic footwear.

Skateboarding got gnarlier in the 1990s, and footwear followed suit, adding air bubbles, plastic shell reinforcement, and whatever bells and whistles skaters thought they needed to protect themselves and their shoes. Shoe companies spent more money trying to create indestructible shoes, and the market was there for them—more and more skaters were buying shoes, even if the shoes lasted longer. The Etnies Vallely shoe is an extreme version of this progress: an indestructible fortress of rubber, hard plastic, and foam.

The Rowley was a pointed rebuke of that excess, a return to board control and purity. Weirdly, with all the webbing and extra reinforced layers of padding, it looks complicated today, almost outdated. That's how culture works: what was once radically simple and daring later appears clunky and Byzantine.

It's a familiar tale: something expands by appearing to retract. Skateboarding began to celebrate its core roots as it accelerated into the future. If this sounds like the sort of language used by corporations, that's exactly what it was.

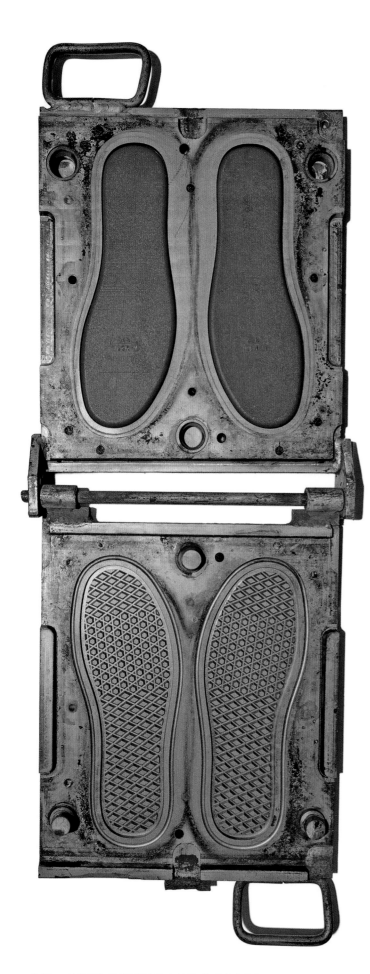

Skateboarding became corporate, a caricature of itself, while the activity itself, bolstered by newly available incubator skateparks that fostered better and better skateboarders, progressed. Activity moved forward; culture moved backward.

Even if skateboarding has always had an industry, there has nonetheless been a strong resistance to institutions within skateboarding, an "us versus them" tooth-sucking defensiveness that comes from riding the turbid tides of a teen-driven market. Let's face it: skateboarding has been cool since the mid-1980s, but the efforts of outside corporations to cash in on that cool throughout the 1990s remained laughably thwarted. Things changed by the turn of the century.

But it's not all bad. At the same time corporations tried to mold the public image of skateboarding into something simple that conformed to the public's expectations, skateboarding resisted—not the industry but the activity. If skateboarding looked homogenous (straight, white, male) at the end of the 1990s, it no longer looks like that. The mixed blessing of corporate interest has resulted in promoting the sport in unexpected places and making skateboarding more accessible and relatable to more potential skaters.

That's the thing—skateboarding has always danced on that knife's edge of rebellion and respectability. As it ages, its practitioners age too. Both radical and retrograde (depending on who is doing it and why), skateboarding has, from its inception, relied on mass culture to redefine the avant-garde. Our cultural currency is built from tricks and the stories and friendships built around them, and yet we hoard our ephemera like relics.

At the Pushing Boarders conference in 2019, someone questioned the role of museums as stewards for skateboarding's history. As skaters, we hoard as much as we destroy, and thus the relics we keep are themselves keepers of our stories. This is what we can learn from some rubber, some cloth, some plastic, and maybe some airbags.

Vans used this 1968 mold to create its famous "waffle" pattern sole, giving skaters shoes that provided greater traction. The outsoles (opposite) were made from this 1968 mold.

TIM BRAUCH AND THE BEGINNING OF THE SKATE COLLECTION

JANE ROGERS

In early 2000, Frank and Joan Brauch contacted the Smithsonian and asked if it would be interested in a collection of their son's items from his professional skateboard career. Tim Brauch, a successful pro skater, had recently passed away at age twenty-five from sudden cardiac arrest, and his parents were looking for a way to share his memory. Up to this point, the Smithsonian skateboard collection consisted of only three skateboards. The Brauchs were very gracious, offering to donate whatever interested the Smithsonian. The variety of items being offered proved a wonderful opportunity to begin building the skateboard collections and also to represent Tim's legacy.

Born with a heart condition, Tim didn't let that keep him out of the action. Following in his father's footsteps, Tim began skating at a young age, winning numerous recreational league trophies and the California Amateur Skate League competition in 1990. At fifteen, he was sponsored by Sessions, an action sports apparel company founded in 1983 by pro skater Joel Gomez. Realizing his potential, more sponsors quickly followed, including Vans, Independent, and New Deal. Santa Monica Airlines gave Tim his first pro model board in 1992, and soon he and fellow skater, Salman Agah, launched their own shoe and clothing line, Este. One of the first lines designed by pro skaters,

it proved a sign of the times as skaters began taking control of their own branding. A year before his death, Tim won the Vans Triple Crown Street Competition, one of the biggest contests of the day.

Curators thoughtfully created what would become the seminal collection of skate objects, chosen to document Tim's meteoric rise through small competitions in the late 1980s to his 1998 victory in the Vans Triple Crown Street Competition. The collection ranges from safety equipment, trophies, posters, and a large promotional check for the Vans win to skate magazines featuring articles praising his skating abilities and tributes after his death.

Clothing collected by the museum for the sports collections consists primarily of uniforms or costumes. The skate clothing and shoes collected from Tim were the first to represent the pervasiveness of the skate style on American culture, offering a sense of 1990s skate clothing styles and the different brands flooding the market. Examples of the Este line were the first in

This shot of Tim Brauch in an ad for the Este brand was taken by photographer Lance Dalgart. Brauch and fellow skater Salman Agah created Este in the mid-1990s when skaters were beginning to try new ways to expand their earning potential.

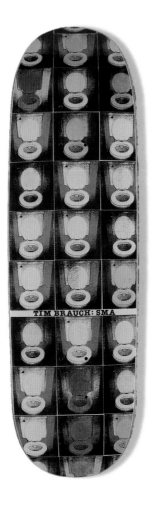

the collections to document the growing business acumen of skaters.

    The skateboard, on which Tim won the Vans competition, and the decks added to the collection—his father's first board, from which Tim took inspiration; his first pro model; a tribute board created by his sponsor Santa Monica Airlines after his death chronicle his legacy. Through these material objects, now accessible as primary sources to scholars, researchers, and skaters worldwide, curators seek to discover and interpret skate's rich history and its influence on American culture.

Top left: *This Santa Cruz skateboard with Independent trucks was used by Tim Brauch at the Vans Triple Crown Skateboarding Championship in 1998.*

Top middle: *This Tim Brauch pro model deck by Santa Monica Airlines dates from mid-1992.*

Top right: *These black, gray, and yellow Etnies shoes were worn by Tim Brauch. In the mid-1990s, Brauch left Vans for Etnies, though he remained close to Steve Van Doren for the remainder of his life.*

Right: *This award was presented to Tim Brauch at the 1998 Vans World Championships of Skateboarding. Held in Huntington Beach, California, it attracted skaters from around the world and was one of the biggest contests in skateboarding in the late 1990s.*

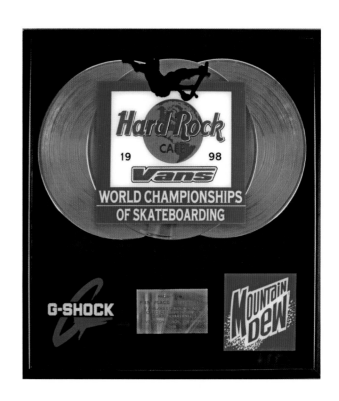

SKATING WHILE BLIND

DAN MANCINA

In 2000, when I was thirteen years old, skateboarding took over my life. Although I was pushing around on a board at seven, it was not until middle school, when I met a group of like-minded skaters, that I understood how important it was to me. This realization of my love for skating has happened twice in my life: once then and again when I lost my sight. Diagnosed with a genetic disorder known as retinitis pigmentosa (RP), my vision deteriorated throughout the first thirty years of my life until I became totally blind.

In 1998, my family moved from a rough neighborhood to a more suburban setting. Surrounded by kids with whom I had little to no connection, skating became an outlet for my inner feelings and gave me the ability to express myself in a unique way. After finishing high school, I moved to California, got a job at a local skate shop, and became fully involved in the skateboarding industry. I never thought that anything could stop me from rolling.

Many years later, as I lost my vision, everything in my life changed, and skating slowly became a memory. Along with my sight, I had lost my self-confidence and identity. For the second time in my life, I felt like an outsider. Like a prisoner, I was forced to wear a uniform as part of my new identity: a white cane. As a blind person living in the sighted world, I was again surrounded by people with whom I had little to no connection. Skating was everything to me, and without it, there was a void. After a few years of coping and training, I was able to regain some of my self-worth. I tried, in every way, to push against the stigma that others attached to me.

One motivated afternoon, I decided to build a skate bench. This was the rekindling of my passion. Incrementally, I relearned my old skate habits. More importantly, I was able to control the way others viewed me, not as a person who is blind but as me. How I skate has changed, but why I skate has not.

I try to use the least number of adaptations when skating. My board needs a marker so I can differentiate the nose from the tail. After many DIY attempts, I started to roll up a tiny sticker and place it under the griptape in the position where my thumb lies as I naturally grab the board.

Working in collaboration with REAL Skateboards, I created a board design for skaters who are visually impaired. On the bottom side of the board, an indented groove is placed where a person's fingers lie as they grab the board. This makes for quick identification of the nose, though I still use my sticker technique

Photographer Zander Taketomo captures Dan Mancina doing a 50-50 pop on a windowsill in Detroit, Michigan, in 2020.

as well. The board graphic has been adapted using braille that reads "Dan Mancina REAL Skateboards" and also identifies the nose and tail.

When skating, I rely on my remaining senses to keep me oriented: my nose and ears to help identify direction and my sense of touch for recognizing my environment and direction. I may use the scent of a doughnut shop to help find a local spot and the sound of a road to keep me heading in the right direction. Sound can be very useful when skating fast, as staying in a straight line is exceedingly difficult when rolling through open surfaces without landmarks to feel. I rely on a speaker to guide me toward skate obstacles. The speaker is stationary at the top or bottom of an obstacle. Primarily used for gaps when I have to start farther away, I use the sound as a reference and skate toward it. It also keeps me from veering too far left or right and helps keep me centered on the face of a quarter pipe or ramp. The sense of touch is the most useful, as I am constantly taking in information from what I feel under my feet and with my hands.

Above left: *Dan Mancina used this 2019 folding cane to examine potential skate spots.*

Above right: *In between tricks, in Detroit, Michigan, Zander Taketomo captured this 2020 portrait of Dan Mancina.*

Large cracks give me information about where to go or when to pop, and my hands help judge ledge heights.

The most valuable adaptation is my white cane, which allows me to judge the distance from myself to skate objects and identify drops and landmarks. Before I start skating a spot, I use the cane to scan the environment for any hazards or out-of-place objects, which I encounter often. One of my local parks has a bike rack that can be found anywhere within the park depending on the day. I also use the cane to help align myself with skate obstacles like a ledge. I will run it along a ledge to gain an idea of the direction I should start and the line I should follow.

A new cane is like a new pair of shoes and takes a couple of days to break in and feel just right. The size of the cane depends on what I am skating. A fifty-four-inch cane is my standard for most skating aside from gaps, which calls for lengthening it to fifty-eight inches. A longer cane allows for more distance between me and a skate obstacle, which gives me more reaction time. More time is needed when I am skating faster toward obstacles like gaps.

The style of tip attached to the bottom of the cane is crucial as well. A big tip can be heavy and cumbersome, causing drag. A small tip is light and easy to maneuver but gets caught on

Right and opposite left: *This 2019 REAL skate deck was used by pro skater Dan Mancina. He painted braille text in white circles on the top and would roll up a small sticker and place it under the griptape so he could be sure he was grabbing the nose of the deck.*

Opposite middle and right: *This 2019 Braille Actions REALized skate deck, with carved notch on the nose produced by REAL Skateboards, was inspired by Dan Mancina. The front of the deck is inscribed with braille and explains that some of the proceeds from the sale of this deck go toward building adaptive skateparks geared toward visually impaired skaters.*

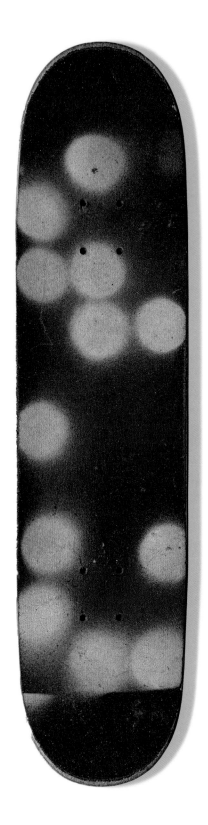

imperfections on the ground. A hard plastic gives the best performance, gliding over rough surfaces. A standard marshmallow-style tip is preferred for everyday skating. This type of tip typically lasts around three weeks, though I've worn one down in a single day. Another helpful tip is the snowball, which is used for skating transitions or gaps. It is a large rolling ball, making it good for gliding across the ground at faster speeds.

A skate cane can last me anywhere from a day to a few months, so I prefer an aluminum cane for its durability and cheap price. Unlike my skate cane, my walking cane is longer, always at fifty-eight inches, and made of a lighter material, preferably graphite. Graphite gives a lot of feedback from the ground and is more flexible. A quiver of canes and tips has become a part of my skate kit for travel, and without them, I feel naked. My cane has truly become an extension of my body, both on and off my board.

Although I use a cane for skating, I do not feel like an adaptive skater, just a skater. Naturally relentless, if there is nothing to skate, we build it. If a spot has skate obstacles, we fix them. Battles for tricks take days, but no fence or obstacle or amount of effort will keep us from pushing. The drive to skate encompasses much of what is needed to overcome the challenges we face in life.

Skateboarding helped me prepare for my blindness by simplifying the struggles into skate obstacles through which I can express myself. No matter what happens, we keep pushing.

SKATEBOARDING AS A CAREER

ALEXIS SABLONE

The word *career* was never part of it. At the time, I just wanted to get really good, and that meant skating all the time. As I got older, I realized that if I wanted to have the time to skate or the freedom to travel for skateboarding, I either had to have a different career or something had to pay for skating.

In 2002, my best friend, PJ, and I put out a video called *PJ Ladd's Wonderful Horrible Life*. PJ would pick me up from high school and take me to Boston, where we'd skate every weekend. I didn't know the video was going to be a big deal. I wasn't even conscious of the fact that I was being filmed for the video.

I was part of this crew, which was what I wanted. That's what I thought was cool about what I saw in Elissa Steamer's *Welcome to Hell* video. And now I was a part of this thing with these other great skaters, and we're skating the city and going on these missions.

In my opinion, PJ was better than the pros. He was doing tricks that no one else had done before, and yet no one knew who he was. It was exciting for this video to come out because, in my mind, it was about PJ, and the world was seeing what PJ could do. I wasn't thinking of it as something for my career. I didn't even see what I was doing as a career.

I started skating for The Firm and éS right around the time the video came out. éS sent me my first check. I didn't know I

was going to get it, and then I felt anxious. Suddenly, it felt like there was more pressure on me. All the skateboard companies were trying to get PJ, and he chose Flip and moved to the West Coast. All the skaters in the *Wonderful Horrible Life* video were moving to California.

Around this time, I was deciding whether to apply to college. It was stressful. Was I just going to skate all day? I didn't get it. I wanted nothing to do with that. I thought I would be so bored. I had never lived in California and just didn't see myself living there. I wasn't a perfect student by any means, but I was good at the subjects I liked and was obsessed with projects. Then I had skateboarding, and I was always balancing the two.

I wanted to move to New York, and I wanted to go to school. I also wanted to skate, but I wanted it to be for fun. I applied only to Barnard, and I got in, so I moved to New York and quit my sponsors. I studied architecture but hated working at an architectural firm. I worked at a restaurant to help pay the bills, but then the restaurant closed due to a fire, and I needed money.

Enter the Maloof Money Cup in 2009, which was held in Costa Mesa, California. The girl's purse was $25,000. Through

On August 1, 2010, at the X Games in Los Angeles, Alexis Sablone performs in the women's skateboard street final on her way to the gold medal.

my skate contacts, I hooked up with Organika and started skating for them four days before Maloof. It didn't go so well. My wheel fell off, and I hit my head twice. I won a Zumiez Destroyer Award. I asked, "Was that for destroying the course but not really winning or for destroying my body?" because my body was a mess. I hadn't skated with the girls in so long. Vanessa Torres and Amy Caron were there. Both of them said, "We remember you from Huntington Beach." They told me that later, but I felt I'd never met any of those people. Elissa Steamer was there, but I was too scared to talk to her.

That was the first time I met other girl skaters and actually started to get to know them. A week after that, the Dew Tour was in Boston. We all went to Boston and skated the Dew Tour, where I placed third. All those girls wanted to stay at my apartment in New York, so we drove to New York, and then the X Games happened a couple of weeks later.

These three contests all took place within a two-month period. I had moved to California while skating for Organika and

This is the first pro model shoe for professional skateboarder Alexis Sablone. They were supposed to be worn during the 2019 Shanghai X Games, but Sablone left her shoes at the hotel, and there was no time to retrieve them. A spectator was wearing the same model shoe and let Sablone borrow their shoes to compete. Sablone went on to win the competition.

was an alternate at the X Games. Lorena Lima, who was in the contest, sprained her ankle and couldn't skate. She was going to skate anyway because even last place at the X Games would win her some money. I told her that if she let me skate instead of her, I would write her a $1,500 check no matter what place I got. We shook on it, so I skated and got second. I won $20,000, and Lorena got her $1,500.

There were only two or three contests a year for a couple of more years. They were Maloof, Dew Tour, and X Games. Then Dew Tour was out and it was just Maloof and X Games, and then Maloof was out. Then there was the Kimberley Diamond Cup in South Africa, but the X Games was the only consistent one.

Fortunately, I won the X Games in 2010, the second year there was equal pay for men and women. For years, women had been getting almost nothing. In 2009, I got $20,000 for second place. In my second X Games, I skated and placed first and won $40,000, so I was rich. I now had enough money to go back to school and skate for fun. I convinced my girlfriend at the time that we should head back to New York, so we moved to Brooklyn, and I applied to school the next year. I remember not even giving Organika my new address in New York because I had had enough boards to last forever.

FIGHT FOR FAIR PLAY

MIMI KNOOP

The first time I stepped onto a skateboard was in 1985 when I was only six years old. I remember in vivid detail that first moment of rolling down the road. It was the closest thing to flying I had ever experienced. I was in love and became instantly obsessed.

My childhood was speckled with moves to new cities every few years. No matter where we ended up, skateboarding was always there, comforting me like an old blanket. It was my outlet for physical expression, exploration, and, later, teenage angst.

After 9/11, when I was twenty-two, I moved to Southern California to surf with a friend. Little did I know that I had ended up moving to the epicenter of the skateboarding industry. I had access to several skateparks, which was something I never had growing up. One thing led to another, and I quickly found myself rubbing shoulders with such icons of the sport as Cara-Beth Burnside and Jen O'Brien. I dropped in on a vert ramp at the age of twenty-four. Two weeks later, I entered my first pro vert contest, the Soul Bowl in Huntington Beach, and I placed fifth, which was second-to-last place. I couldn't have planned this if I had tried.

In the summer of 2003, I received an invite from ESPN to skate in the Summer X Games, which was skateboarding's most prestigious contest of the year. I quickly learned the limits to

earning income as a female skater. In 2004, the men's first place purse at the X Games was $50,000, while the women's first place purse was $2,000. Even if you were the best female skater in the world, you could barely cover the costs of your trip to the biggest competition of the year.

At the end of 2004, I met sports coach and former IMG agent Drew Mearns. The following summer, and under the guidance of Drew, the women skateboarders spontaneously chose to boycott the Summer X Games in an effort to create a voice for women's skateboarding. It worked. ESPN promised us a meeting in exchange for getting the skaters to show up for its events. The skaters showed up and skated. And then we waited for our meeting.

The promise to meet with the women skateboarders took ESPN one full year and a very glaring *New York Times* article by Matt Higgins to come to fruition. But in the summer of 2006, Cara-Beth, Drew Mearns, and I finally sat down with the vice president of ESPN in a room at the top of the Staples Center. We asked ESPN for three things: prize purse parity over the span of a few years, increased media coverage and exposure for

Mimi Knoop competes in the women's skateboard vert final during the 2007 X Games at the Home Depot Center in Carson, California. Her father, Kevin Knoop, took this photo while watching her compete.

women's events, and to be the organizers of our own competitions. ESPN agreed to all the terms, and in 2009, they announced equal prize purses for all men and women competitions at X Games at both summer and winter events.

This reset the bar for event organizers worldwide, though it would take the next decade for major contests (Street League Skateboarding, Vans Park Series, Dew Tour, and others) to offer equal purses at their events. The commencement of the first ever Olympic qualifiers in 2018 played a big role in this as well, as Olympic events cannot be gender biased. Today, almost all major televised skateboarding contests have equal purses for men and women.

Over the past fifteen years, it has been an honor to have witnessed women's skateboarding mature from being an underground counterculture to a full-blown worldwide phenomenon. Skateboarding is for everyone, and now women can carve a path as professional skateboarders better than ever before.

Above: *Mimi Knoop and Drew Mearns having dinner after the summer 2006 meeting with ESPN executives at which they struck a prize purse parity deal.*

Right: *Mimi Knoop won bronze at the 2004 X Games with this board, which was the first of her five total medals earned at the X Games in her professional career.*

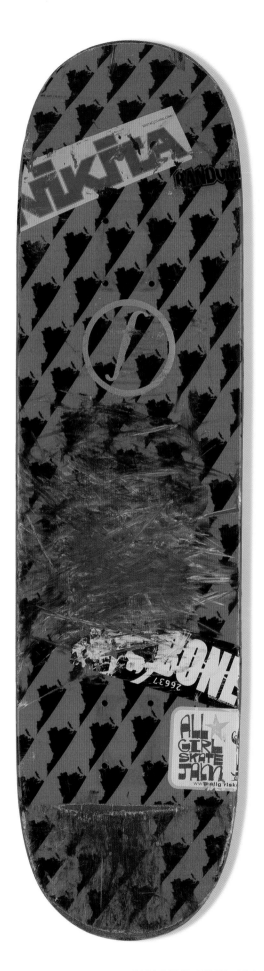

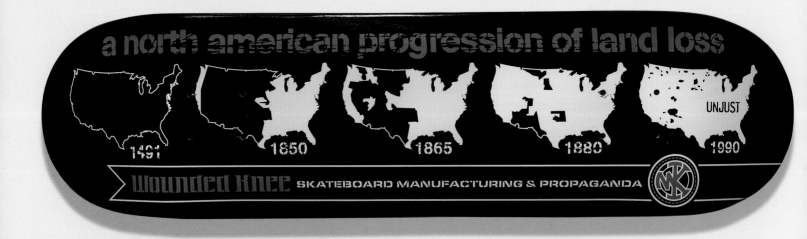

NATIVE AMERICAN SKATEBOARD HISTORY AND CULTURE

BETSY GORDON

When the Smithsonian opened the exhibition *Ramp It Up* about Native American skateboard culture, many visitors' first reaction was something along the lines of, "Wow, I didn't know Native kids skated!" Their surprise and interest, albeit genuine and welcome, betrayed a huge blind spot in America. Native words serve as the name to many things, from lakes and cities to helicopters and baking soda. Images of Native Americans are everywhere in American culture, usually depicted by broad stereotypes of "warriors" or "Indian maidens" appearing as sports mascots or selling butter. No wonder most people can't understand that Native Americans skateboard.

The truth is, Native people have been skating just as long as any other group of skaters in America. Contrary to assumptions, most Native people in the United States do not live on reservations. In fact, most live in urban or suburban localities, giving them access to the country's concrete and asphalt infrastructure of sidewalks, roads, drainage ditches, and skateparks.

C. R. Stecyk remembers seeing Native kids on skateboards in the 1960s as he drove east on Route 66 from California to New Mexico. Brothers Jimmy and Ricky Tavarez (Gabrielino-Tongva) skated with the Z-Boys in the mid-1970s, and *National Geographic* featured Duwayne Mark Johnson (White Mountain Apache) on his skateboard in 1980. Just like their non-Native counterparts,

they competed in contests, devoured skateboard magazines, and built ramps to emulate what they saw in those magazines. Yet unlike most non-Native skaters, many had deep cultural traditions to draw from when starting their own skate brand or creating graphics for their skate deck. It is impossible to determine who started the "first" Native American skateboard brand. Among the firsts were Dustinn Craig's (White Mountain Apache) 4-Wheel Warpony and Douglas Miles's (San Carlos Apache/Akimel O'odham) Apache Skateboards, both launched in the early 2000s. Craig's brand name references the traditional presence of horses in Native life to create a strong metaphor of twenty-first century Native identity—the skateboard replacing the horse for many Native "riders." Following these nascent brands were a number of others, including Native Skates, Full Blood Skates, and Remnant Skateboards. Native Skates often commissioned well-known Native artists to produce the artwork for its decks, including Bunky Echo-Hawk (Yakima), Traci Rochelle Rabbit (Cherokee Nation), Joe Yazzie (Diné), and David Shananaquet (Odawa, Little Traverse Bay Bands). While Shananaquet,

Founded by former Alva pro Jim Murphy, Wounded Knee Skateboard Manufacturing and Propaganda works to create skate graphics that inspire and educate the public about the history of Native Americans. This 2004 Progression of Land Loss model deck is part of that effort.

This image, taken by C. R. Stecyk near Gallup, New Mexico, in 1969, captures an early Native-designed skateboard. The "whirling logs," or "four directional winds," design is common in Navajo weaving and ancient Pueblo pottery. The symbol is often used in Navajo healing ceremonies.

Yazzie, and Rabbit featured traditional Native iconography on their decks (Medicine Wheel, dance regalia, and feather bundles), Echo-Hawk used the opportunity to make a biting statement about the storing of nuclear waste on Native lands.

Although not an enrolled member of a Native tribe, Jim Murphy received approval from Arvol Looking Horse (Oglala Lakota), the nineteenth-generation keeper of the Sacred White Buffalo Calf Pipe and Bundle, to use the name Wounded Knee Skateboards. Many of his graphics act as a visual primer to educate the non-Native public about Native history and politics. Murphy and his partner, Walter Pourier (Oglala Lakota), formed the nonprofit Stronghold Society to build skateparks in or near Native communities. To date, they have built two world-class concrete skateparks, the Wounded Knee 4-Directions Toby Eagle Bull Memorial Skatepark on the Pine Ridge reservation in South Dakota and the Wounded Knee 4-Directions Skatepark in Manderson, South Dakota. Murphy and Pourier insisted that the skateparks be of high quality to attract professional skateboard contests and team demos.

In sharp contrast to many non-Native communities, many Native Nations actively pursue and encourage the building of skateparks on their land. Tribal leaders have responded to skateboarding's popularity by building skateparks, sponsoring skate teams, and hosting skate events as an investment in their youth. The Pala Band of Mission Indians in northern San Diego County, California, commissioned legendary skatepark designer Wally Hollyday to design a 22,000-square-foot park in 2008. Numerous other Native Nations, including the Pascua Yaqui (Arizona), Southern Ute (Colorado), Chippewa Cree (Montana), Blackfeet (Montana), S'Klallam (Washington), Tulalip (Washington), and the Eastern Band of Cherokee Indians (North Carolina), have built parks for their citizens and the public. Recently, the Toadlena/Two Grey Hills Chapter of the Navajo Nation has partnered with the Skatepark Foundation and the singer Jewel to raise funds for the Diné Skate Garden. Spearheaded by Naiomi Glasses, a Diné skateboarder and a seventh-generation textile artist who has been featured in *Teen Vogue* as well as the prestigious Santa Fe Indian Art Market, the new park is very close to its funding goal.

As tribal support strengthens, a strong intertribal skate community has developed, uniting reservation, urban, and suburban skaters. Native skateboard competitions such as the

All Nations Skate Jam in Albuquerque, New Mexico, bring together many Native skaters during the Gathering of Nations Pow Wow. This competition has been going for nearly twenty years, canceled only once because of COVID-19 restrictions in 2021.

Skateboarding's roots are Indigenous, stretching back to the ancient Polynesian practice of surfing. Native Americans—American Indians, Native Hawaiians, and Alaska Natives—have always been part of the history of skateboarding and continue to contribute to its history and culture. Most recently, Native Hawaiian Heimana Reynolds competed in the men's park skateboarding event in the 2020 Summer Olympics in Tokyo, becoming the first Indigenous skateboarder to compete as an Olympic athlete. As Native Nations continue to support their citizens with skateparks, it seems likely that there will be many more champions to come.

Right: *This 2007 skate deck, with a graphic by Dustinn Craig (White Mountain Apache), was produced by 4-Wheel Warpony, one of the first Native American skateboard brands.*

Opposite left: *This Pala deck was issued at the opening of the Pala Band of Mission Indians skatepark in 2007. Many men from Native communities in Southern California wear bandannas at tribal events. The color of each man's bandanna is based on the colors of his tribal flag. In this case, Pala identifies with the green bandanna.*

Opposite middle: *Artist David Shananaquet (Odawa, Little Traverse Bay Bands) places a skateboarder within the Medicine Wheel, a symbol common to many Native nations in North America, on this 2004 Medicine Wheel model deck from Native Skates.*

Opposite right: *Artist Joe Yazzie (Diné) uses Native images and symbols in his deck graphics, as illustrated in his 2008 Apache Mountain Spirit Dancer model for Native Skates.*

MAKING A LIVING AS A PRO SKATER

LEO BAKER

I was ten years old when I got my first sponsor. At eleven, I started competing in the California Amateur Skate League (CASL) and was usually the only girl among the contestants. At one contest, I got second place against all the boys. They weren't used to competing with and getting beaten by a girl.

Around this time, I met Ryan Miller, who was teaching skate classes in the area. He told my mom that I was too good to be in a class and we should do private lessons. He was the one who suggested I compete in CASL. I entered CASL competitions for the next three years, and then I started skating in the Amateur (AM) contests, Damn AM and Tampa AM. At thirteen, I was invited to skate in an all-women's competition, and that's where I met Jaime Reyes, Lauren Mollica, Jessie Van Roechoudt, and Lisa Whitaker.

I couldn't believe there were all these girl skaters. The whole time I thought it was just Elissa Steamer and me. This mysterious Alexis Sablone person whom I had never seen before was also there. I ended up winning that contest, and the prize was a trip to Australia to compete in the Global Assaults. That's how I started skating in World Cup competitions. I was skating in "pro women contests" and in AM contests against guys. Those paths were parallel for a while.

I knew I wanted to go pro, and the people who run the World Cup contest said that if I had won money, that made me a pro. But I was thinking that's not how it works in skating. Until I get a pro board, I'm not pro. To be a pro skater, it's the company that turns you pro—you get your name on a board or a shoe. Nowadays, it's a little different because a lot of companies just do colorways (a shoe is given a new color design associated with a skater, but the skater's name doesn't go on the shoe). In the past, skaters got to design the shoe with their name on it. When I was in the third grade, I had the Cara-Beth Vans. I didn't even know they were Cara-Beth Vans, but I really liked them.

I was skating all the time but not making much money. If you're a pro skater getting a paycheck, you can at least pay your rent, but I got paid only about $800 from two of my sponsors. Then around 2009, sponsors started cutting all their skate programs. The skate industry as a whole didn't have a lot of money, and the first thing to go were the women's contests.

I think the only woman making a living wage skateboarding at the time was Leticia Bufoni. The companies were continuing to dump buckets of money on the guys. I was working a full-time

This rose was drawn by professional skateboarder Leo Baker, who then used it as their signature design on much of their merchandise in the late 2010s.

job and skating, filming video parts, and doing well in contests, but I was getting nothing. I worked hard and felt I should have at least earned a spot somewhere because I was extremely dedicated and loyal to my sponsors. It all felt fake: I was working for something that just wasn't there.

I had to do a lot of self-searching because there was a time in skating when I was really depressed. I was in school working toward a bachelor's degree, and I needed a job now. So instead, I graduated in two years with an associate's degree, which I think was a good move.

Contests were the means for survival. Even when there were lots of competitions, women weren't getting paid enough to skate. That was why I was on the path of doing skating contests for just so long. I was still pushing through to skate because I didn't want to give up. It's what I love to do. Even if I had to work a full-time job, I was still a skateboarder. Then in

2017, I filmed the *Thrasher* video part in *My World*. Doing the *My World* video was one of my biggest accomplishments; a lot of great footage came from that. We were just present, exactly the way that I feel comfortable. I didn't have a clothing sponsor, so I didn't have to dress a specific way.

I didn't have any sponsors or other people to tell me how I needed to look. I was able to skate and to do whatever I wanted. But then, people started to notice me. Plus, right after the footage came out, I also won the Street League Skateboarding contest.

Those two things happened close to each other, and the industry was suddenly interested in me. That's when I got a manager because I wasn't able to negotiate these deals— I was asking for money and everyone told me no. With a manager I was given a certain level of respect, and dealing with the different companies that were asking for my endorsement was much easier. I was excited about the negotiations going on with Nike because I considered them one of the best brands to be associated with. Once I landed that deal, everything just turned around from there. I received better endorsement deals and more money. I was finally earning enough to be able to quit my job as a graphic designer and focus on my skating, placing second at the 2018 X Games and earning a spot on USA Skateboarding's inaugural skate team in 2019.

Above left: *Leo Baker designed these Nike SB Bruins, the first skate shoe the company produced specifically for women, and the eye design represents visibility, something Baker strives for in the LGBTQ community.*

Above right: *The various patches and pins on this backpack, which was used by pro skateboarder Leo Baker in 2017 and 2018, show where Baker's interests were at the time they carried this pack.*

CHAPTER SIX

2010s TO PRESENT

DIVERSITY, INCLUSION, AND THE OLYMPICS: SKATEBOARDING'S SIXTH DECADE

By 2010, the ability of the Internet to provide instantaneous distribution of everything, be it momentous or minor, created an oversaturated environment of information. There was a channel, app, network, group chat, Wiki, or podcast for anything ever thought, done, or created. Communication proliferated at unprecedented speeds, adopting the term *viral* to describe its rapid spread. Change seemed to accelerate, with "new" becoming a matter of days or even hours before being replaced by something even more novel. Life seemed to be at warp speed until a real virus, a biological one, caused the world to halt.

The skateboarding trends first glimpsed in the early 2000s grew exponentially during this decade. They became completely enmeshed in the world of online content. Instagram replaced YouTube as skateboarding's 24-7 news channel. Corporate buyouts became augmented with collaborations as skate brands partnered with non-skateboarding entities to redefine what a skate brand looked like. Supreme enlarged its vast collaboration portfolio by working with brands such as Fender, Comme des Garçons, Everlast, and Spalding. Olympian skateboard bronze medal winner Cory Juneau chose the Italian luxury footwear manufacturer Golden Goose for his first skate shoe sponsor, bucking the trend of launching with Vans, Nike, or Converse. As research into skateboarding became more

embraced by universities, an international skateboarding conference, Pushing Boarders, formed to provide a forum for scholars of skateboarding as well as skaters interested in academic discourse. Skate-centric nonprofits and NGOs proliferated globally. A 2020 survey conducted by the Goodpush Alliance, an initiative by the NGO Skateistan to provide training and advice to skateboarding projects around the world, tracked 117 skateboard projects in 61 countries.

Skateboarders with differing abilities joined the skateboard community in growing numbers in the 2010s as more skateboard competitions included adaptive events. Although adaptive skaters have been involved in competitions since the mid-1990s, the inclusion of skateboarding in the Olympics opened up more opportunities to compete. The 2021 Dew Tour, which featured Olympic qualifying events for the Tokyo Olympics, also featured a street and pool event for adaptive skaters. Whether riding a skateboard or dropping in with a wheelchair, adaptive skaters are growing in numbers and the skate community has welcomed their effort. And while they are still waiting for skateboarding events in the Paralympics, Oscar Loreto Jr., an adaptive skater, is an athletic director for USA Skateboarding and a vocal advocate for skateboarders with differing abilities.

COVID-19 had a devastating effect on many in the skateboarding industry and community. Since many skateboard and truck manufacturers get their products from China, there was

Opposite: *A family poses for an informal portrait by photographer Ian Logan during the Venice Beach, California, skateboarding community's Black Lives Matter protest on June 14, 2020.*

an immediate disruption in the supply chain, creating a lack of available skate goods to sell. Ironically, this lack of supply met with an unexpected increase in demand from the American consumer. With offices, schools, and gyms closed and team sports programs suspended, individuals and families looked for a way to continue being physically active. For many, a seemingly easy alternative was to find a skateboard and skate outside on the omnipresent asphalt and concrete.

While the latter part of the decade will be forever defined by COVID-19, many other major events left their mark. From 2011's Occupy Wall Street, to the Women's March and Charlottesville protests of 2017, to the Black Lives Matter protests of 2020, this was a decade of protest and outrage.

Skateboarding and skateboarders took notice and participated in these social justice movements, demanding change not only from outside systems and institutions but also from the skateboard industry itself. They urged their fellow skaters to participate in the national presidential elections. They directly challenged the pervasive myth that skateboarding was inclusive and welcoming, color and class blind. They revealed that racism, sexism, and homophobia had always been part of the industry and the culture, and although they had vacillated between covert and overt, they have been overwhelmingly tolerated.

While some argued that skateboarding mirrored the sexism, racism, and homophobia underpinning American culture, there was a notable disconnect and dissonance between what was happening in America and what was being seen and promoted within the skateboard community. Women around the world continued to garner significant achievements in the arts, sciences, and politics while remaining largely unacknowledged in skateboarding until recently. In *Thrasher*'s forty-year history, women have been featured on only four covers out of five hundred. That is less than 1 percent representation for half of the population.

Although telling history via *Thrasher* magazine covers is not exactly scientific, it is an aperture into how the skateboard industry and community recognize women. In short, they don't—not on any scale comparable to the recognition given to men. The same goes for the BIPOC and LGBTQ skaters, who have been skating for as long as there have been skateboards, though largely without acknowledgment, representation, or

This WCMX wheelchair was used by Aaron "Wheelz" Fotheringham during Nitro Circus performances and to kick off the 2016 Paralympic Summer Games in Rio. Paralyzed below the waist, Fotheringham founded WCMX, or wheelchair motocross, a sport that combines tricks adapted from skateboarding and BMX that are performed in skateparks.

Top: *Skate Like a Girl is a nonprofit organization that promotes inclusivity and empowers skaters, especially women and trans people, by promoting social equity throughout the skate community. (Middle) The Abolish ICE movement gained traction during the Trump administration and was a popular choice among skaters. (Bottom) Skate stickers are an important aspect of skate culture, and with the broadening of the skate community, politics have come into play. Skaters proudly display their social and political views on their skateboards. During the 2020 presidential campaign, many artists began using Bernie Sanders in a series of stickers and memes that expressed their faith in the candidate.*

Right: *Created during the global pandemic, this 2020 COVID-19 Social Distancing Device skate deck by Pocket Pistols is the seventh of nine decks painted and signed by Barret "Chicken" Deck and distributed by Scream.*

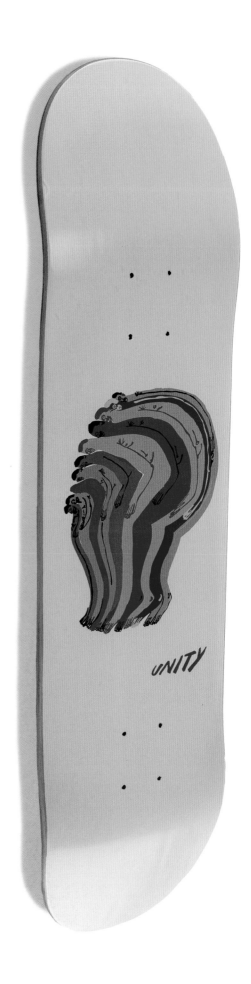

acceptance from skateboarding. While the industry believed in the marketing magic of the straight white male to sell skateboards, Black skaters were told by their friends that skateboarding is a "white boy" thing. Indigenous skaters saw their imagery appropriated by non-Native skaters to reinforce stereotypes of the "stoic warrior." Nonbinary skaters were told to dress more gender conforming. Queer skaters routinely heard slurs on skateboard tours and went to great lengths to hide their sexuality.

As skateboarding continued to pretend that all were welcome, the skaters who did not feel at all welcome took matters into their own hands. They created spaces and

Top: *Pro skateboarder Judi Oyama used an Independent Trucks T-shirt to make this COVID-19 face mask in 2020.*

Above: *This Black Lives Matter protest poster was made by skateboarder Cindy Whitehead and used at Pershing Square in Los Angeles on June 21, 2020, and during the Venice skateboarders support of Black Lives Matter at Venice High School and Venice Skatepark in Venice, California, on June 14, 2020.*

Right: *Unity Skateboards founder Jeffrey Cheung created the graphic on this 2018 Unity skate deck. His androgynous characters on this deck blend together nonbinary forms without the traditional markers of gender and race.*

opportunities for women, BIPOC, and LGBTQ skaters to skate without harassment and intimidation. They formed their own companies, created their own media, declared their correct pronouns and nonbinary status, and courageously came out to an industry they feared would reject them. This created a momentum of change, first within the community of skateboarders and, finally, within the large skateboard companies. Brands such as Unity and Pave the Way created deck graphics that celebrated queerness and advocacy for equality and hosted skateboard meetups specifically for the LGBTQ community. froSkate, a Black women–founded and queer-led collective based in Chicago, provided "inclusive experiences, resources and equity for the BIPOC, non-traditional skateboarding community."

Above left: *Filmmaker John Waters, one of the many pioneers who "paved the way" for queer people, is featured on this 2018 sticker by Pave the Way Skateboards as well as other merchandise.*

Above middle: *This 2018 flyer was created by Unity Skateboards, which was founded in January 2017 by Jeffrey Cheung, a Northern California–based multidisciplinary artist who wanted to provide a safe environment for queer skaters who often face ridicule and shame in their local skateparks.*

Above right: *Founded by skateboarder, photographer, and filmmaker Lisa Whitaker, Meow is a brand "focused on having fun and creating high-quality products that will help support an all-female team."*

Recently, there has been a growing consciousness of how harmful the accepted paradigm has been and how long overdue accountability and apology are. In 2016, skateboarder Brian Anderson used a twenty-six-minute video on Vice Sports to come out as gay. In 2019, in the wake of the #MeToo movement, *Bigfoot* magazine published a groundbreaking article that addressed the occurrence of sexual abuse within the skateboarding community. Written by skateboarders Alex White and Kristin Ebeling, "Coping with Creeps: Concrete Action You Can Take" states unapologetically that "The hashtag lately has been #MeToo but it's clear that it must be #All-In if we ever want things to change." Shortly after the murder of George Floyd and subsequent BLM protests, *Thrasher* magazine published its September 2020 issue with thirty-seven images of Black skaters on the front and back covers. Guest editor Atiba Jefferson declared, "This issue is a celebration of one of many cultures that have made an amazing impact on skateboarding."

And then there was the Olympics. For much of this decade, the Olympics was promised and fought over. COVID-19 further complicated this. Skateparks were shut down and competitions—national and international—were canceled. The competition-based process of qualifying for the Olympics was placed on indefinite hold, and the 2020 Summer Games were postponed until 2021.

Marred by organizational missteps and delayed for a year by COVID-19, skateboarding nonetheless made its Olympic debut in August 2021. Although Team USA did not win the number of medals they hoped for, the team, which included two Black, one Native Hawaiian, and one gender-nonconforming member, represented the new, aspirational face of skateboarding—diverse and inclusive. For many, seeing the diversity of the Olympic skaters on an Olympic podium defined skateboarding as something they could participate in. In particular, many skateboard shops saw a noticeable increase in demand for skateboards from young women. The International Olympic Committee's addition of skateboarding into the 2024 and 2028 Olympic Games seems to have cemented its future as an Olympic sport.

During this past decade, skateboarding found itself again in the vanguard of using social media and the Internet to create and distribute content. It redefined what it meant to be a skate brand, adding haute couture and pinball machines to its product drops. It advocated for social justice and appeared in university course offerings. As it enters its seventh decade, it is bound to reinvent, redirect, and readdress, exasperating some who will resist these changes as deviations from the "core" of true skateboarding. However, what seems to be at the core of skateboarding, no matter what decade, is polymorphism and creativity. It started as a fun diversion for kids, and it will remain a fun diversion for kids no matter what their age.

—Betsy Gordon and Jane Rogers

Above: *At the beginning of the COVID-19 pandemic in 2020, photographer Ian Logan used a drone to document how skateparks were being filled in with sand to prevent skaters from congregating to use them. Shown here is the Venice Skatepark in Venice, California.*

Opposite: *The September 2020 issue of* Thrasher *featured thirty-seven portraits of Black skaters on the front and back covers.*

The 2010s to Present

2010

- Rob Dyrdek inaugurates Street League Skateboarding (SLS), a competition series with the goal of "[redefining] the way skateboarding competitions are done."
- Elena Kagan becomes the fourth female US Supreme Court justice.
- Instagram is founded.

- The Deepwater Horizon oil rig in the Gulf of Mexico catches fire and explodes, sending millions of gallons of oil into the sea.
- The Affordable Care Act, extending health-care benefits and insurance to most Americans, is passed. It will take four years to go into effect.

2011

- Osama bin Laden, leader of al-Qaeda, is killed in Pakistan by the US Navy SEAL Team Six.
- *Jenkem*, an online skateboard magazine, is launched by Ian Michna in Brooklyn, NY.

- *Thrasher* magazine turns thirty.
- The RIDE Channel, a "digital destination for skate culture and conversation," debuts on YouTube.

2013

- Edward Snowden leaks highly classified documents from the National Security Agency.
- Terrorists detonate two bombs at the finish line of the Boston Marathon, killing 3 and injuring 283 runners and spectators.

- Black Lives Matter emerges as a political movement to protest against racial profiling, police brutality, and racial inequality in the United States.
- Ishod Wair is the first Black skater to be named Skater of the Year by *Thrasher* magazine.

2016

- Samarria Brevard becomes the first Black woman with a signature skate deck and the first Black woman to get a video part in *Quit Your Day Job*.

2017

- Donald Trump becomes the forty-fifth president of the United States.
- The Unite the Right white supremacist rally in Charlottesville, VA, results in three deaths and introduces the term *alt-right* into the vocabulary of the American public.

2019

- The longest government shutdown in American history (December 22, 2018, through January 25, 2019) officially ends.
- The first image of a black hole is taken.
- The Dow Jones Industrial Average closes above 28,000 for the first time in November and reaches its highest level in history on December 27, 2019.

2020

- The World Health Organization officially declares COVID-19 a global pandemic.
- Nationwide protests and riots erupt after the murder of African American George Floyd during an arrest.
- Joe Biden is elected the forty-sixth president of the United States, defeating Donald Trump. Biden's running mate, Kamala Harris, becomes the first female vice president.

- Welcome Skateboards is founded by Jason Celaya. The brand statement reads, "We believe a skateboard company should make decks that stand apart from the brand next to them, beyond just a variance in the graphic or logo on the bottom."

- Penny Skateboards launches with a line of brightly colored, plastic cruiser skateboards meant specifically for the casual, non-trick-executing skater.

- Apple introduces the iPad, a tablet-style computer.

2012

- Barack Obama is reelected president of the United States.

- At the Sandy Hook Elementary School in Newtown, CT, a gunman kills twenty-six people, including twenty children.

- Instagram is sold to Facebook for $1 billion in cash and stocks.

- Lisa Whitaker founds Meow Skateboards, a skateboard brand exclusively for women skaters.

2014

- Eric Garner, an unarmed African American, dies after a New York City police officer puts him in a chokehold. Garner's words, "I can't breathe," become a rallying cry for activists everywhere.

2015

- Same-sex marriage is legalized in all fifty US states.

- The Paris Climate Accord is signed by 195 countries.

- The *New York Times* publishes an exposé on film producer Harvey Weinstein and accuses him of rampant sexual harassment. The #MeToo movement is launched.

2018

- *Skate Kitchen*, a feature-length film by Crystal Moselle, fictionalizes the lives of a real New York City skate collective called Skate Kitchen.

- *Minding the Gap*, a documentary that chronicles twelve years of Bing Liu and his two skateboarding friends, debuts at Sundance. It wins a 2019 Peabody Award and is a 2019 Academy Award nominee.

- VF Corporation, a US-based apparel and footwear company, buys skate and street-wear brand Supreme for $2.1 billion.

- Luxury couture brand Louis Vuitton collaborates with Jamaican-born skateboarder Lucien Clarke to produce A View, the company's first skateboard shoe.

- Samarria Brevard becomes the first Black woman featured on the cover of *Thrasher* magazine.

2021

- Rioters storm the United States Capitol in a failed attempt to challenge Joe Biden's presidential victory.

- Skateboarding debuts at the Summer Olympics in Tokyo, Japan.

EXPOSING FOR THE SHADE: SKATEBOARDING, GORDON PARKS, AND ME

NEFTALIE WILLIAMS

On a scorching day in mid-July in the mid-2000s, I'd scored my first assignment shooting photos of an uncharacteristically open public skateboarding contest in Venice, California. The "open" element of the Venice Beach boardwalk allowed for a merger of elite skateboarding and Hollywood elite. Cameron Diaz rolled straight from surfing the waves into the audience. The casual chat observed between the Albas (Jessica and pro skater Steve) and the arrival of Tony Hawk suggested another day on the West/Best Coast.

The proximity to the limelight situated me in the company of elite photographers. Rubbing elbows with these pros from the "paper of record" and the hippest LA publications made my first shoot feel considerably more critical. I envisioned what photos might derive from this menagerie of talent.

Nervously, I entered the credentialed media booth. Faced with the new environment (coincidently the only African American), I reverted to tactics employed by all "newbie" photogs facing the "big dawgs"—nerding out on camera gear. I'd lived on Top Ramen long enough to acquire a Nikon D700, a monster for its time, while attending photo classes at Santa Monica College. My seasoned cohorts recognized the equipment as a serious investment in the craft and commitment to the game. One noted photographer proclaimed that I "showed promise" and discussed capturing the elusive Tom Cruise with a similar Nikon. I'd never even heard the word *capture* used that way before. (More importantly, who "captures" Ethan Hunt—surely impossible?)

Despite the terminological confusion, I hurriedly scribbled names, locations, and future shoot invites. Surmising that significant time passed since this cadre last schooled a "new-comer," the gravity of this intergenerational knowledge transfer did not escape me. My uniqueness seemed to grant successful access to this exclusive troop propagating and supporting the most sought-after stories worldwide.

Until it didn't.

Hoping to snap a good photo of the innovative African American female skater Samarria Brevard, I aligned my lens and strobes and prepared to work. Brevard's arrival heralded a return of Black excellence in women's skateboarding (Stephanie Person, the first African American female pro skater, had departed for Europe years prior). Suddenly, an ace paparazzo appeared and inspected my configuration.

Neftalie Williams captures Lucien Clarke doing a heel flip-varial in Havana, Cuba, during a skateboard diplomacy mission with the Skate Cuba NGO in 2016. Clarke became the first skateboarder to have a signature pro model skate shoe for Louis Vuitton, which he designed in collaboration with African American fashion designer Virgil Abloh.

"What are you doing all that for?" he asked. "You look like you are working hard to make something happen in your frame!"

Indeed, I was. "Nailing down the exposure," I answered. "Don't want her face to be underexposed mid-trick with all this harsh sun."

"Dude, it's skateboarders and skateboarding. No one cares who it is or what it looks like."

"Wait, what?" I asked.

"Seriously, it's skateboarding, man! No one cares what it looks like or who it is."

Damn.

Although the statement might not have triggered others, the words stopped my heart as a Black man chronicling a young Black woman and other diverse skaters. The sentiment from these arbiters of taste signaled I had the skills, but my subject of study was insignificant. Sadly, my colleague's response correlated to my recent studies on photography and film. Communities of color, specifically Black people, experienced historical disregard and endured the perception of the BIPOC body as

Samarria Brevard, photographed by Neftalie Williams during the earliest days of her career, competes in the Supergirl Am Jam in Venice Beach, California, in 2011. Brevard went on to join the USA Skateboarding Olympic team in 2020.

"valueless" in front of and behind the camera.

Dejected, I dug deep into divine edicts.

"Landmines be disguised as 'welcome' signs, I'll repeat it so you ain't got to press rewind. The Landmines be disguised as 'welcome' signs." Profound reflections by the mighty Mos Def/ Yasiin Bey.

To his credit, the photographer stated no one cared. However, what I heard was skateboarders don't matter. Extended, it meant the living, breathing BIPOC individuals with histories, families, and hearts sweating in front of our collective lenses didn't matter.

Gutted and recoiling from the interaction, I did what all Black people and marginalized communities do when their hearts are left bloody in moments of casual racism or disregard: seek an ancestral thread with the appropriate tensile strength to suture the wound. Reaching out, my spirit found Gordon Parks.

We'd just begun learning about the legacy of the preeminent Black photographer in class. Since all origin stories slip into fables at each retelling, I'll stick to the key notes. Gordon Parks lived during a period that attempted to reject him and his potential contributions to photography because parties in the United States could not imagine a Black man with a vision and perspective that might contribute to the cultural zeitgeist. In

fact, he could add a unique tone to every outlet, from the Farm Security Administration to the pages of *Vogue*, *Life*, and eventually the silver screen. He uniquely transformed BIPOC experiences from tales about poor people and the other into stories inspiring and connecting viewers to the joys and humanity in one another worldwide. His groundbreaking efforts provided a voice that inspired many and demonstrated that someone should always endeavor to archive diverse human experiences because they deserve documentation, not exploitation.

Parks desired for Black people—and ultimately all people—to be "seen." Incorporating a high level of care into his images, he disrupted fallacies and evidenced the beauty in simple lives and the humility within extraordinary ones. Despite initially facing rejection, Parks continually pushed forward to learn and expand his networks with those willing to provide him the opportunity to work. I'd found similar solace among the skateboarding community—a place to work and learn the craft.

Drawing on him at that moment, I reflected on my mission: to provide the same level of recognition to the remarkable space provided by skateboarding and to nurture the seeds first planted by Parks and others, which might bring BIPOC and non-BIPOC together through mutual love and experience.

Top: *Sal Barbier, photographed in 2022 by Neftalie Williams with his signature sneakers around his neck, is currently working under the label S. L. Barbier, designing reissues and cobranding his current projects. The deck shown here include his logo of a snake wrapped around a wrench, which is hand-screened with a flocked treatment giving the deck a rich look.*

Above: *This SLB 97 from éS is the first sample for Barbier's third signature shoe. The sole was not yet developed, so the factory used an existing sole from another shoe company (Brooks). This shoe had one correction and then went straight to production.*

Opposite: *In this 2019 photograph by Neftalie Williams, Skateboarding Hall of Fame inductee Kareem Campbell performs his textbook shifty-ollie to fakie at the seminal Brooklyn Projects skate shop mini-ramp in Los Angeles, California.*

I exhaled and finished setting up, sober and thankful for having Black history to draw on and for skateboarding's ability to act as a fluid instrument for my deliberations on race culture, community, and power. Ever gracious, Brevard accepted my request and allowed me to archive her image.

When retelling this story to students, many ask if the interaction still hurts me. It does not. I'm forever grateful to that photographer because he gave me the shot: a shot to see inner sanctum and a shot at recognizing that BIPOC men, women, LGBTQ, and nonbinary skaters were beyond the scope of those with an authoritative voice and in positions of power to make our community visible. While perhaps well-intentioned individuals collectively, they could not recognize themselves in the miraculous union of disparate souls sharing a practice.

Fire from that incident spilled over into all my endeavors, from the books on the history of skaters of color to my academic scholarship at the University of Southern California (USC) and Yale Schwarzman Center and the skate diplomacy projects. It all stems from that day and the need to feature skateboarding as a site of awe, awesomeness, and allyship manifest.

The broader skate community joins me through the organic discussions of mental health made possible by the Ben Raemers Foundation and the USC skate study, the work of SKATEISM and The Skatepark Project, all building inclusive communities via skateboarding. Together we have formed initiatives to push against racism with Surf Ghana, kept Skateistan rolling, and generated honest dialogue at Pushing Boarders, while Virgil Abloh's collab with Lucien Clarke tangibly dismantled "borders." Beyond this, just as in Parks's time, Black women lead, challenging norms through Proper Gnar, froSkate, Black Girls Skate, Briana King, and others seizing the malleable clay of skate culture. The magic within our collective became further evident to the masses when our world was brought to light by the writers and photographers who witnessed the beauty of a supportive multiracial, multigendered, and nongendered skateboarding community during the Olympics.

Our skate family has created a stir undeniable by those who once deemed us insignificant. We break cycles of exclusion and sustain ourselves through a process of love, documentation, reflection, and action, just as Parks prescribed. May those who dare to stand tall and proud and to break barriers with their skill, determination, and allyship roll forever!

Professional skateboarder Ishod Wair demonstrates a frontside cooked grind, as captured by Neftalie Williams in Havana, Cuba, in 2016. Wair was named the 2013 Thrasher *magazine Skater of the Year.*

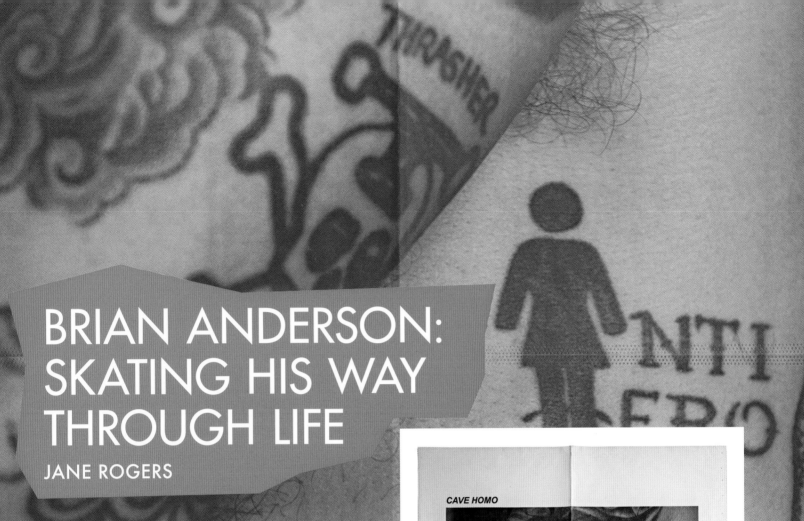

BRIAN ANDERSON: SKATING HIS WAY THROUGH LIFE

JANE ROGERS

Brian Anderson's aggressive yet graceful and lithe skating style belies his massive six-foot-three frame. To see Anderson twist, turn, and grind his way over stairs, railings, and just about any other structure he can skate over, under, or through is like watching a ballet dancer.

One of the best street skaters of his generation, Anderson first gained notoriety in 1996 with his appearance in Toy Machine's *Welcome to Hell* video. Three years later, while skating for Toy Machine, he won the World Cup of Skateboarding and was named *Thrasher* magazine's Skater of the Year. Joining Girl Skateboards in 1999, Anderson skated for them for over ten years before leaving in 2013 to start his own skate company.

Wanting to express his creativity in fashion and board design, and to have something to fall back on when he could no longer rely solely on skating as a source of income, Anderson created 3D Skateboards. That same year, Anderson collaborated with Nike SB, another of his sponsors, to produce his signature shoe. Using sketches drawn by Anderson, Nike designers created a skate shoe with a "runner-like upturned toe" specifically designed for flip tricks.

His venture into the business side of skate lasted three years, and though it was successful, living on the East Coast while the business was on the West Coast didn't work out well. In 2016, 3D folded and Anderson was picked up by Antihero Skateboards.

Included in a 2017 issue of Cave Homo, *this poster art is an assembly of Brian Anderson's tattoos, which illustrate his skate story.*

Although Anderson is known for his powerful skating, it was his coming out as gay in 2016 that has earned him accolades from the skate community. He became the most high-profile and most successful professional skater to come out as gay, something he never thought he would do while still skating. Historically, skate has been known for its homophobic views, and coming up in the mid-1990s skate scene, Anderson witnessed antigay behavior from his fellow skaters.

In an interview with *Vice,* Anderson remembers hearing gay slurs all the time, which made him think at a young age that it was dangerous to talk about his sexuality. Knowing it would have a negative effect on his career in such a male-dominated and macho community, Anderson put his rage and frustration into his skating. "I think a part of me was so irritated and angry from holding that in, so it made me more of an animal on my skateboard," he recalls.

Skate has made progress in recent years to be more accepting, and Anderson's recognition has made him a symbol for the LGBTQ community, leading him to take an active role in public awareness. Designer Luke Williams, a friend of Anderson's, asked if he wanted to collaborate on a project with photographer Christian Trippe. This idea grew into what is now *Cave Homo,* a queer art-focused zine based in New York that aspires to "showcase members of our community who inspire us to be our complete selves unapologetically." Proceeds from its sale are donated to the LGBTQ suicide prevention nonprofit, The Trevor Project.

Top left: *This Brian Anderson pro model Girl skate deck, with graphic by Andy Jenkins, came out in 2002.*

Top right: *In 2013, Brian Anderson collaborated with his sponsor, Nike SB, to create this signature pro model shoe.*

Bottom right: *Brian Anderson's love of hockey jerseys inspired this 2017 Nike jersey with his own cheetah head design. The cheetah reminded Anderson of typical US high-school logos.*

Tony Hawk used his 2016 signature model skateboard by Birdhouse on the last 900 he completed. A testimony to Hawk's tenacity, though hard to see, the top of this board is nearly cracked all the way through.

MY LAST 900

The first 900 I ever made—and the first ever done—was at the X Games in 1999. It was the culmination of more than ten years of failed attempts and marked the end of my competitive career. It was also the first time that skateboarding was featured on mainstream-sports highlight reels. I didn't imagine that one trick would resonate so widely, and it became synonymous with my name—and with skateboarding to newcomers—in the years that followed. I did the trick dozens of times over the next ten years, until finally realizing that the impact of failed attempts was starting to shorten my overall career arc.

On the seventeenth anniversary of that first 900, feeling physically capable and mentally prepared, I decided to do it one last time. It took much longer than I thought, and the failures hurt more than ever. But I finally made one. I felt a sense of great relief and closure when I found myself riding away.

I kept the board I was riding, unsure of what to do with it for months afterward, until the Smithsonian reached out to see if I had any items to donate. I was honored to hand it off, knowing that it gave me the opportunity to prove myself at an age when most people wouldn't believe that I could even skate anymore. I'm still here, skating as much as possible. But my 900s ended with that skateboard.

—Tony Hawk

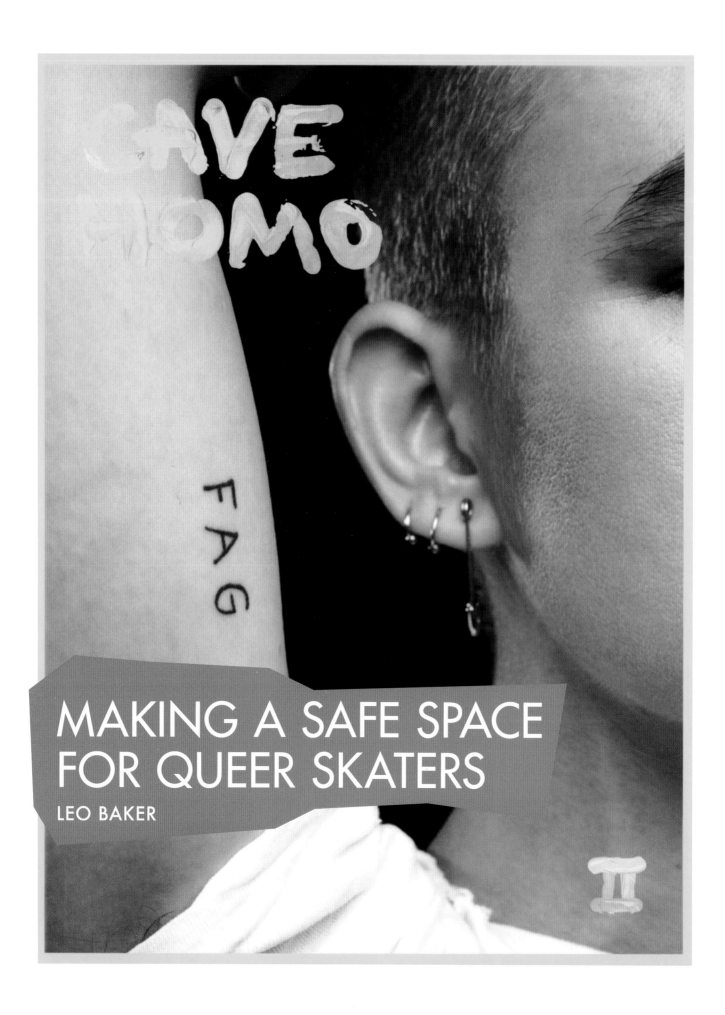

MAKING A SAFE SPACE
FOR QUEER SKATERS

LEO BAKER

No more competitions for the rest of my life. But at the same time, it was hard to make that decision because this is what everyone is doing right now. Am I crazy for not wanting to compete? Through the Olympic qualifiers, I just didn't want to be there for so many reasons.

Don't get me wrong, skateboarding for the Olympics and Paralympics has created space and more opportunity for women and skaters with disabilities, which is incredible. I cannot argue with that. But at the same time, my actual experience hasn't been positive. I've battled with being a trans person in this space.

Getting categorized as a woman when I'm a trans person was the number one reason why I stepped away from competing and didn't try to make the Olympic team. I wrestled with my decision to drop out of competitions. My sponsors and I talked

Opposite: Leo Baker collaborated with Brian Anderson on this second issue of the skatezine Cave Homo.

Above: This complete includes a Meow Skateboards deck, Independent trucks, and Lacey Baker Spitfire wheels also shown on top, illustrating Baker's journey of self-discovery.

a lot about the fact that I can compete. I didn't want to go back on my word to my sponsors. But I'm human and humans change. I told my sponsors that I know what my impact is, and it is not going to be fully realized if I'm in the competition setting.

My impact is outside that, and right now is the time. It feels political just to be out as trans and use my privilege to lift up my community.

I'm doing what I want to do. I created a board company, Glue Skateboards, with two queer people who also don't feel they fit anywhere in skating. I, and other people, have done things to create space for queer people to skate, but it is a beginner space. There hasn't really been a specific safe space in skating that has celebrated the queer skateboarders who have been here doing it for so long.

Queer people have been fragmented out in different teams. There is no empowerment in that situation. I want to create a space with people who understand me as a person. Cher Strauberry, Stephen Ostrowski, and I are the first three, and we want to get people on Glue's team who are like us and who have the same dedication to skating we do.

AN ELECTRIC PUSH

Ever since I first pushed a skateboard across America in 1976 using a relay method, I'd wanted to make a solo crossing.

In 2012, my father passed away from complications due to Alzheimer's, and I thought about making a solo push to honor him and to raise funds for Alzheimer's research. As I was still running the Morro Bay Skateboard Museum, taking off enough time to do a solo push just wasn't going to happen. It would have to be another leapfrog relay effort. The first two people I asked to join me were my wife, Cathy, as the support team leader, and Dylan, my son, as a skater. Dylan had grown up hearing my cross-country stories, and now it was time for him to create some stories of his own.

We rounded out the team with Melanie Leilani Castro, Colleen Pelech, and Marc Juvinall, and then recruited a photographer, Dylan Baumann. We connected with the Alzheimer's Association and worked out a plan to raise funds for the organization. The longboard and skateboard industry and the worldwide skateboarding community all offered incredible support.

Our push began in Waldport, Oregon, and finished twenty-three days later in New York City. It would take pages upon pages to describe the ride thoroughly, but what really stood out to me was that these young people were willing to take a month out of their lives to support the fight against this terrible disease. It was also the first time that my teammates were all young enough to be my children. I felt a huge responsibility to make sure they returned home safely. Sometimes it was like herding cats, but with the calmness that Cathy exhibited and with Dylan acting as a bridge across the generation gap, we accomplished our goal and had a heck of a lot of fun doing it!

Okay, back to wanting to do that solo ride. In 2016, I decided to give it a shot, but at age fifty-nine, I chose to use an electric skateboard.

Evolve Skateboards agreed to sponsor me. I selected a route similar to my 1976 path, and Hall of Fame skateboarder Ed Nadalin came on board as my support team. We began our journey in Eugene, Oregon. Eight days later, we arrived in Mountain Home, Idaho. Due to some frighteningly close encounters with vehicles, I decided to abandon the ride, and we returned home.

Top: *Jack Smith makes his way along a quiet stretch of asphalt somewhere between Kemmerer and Farson, Wyoming, during his solo push across America on an electric skateboard in 2018.*

Above: *Jack Smith wore these Vans shoes during his 2012 cross-country push. The bottom of the right shoe has a hole worn through the heel due to his braking with his right foot.*

Over the next two years, it really bothered me that I had quit. I thought about it every day. In addition, I kept hearing my late father's words in my head, "Finish what you start." Cathy, who had retired from teaching in 2018 and knew how much finishing the ride would mean, said, "Let's go," so we did.

Inboard Technology supplied me with the gear I would need, and a local company, GoWesty, loaned us a 1990 VW Westfalia as a support vehicle. We decided to make the ride a fundraiser for the Morro Bay Skateboard Museum.

We began the ride in Mountain Home, where Ed and I had stopped in 2016. We made our way across the high desert of Idaho, climbed and descended the Rockies, rolled across the beautiful Great Plains, and made our way over the always difficult Appalachians. Forty-five days later, we rolled up to the front steps of the Smithsonian in Washington, DC. Even though I was propelled across America by an electric motor, standing in the same position for long periods of time, the intense vibrations caused by rough roads, headwinds, the ever-present stress of vehicles roaring by just feet away, and the extreme heat and cold all contributed to making the ride much more demanding than I thought it would be, both physically and mentally.

I often tell people that I had the easy job on this ride and that Cathy's was much more difficult. She was always on the lookout for poor road conditions and hazards, driving ahead anywhere from five to ten miles. She also had to find safe places to park in what were sometimes very isolated and sketchy locations. She kept the support vehicle fueled and stocked and kept the board's batteries as well as mine charged! Most importantly, Cathy buoyed my spirits when I felt like giving up. This wasn't her first rodeo, as she was the support vehicle driver on my 2013 push across America. I could not have made this trip without her love and support.

Completing this journey at the age of sixty-one was the realization of a nineteen-year-old boy's dream to make a solo crossing of America by skateboard. Although it ended up being on an electric skateboard, it was, as were my previous rides, a magical way to experience this amazing country. Cathy and I will never forget this ride of a lifetime.

—*Jack Smith*

Top: *Jack Smith was riding with a few younger skaters on his 2012 push across America, and safety was paramount. Everyone on the team wore one of these yellow vests while riding for greater visibility on the road. (Middle) Jack Smith rode this 2018 Inboard Technology electric skateboard with handheld remote on his solo ride from Mountain Home, Idaho, to Washington, DC. It took Smith and his wife, who followed in a support van, forty-five days to travel 2,394 miles. (Above) On his 2018 solo electric-powered ride across the country, Jack Smith was in his early sixties and has said he could not have made it without these knee braces.*

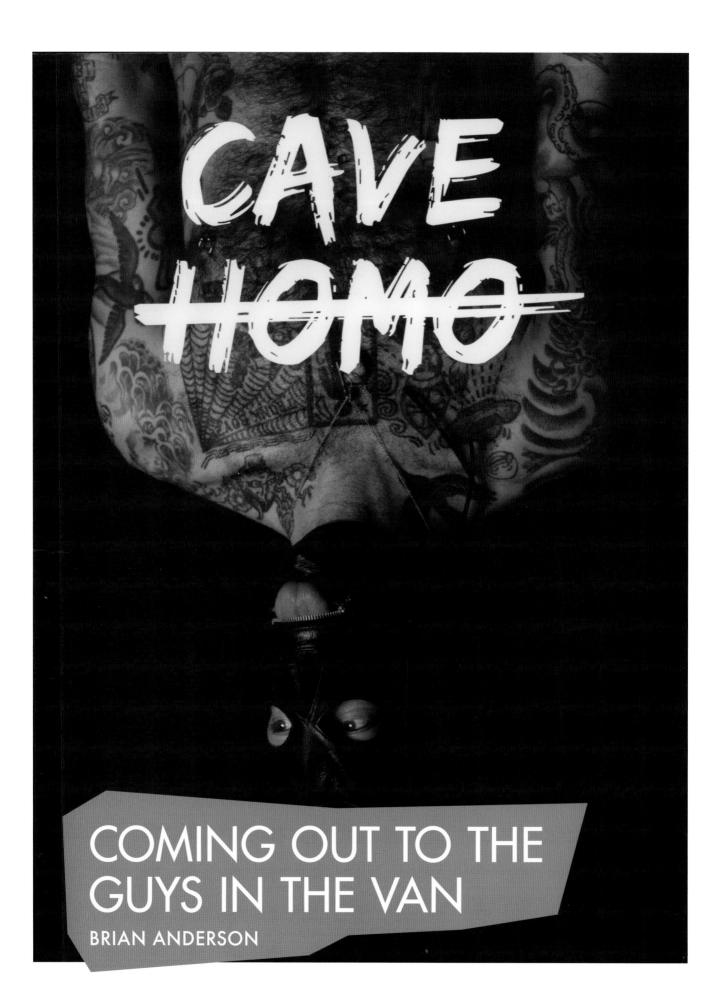

CAVE ~~HOMO~~

COMING OUT TO THE GUYS IN THE VAN

BRIAN ANDERSON

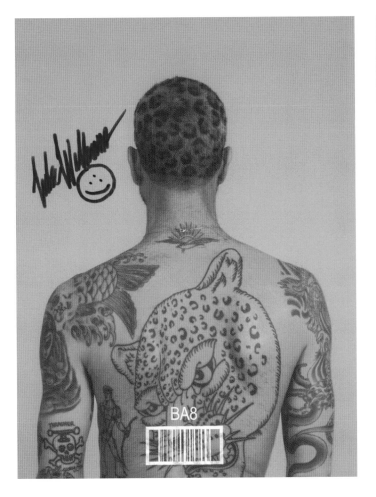

It was fun all day long—the camaraderie of the skate team, high-fiving, and having smokes and drinks together. But at the end of the day, as the years went by, I felt increasingly depressed and alone when all my buddies were off chasing girls or out with their girlfriends. That was hard. I always had my sketchbook and music—my Walkman, CDs, and a good pair of headphones. But I had gotten to the point where I knew I had to tell the people I was working with—the people closest to me—that I was gay. I loved those guys, and them not knowing was killing me inside.

Opposite and above left: Cave Homo was a collaboration between Luke Williams and Brian Anderson that gave Anderson a platform to express himself as an openly gay man for the first time.

Above right: Skateism is a nontraditional media platform for the skate community that focuses on diversity and features "women, LGBTQ+, DIY, non-western and charity organizations." The theme of this July 2019 issue of Skateism magazine was "pride."

They were solid, understanding, intelligent people, and I knew that telling them would make our lives together more fun.

I am six foot three and have a fairly deep voice—not the stereotypical gay man in appearance, so I figured their first reaction would be, "What?" And that's exactly what it was. Then I watched as they moved from surprise at what they had just heard to thinking, Hey, we love this dude. Then I got hugs from all of them. What happened that day changed the minds of a lot of my van mates about what a gay person is—about what that means. I was lucky that I got to slip right into this new feeling of everyone knowing and of being confident that they would hide my sexuality from the outside world. I knew what I had told them wouldn't leave the van.

Skateboarding ended up being very punk rock and more open than was the case in other organized sports back then—and now.

PAVE THE WAY SKATEBOARDS

MIRIAM KLEIN STAHL

I don't remember not skateboarding. That's probably because I grew up by the beach in Los Angeles in the 1970s and 1980s and was, and still am, a tomboy/butch dyke. I lived near a pro skater named Steve Rocco. His house was the hangout for pros who were younger than he, like Mark "Gonz" Gonzales, Rodney Mullen, and Natas Kaupas. Steve took me in as one of the boys, and we would skate nonstop. He had us practice ollies on a carpet, so when we went outside, our tails would slap really hard because we were used to the softness of the fabric. He also had us ride tiny freestyle wheels and flip the bolts on our top truck so our foot would catch on the nut, and we could ollie higher that way. We still tore up our shoes, but we could all ollie without bolts hurting our feet.

At eighteen, in 1989, I left Los Angles and my skate pals for the San Francisco Bay Area and never looked back. Although I didn't find a skate community in the Bay Area, I did find a queer punk underground that kept me busy for the next thirty years. The first time I met Tara Jepson was in the Mission District of San Francisco in the 1990s. We were both part of a vibrant queer arts scene that was happening at that time. The first time we met was at a reading and cabaret she was doing at Red Dora's Bearded Lady Café.

But skateboarding is in my bones. I got back into skating when my daughter was five and wanted to learn how to skate. We'd go to the skatepark, where I would teach her all the tricks I knew from the 1980s. She picked up skating quickly and left me wanting to learn more. My fifty-year-old body can't do what my teenage body used to do, but I still have that stoked feeling when I land a trick or drop into a bowl, or just skate really fast down a hill.

Tara Jepsen and I reconnected after she moved to Los Angeles. Tara started skating in her forties, even cleaning pools so she could skate in them. We inspired each other with our skate photos and videos on Instagram. Together, we decided to make a skateboard deck that celebrates our love of skating and our queer lives and icons. I never thought those two subcultures would merge, but now I can go to a queer skate meetup almost every week thanks to our friends at Unity Skateboards, who are bringing generations of queer skaters together.

Tara and I approached making skateboards through a shared DIY work ethic we learned from our punk community. We had an idea and made it happen with the resources we have: creating

This papercut illustration, created by Miriam Klein Stahl, outlines the moves needed to do an ollie.

art, writing, and our passion for skating. Our queer skate culture thrived through meetups, and we were able to offer a skateboard that celebrated our queer icons, both past and present. The manifesto for our company, Pave the Way Skateboards, was printed on the underside of our first deck: "Skateboarding and being queer have always aligned for us spiritually. We believe in living and working outside the mainstream to create a beautiful and meaningful world. We believe in outsiders and weirdos and people that don't align with socially legible life paths. DIY culture exists robustly within both queer and skate cultures because they share the same values." We were also very fortunate to work with genius queer skater and board shaper Joi Tillman.

Pave the Way Skateboards has been an incredible joy for me. Through the project, I've connected with other skaters and am able to contribute to skate culture through art, friendship, and love of rolling around.

Above: *Miriam Klein Stahl doing a bomb drop off a truck in San Pedro, California, in 1984.*

Right: *This 2018 Potluck Fundraiser model deck by Pave the Way Skateboards features a graphic by Miriam Klein Stahl that includes portraits of Laverne Cox, John Waters, Susan Sontag, and other icons who helped raise awareness of gender equality and queer culture.*

FROM APOLLO 11 TO *THE SHINING*

July 16, 2019, marked the fiftieth anniversary of the Apollo 11 Moon landing. This remarkable achievement was celebrated around the world. Perhaps no event honored it as spectacularly as the full-size projection of the 363-foot Saturn V rocket on the east face of the Washington Monument. From July 16 through July 20, over a half million people joined the Smithsonian's National Air and Space Museum on the National Mall to memorialize the first-ever walk on the Moon.

StrangeLove Skateboards offered its own homage to the Moon landing by issuing an Apollo 11 skate deck with artwork by Todd Bratrud. Rather than a simple salute to the anniversary, the deck's graphics allude to the fifty years of crackpot conspiracy theories that claim the Moon landing was faked.

According to some, the landing was a scam perpetuated by the US government and created by a top-secret team of cinematographers. Bratrud makes the film director Stanley Kubrick the protagonist of this alleged fraud, placing him in a director's chair with the name Kubrick clearly visible on the back. In addition to showing the Apollo module on a sound stage with lights and other film equipment surrounding it, Bratrud throws in an empty Coke bottle (someone once claimed that they saw a Coke bottle fall out of the space module as it landed) and a coffee mug with the NASA logo on it to create an Illuminati-approved tableaux of "evidence."

As if this isn't enough, Bratrud populates his deck graphic with specific references to Kubrick's film *The Shining*: the orange Hicks's hexagon-pattern carpet underneath the director's chair on the back graphic is seen in the hallway scenes when Danny is driving his Big Wheel through the hotel, and the shape and color of the "Apollo 11 USA" on the front is the exact same image found on Danny's sweater worn throughout the film. Some believe that *The Shining* was Kubrick's way of telling the world that he did, in fact, conspire with NASA to create a fake Moon landing.

Lest you think StrangeLove was trying to revive the old Moon-landing conspiracy theories with this graphic, included in the deck's packaging was an actual tin foil hat, a not-so-subtle rebuttal to those who believe in secret shadow forces that collude to deceive the American public. Fortunately for our visitors, the Smithsonian contains abundant proof that the landing was real.

—*Betsy Gordon*

StrangeLove Skateboards included a tin foil hat with its conspiracy-themed 2019 Apollo 11 skate deck.

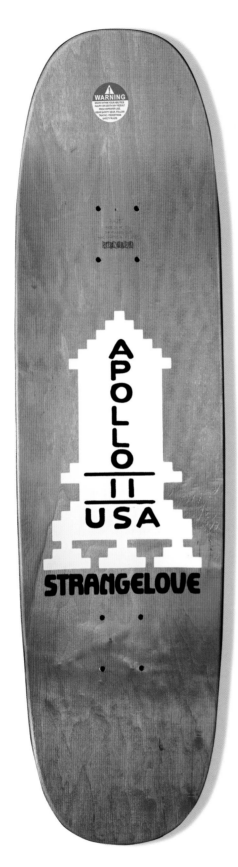

Artist Todd Bratrud created the artwork for this Apollo Moon Landing model deck issued by StrangeLove Skateboards in 2019. Both sides of this deck allude to the conspiracy theory that director Stanley Kubrick created fake footage of the 1969 Apollo 11 Moon landing and that Kubrick's film, The Shining, provided additional proof to support the theory.

QUELL

a skateboarding media outlet

for women, by women

SKATEBOARDING

Issue 005

In 2020, photographer Lanna Apisukh photographed Leo Baker for the cover of issue 005 of Quell Skateboarding magazine. Outspoken about their gender identity, Baker is often asked to talk about their advocacy role in the skate community.

LEO BAKER'S JOURNEY

JANE ROGERS

To be unapologetic about my image and who I am and then to have people acknowledge how important that is in the skate industry . . . I can't even describe how that feels. To bring together girls who skate, queers who skate . . . and let those worlds collide. I'm lucky to be here.

—Leo Baker (*Project-Nerd* blog, 2019)

My first interaction with Leo Baker was when their name was Lacey Baker. When Baker became the first female pro skater to get a Nike SB model shoe in 2018, my colleague Betsy Gordon and I reached out to their agent and asked if they would be interested in donating something to the museum, specifically a pair of those Lacey Baker pro models. In addition, we wondered if they would be willing to donate other items that represented their career path as a pro skater, from fifteen-year-old phenom to a more reflective twenty-seven-year-old.

Baker sent a wonderful array of objects. Included were those pro model shoes, their signature Meow Skateboards deck with a rose graphic, a computer-generated sketch of that graphic that they designed, and a package of "Lacey Baker" Spitfire wheels, all typical representatives of the sponsors and merchandise pro skaters tend to have. What was not typical in their donation was the inclusion of a chest binder. When I had mistakenly identified it as a sports bra, Baker clarified for me in an email, "I use it to appear flat chested. Important for me to share because I'm very passionate about gender expression and binders are a staple for me."

Gender in sports is a complex issue. Most competitive sports use the traditional binary gender definitions of "male" and "female" to organize and regulate participation. As many museum professionals try to address the limitations of the gender binary, Baker's binder stands as an illuminating object that can educate in ways that words cannot.

A copy of the zine *Cave Homo*, with Baker on the cover (see page 206), demonstrates Baker's continued journey into self-discovery. In a 2018 article in *Huck* magazine, Baker relates, "*Cave Homo* helped me feel validated and seen for who I am beyond my skateboarding identity. That's really important for me, because for a long time the industry wanted to shape me in a way that wasn't me." As Baker's journey as a nonbinary athlete continued, it was documented through their subsequent donations to the museum.

Top: *Leo Baker, who identifies as nonbinary, used this chest binder to appear less gender specific, so as not to be defined by their gender.*

Above: *Leo Baker wore this T-shirt during their appearance in* Mother's Daughter, *the 2019 Miley Cyrus video. Baker was initially wearing a plain white T-shirt for the video shoot and at the last minute decided to hand write "They/Them" on it, introducing the gender identity they are most comfortable with.*

Above right: *Baker's signature rose graphic is still visible through the wear on this 2016 Meow Skateboards Lacey Baker model deck.*

In 2019, Baker changed their name briefly to Lee. It was then that I contacted them to collect the "They/Them" T-shirt Baker wore in the Miley Cyrus video *Mother's Daughter*, signaling their public coming out as nonbinary and acknowledging their gender identity beyond skateboarding. In a POPSUGAR interview shortly after the video debuted, Baker explains, "Obviously standing in my power and sticking to who I am and being authentic really spoke volumes more than just winning a competition because I think it's paying off now. What would it be like if I was living as Lacey Baker? There's nothing there, it's just hollow."

The next time I contacted them, it was Leo Baker who I asked to participate in an oral history for this book. More items followed, documenting the place Baker was in their journey: a vest from fellow skater Elissa Steamer's brand Gnarhunters, a T-shirt Baker designed for Meow Skateboards, and another pro model shoe from Nike SB. This time, the words *Leo Baker* were imprinted on the shoe, symbolizing full circle if you will. The Smithsonian is grateful that Baker has found a safe and accepting space for their legacy.

PAISLEY GRABS BACK

BETSY GORDON

On January 21, 2017, the day after Donald Trump's inauguration and the first full day of his presidency, hundreds of thousands of people marched in the streets of Washington, DC, to protest the Trump administration and to advocate for women's rights. They were joined by similar protest marches across all fifty states and more than thirty foreign countries, ranging from Antarctica to Zimbabwe. In total, more than 4.3 million people took part in these protests, making it the largest single-day protest in US history.

Many people who protested wore homemade pink knitted hats embellished with cat ears in reference to Trump's vulgar remarks that women would let him "grab them by the pussy." Nicknamed the pussyhat, it soon became a potent symbol of dissent and activism.

Skateboarders took notice. Shortly after the Women's March, Paisley Skateboards issued its Paisley Grabs Back deck featuring the artwork of Winston Tseng. Although a short-lived brand, Paisley produced other politically charged decks, including one portraying Donald Trump and Satan and another one of police shooting children. On this deck, Tseng depicts profiles of people of all genders and races wearing the pussyhat. Sometimes a skateboard is just a skateboard, but for Paisley and Tseng, it becomes something more than seven plies of maple.

Top: *Hundreds of thousands of people took to the streets of Washington, DC, on January 21, 2017, to advocate for women's rights.*

Above: *This pussyhat was worn at the 2017 Women's March in Washington, DC.*

Opposite: *This 2017 Paisley Skates Paisley Grabs Back model deck includes a Winston Tseng graphic depicting a diverse array of people wearing the pussyhat.*

TOKYO 2020

THE OLYMPICS— ARE YOU KIDDING ME?

ALEXIS SABLONE

No one in skateboarding ever thought they'd see it in the Olympics. That was a crazy thought. But skateboarding has changed a lot. Before it was included, I wondered what it would be and how it would be scored. Suddenly, there was the Street League series, and I had an idea what the numbers would be like. I could see how at least that one part of skateboarding might work in the Olympics.

The contest part of skateboarding is like a branch. I've never felt comfortable referring to it as a sport. It was an anti-jock thing, and there's a part of skateboarding that still feels that way and hates all the organized sport aspect. And then there's the contest side, which keeps growing and becoming more organized.

Even though I am a very competitive person, I've always hated contests. But contests were where I could win $25,000. I didn't know any women who were being paid by skateboard companies, and if you weren't getting paid by a skate company, you couldn't live. I didn't have a contract because there was no path for that. So I started skating in contests, and once I was in, I was invited back. Every year, even throughout grad school, I knew I would get my one chance to try to win a bunch of money at the X Games.

As a result, I've always done contests. Then suddenly there were serious talks about including skateboarding in the

Olympics. When it became official, I couldn't believe it. It's not like I was crossing my fingers for years hoping skateboarding would be in the Olympics. But now it was a potential reality in my life.

I've been doing contests for ten years, so why would I stop the year before I could go to the Olympics? I decided to give it a try, even though I'm not young. I don't feel old, but I'm the oldest person competing in the sport. I've seen other people who were in contests with me retire. I'm the only one from that generation left competing. I'm so lucky that I got the chance to do this, and I would have always regretted it if I didn't try as hard as I possibly could to be there.

I have split feelings, however. Skateboarding in the Olympics is so far from why I started skateboarding. When I began skating in the 1990s, the Olympic Games weren't possible. Motivations to make it to the Olympics will be different than when I first came

Above: *On day three of the 2020 Tokyo Summer Olympic Games, Alexis Sablone of Team USA competes during the women's street final at Ariake Urban Sports Park.*

Opposite: *Photographer Ian Logan captures the entrance of USA Skateboarding's Alexis Sablone, Brighton Zeuner, and Nyjah Huston as they make their way to the stage for the official Olympic team announcement in Los Angeles on June 21, 2021.*

up, and part of me is worried for that. I'm attached to the time that I started skateboarding, and I want everyone to have that.

But then there's the side of me that says it's the Olympics. It's just such an honor. Not everyone gets the chance. I could get to go to Tokyo and wear weird outfits and stay in the Olympic Village. That's a crazy experience.

I'm constantly traveling right now until the qualifiers are done. I'm definitely older than I want to be. I don't want to be almost forty and competing against twelve-year-olds. Not to put down twelve-year-olds, but there's humor in standing next to a little person and this little person is beating me. If I can make it to this Olympics, I don't have to worry about the next one. I can just be there for the first one so I can say I did it.

I'll remember that moment forever, and then skateboarding can morph again and I can focus on filming. I have a list of tricks I want to film. I practice a certain way for a contest because I'm trying to do big things repeatedly under pressure. When I'm filming, I want the spot to look cool, and I want to learn a new trick to do. It's totally different and creative.

Skateboarding has changed so much in the twenty-three years I've been doing it. It's maturing and will continue to evolve even if there's this more organized part of it. When it becomes thought of as an Olympic sport, on some level it will be

unrecognizable, at least the contest part. I think there's always going to be this other branch of skateboarding that is more interested in what pants people are wearing and what size wheels they have. Maybe that part gets more underground because the different veins of skateboarding will have money and no money.

I worry how it's going to change the industry financially and what the industry will see as valuable in the future. Not all corporations in skateboarding will lose touch with what cool skateboarding is about and only see value in contests or athletes. There will always be people skating who don't care about contests and people who do care about contests, and now that means getting into the Olympics.

OLYMPIC DREAM

BRYCE WETTSTEIN

The moment I stood at the Olympics I saw my dream becoming reality. And this moment was unlike any other moment. You don't even realize you're in it. It was right after I had landed my run and realized that the forty seconds of my life that I had been envisioning for an entire two years was over. But somehow it could never be over because my dream still stood there, waiting for me to acknowledge that I had actually done it. I couldn't seem to acknowledge it, however, as I was just too stunned. This moment of being in the height of competition, despite it being only a moment, is forever inside of us.

Poppy Olsen and I did an interview together while we were watching the podium being built. Mid-interview, after raving about what all of this means—which is impossible to describe—we started to cry. We just started tearing up on camera over how unreal this moment was for us.

One of the lasting impacts of the games is the camaraderie of friendship. All of the female competitors became close friends despite being on different teams. When Misugu Okamoto fell during her run, we lifted her on our shoulders and cheered for her. Sakura, Yndi, Isa, Jordyn, and Brighton—we were all there for her.

Bryce Wettstein, member of the USA Skateboarding Women's Park National Team, during her competition run in August 2021 at the Summer Olympics in Tokyo, Japan. Bryce placed sixth in the final.

A POST-OLYMPIC FUTURE

BETSY GORDON

On August 6, 2021, during the Olympic pentathlon finals, the coach of the German team forcibly struck a horse with her hand that Annika Schleu was riding to coerce it to jump. In other words, someone punched a horse during the 2020 Summer Olympic Games in Tokyo, Japan. But that wasn't the weirdest thing seen during those Olympics. Tokyo 2020 gave us positive COVID-19 tests, mandatory athlete quarantines, stadiums devoid of fans, cardboard beds, and megastar athletes withdrawing from competition. In this soup of strange, odd, and unprecedented events, skateboarding made its debut as an Olympic sport.

Why skateboarding became an Olympic sport is easy to answer: money. The largest source of revenue for the International Olympic Committee (IOC) is from television licensing fees. High viewership ratings for televised Olympic coverage mean broadcast corporations can charge more money to advertisers to run their commercials during the games. Increased revenue from advertising fees means more corporate profit. More corporate profit means more billion-dollar deals for the IOC.

American broadcast conglomerate NBCUniversal, owner of NBC Sports, paid nearly $5 billion for the media rights to broadcast the Olympic Games from 2014 through 2020. Unfortunately, this was bad timing for NBC. Watching sports on a TV during primetime is an antiquated practice. Most people under the age of thirty-five get their news via phone or computer screen. Media content consumption has been transformed by young content makers, Instagram influencers, and TikTok stars. NBC needed a return on its investment by promising more viewers to their advertisers. In short, NBC needed Olympic events that attracted younger viewers to assure their advertisers that the fees they paid were justified. Since skateboarding skewed to a much younger demographic than the pentathlon, NBC hoped that it would be its golden goose.

How skateboarding got into the Olympics is much more complex than a corporate balance sheet, however. It used to be that to introduce a new Olympic sport, an existing sport had to be removed. One new in, one old out. That changed in 2014 when Thomas Bach, president of the IOC, introduced the Olympic Agenda 2020 strategic plan that opened a pathway for new sports to become part of the Olympic roster without the requirement of eliminating existing sports.

Even with Bach's rule revisions, the path to becoming a new Olympic sport was not straightforward. Any new sport

Street and park skateboarders of the USA Skateboarding National Team appear at the official Summer Olympics team announcement on June 21, 2020, in Los Angeles, California.

On August 21, 2014, Thomas Bach, center, president of the International Olympic Committee (IOC), poses with skateboarders on his visit to the Nanjing 2014 Sports Lab during the 2014 Summer Youth Olympic Games, held in Nanjing, China.

contender had to be part of an IOC-recognized international federation. An Olympic federation had to have multiple member nations with each member nation having its own governing body, bylaws, and the like. What was required by the IOC—clear delegation of authority, hierarchical organizational structure, rules, regulations, and schedules—was not a strength of skateboarding in the United States or in any other country. Along the route to becoming an Olympic sport were rival international skateboard federations that battled to become the international skateboarding federation, lawsuits, and tremendous animosity from many skateboarders who opposed any effort to make skateboarding a sport with uniforms, coaches, and opening ceremonies that required marching while waving a flag.

Nonetheless, led by American Gary Ream, the International Skateboarding Federation (ISF) was formed in 2004 to begin the process of getting skateboarding into the Olympics. Ream, then president of the Camp Woodward conglomerate, a skateboarding summer camp with eleven sites in the United States and Mexico, stated that the Olympics needed skateboarding more than skateboarding needed the Olympics. He claimed a personal friendship with IOC President Thomas Bach (whose skateboarding son attended Woodward) and fervently believed that the Olympics would be good for skateboarding. It would bring much needed gender parity, requiring that the same number of women competed as men, and bring global recognition to an often maligned and misunderstood sport. He warned naysayers that if the ISF weren't in charge, rival Olympic sports federations like Fédération Internationale de Roller Sports (FIRS) or the Union Cycliste Internationale (UCI) would take the leadership role in presenting skateboarding to the IOC. Bicyclists and in-line skaters? Not on Ream's watch! As he promised that the ISF would run Olympic skateboarding "by skateboarders for skateboarders," some wondered if Ream's fervor was more than a little motivated by the possibility of future profits. After all, with Ream controlling global skateboarding, wouldn't Camp Woodward stand to profit mightily as a potential ISF training facility?

The blurring of lines between Ream's promises and potential for conflict of interest came into sharper focus when the ISF, after years of working with the IOC, was suddenly rejected. In 2017, the IOC failed to recognize the ISF as an IOC federation. A last-minute deal was formed between the ISF and FIRS, the

long-standing, officially recognized Olympic federation for roller sports, the very same federation that Ream promised wouldn't touch skateboarding. FIRS and the ISF formed World Skate, with Ream assuming a senior leadership position within the World Skate bureaucracy. In 2018, former ISF executive director Josh Friedberg became the CEO of USA Skateboarding, which the United States Olympic & Paralympic Committee (USOPC) recognized as the national governing body for skateboarding in the United States, and began to organize qualifying competitions to select the first US Olympic skateboarding team.

The COVID-19 pandemic shut down most Olympic skateboard qualifying competitions and ultimately postponed the 2020 games until 2021. Nonetheless, the ISF named the first, official Team USA.

How did NBC's gamble pay off? The overall television ratings were the worst ever for the network since it began broadcasting the Olympics in 1988. Primetime coverage of the Tokyo Games was 42 percent lower than the 2016 Summer Olympic Games in Rio and 22 percent lower than the 2018 Winter Olympic Games in Pyeongchang.

Ironically, given its heavy stake in skateboarding as a ratings booster, NBC made it extremely difficult to watch the skating competitions. Coverage was provided by NBC during its prime-

time broadcasts and on a myriad of NBC-affiliated streaming platforms. Getting the schedule for the events, times, days, and platforms was confusing. The official website of Team USA did not post a schedule but did have links for donating money and buying merchandise. The USA Skate Instagram account had a link in its bio to access the NBC streaming platform that required scrolling through endless headers before finding the skate information.

Primetime Olympic coverage on NBC didn't show all of the skate events in their entirety and cut away frequently to other sports, like rugby. The streaming services covered the competitions in their entirety but were frequently interrupted by ads and marred by lackluster commentary and poor camerawork. For those viewers used to watching skate competitions like Street League and X Games, the production values of the coverage fell

Above left: *Skateboarder Minna Stess wore this helmet when she became the youngest USA Skateboarding National Champion in 2021. Stess also became the youngest member of USA Skateboarding Women's Park National Team but failed to qualify for the Tokyo Olympics. She continues to compete and strives to qualify for the 2024 Olympics.*

Above right: *This Bridgestone sponsor pin was produced for the 2020 Tokyo Summer Olympics Games, the first to include skateboarding and surfing.*

below what they were accustomed to seeing. The commentator's attempt to explain the basics of the skateboarding vocabulary—goofy, regular, switch, fakie—was unnecessary for the skateboard savvy and baffling for the skateboard uninitiated.

So how did Team USA skateboarding do at its first Olympics? Of the twelve medals given out for Olympic skateboarding, the USA did not dominate, with several top contenders failing to perform at their anticipated peak. Unlike every other Olympic sport where qualifying heats are held days before the final competition, the IOC and World Skate decided that skateboarding would hold both qualifying and final events back-to-back on the same day, with little more than a half hour between the end of the last heat and the start of the final. For the skaters, that meant skating hard to make the finals, then having no time to rest and recover before skating to win a medal. Given the brutal heat and humidity radiating off the concrete skatepark, the

Above left: *Photographer Jamie Squire captured Poppy Olsen of Team Australia and Bryce Wettstein of Team USA carrying off Misugu Okamoto of Team Japan during the women's skateboarding park finals at Ariake Urban Sports Park on day twelve of the 2020 Tokyo Summer Olympic Games.*

Above right: *A sign that says* Skateboarding Banned *is duct-taped to a white wall that obstructs a view of the Ariake Urban Sports Park, site of the skateboarding events at the 2020 Tokyo Summer Olympic Games.*

skaters' performances must have been compromised by this decision, resulting in unexpected finishes among the men. Team USA's Nyjah Huston, favored to win the gold in men's street, finished next to last, in seventh place, while Heimana Reynolds, the top-ranked men's park skateboarder, failed to make the finals and placed thirteenth out of twenty. Cory Juneau won bronze for men's park, and Jagger Eaton won bronze for men's street.

The women's events created most of the excitement around skateboarding's debut. A quartet of young girls produced some of the youngest Olympic medalists ever. Japan's twelve-year-old Kokona Hiraki won silver in the women's park event, while Great Britain's thirteen-year-old Sky Brown won bronze. In women's street, Japan's Momiji Nishiya (age thirteen) won gold, followed by Brazil's Rayssa Leal (age thirteen) winning silver. Their images were splashed all over television, newspapers, and social media, making them the darlings of Tokyo 2020. Team USA's Alexis Sablone, thirty-four, placed fourth in the women's street, losing by 0.92 points to sixteen-year-old Funa Nakayama of Japan.

The American media loves a good Olympic story—a redemption story of coming from behind, returning after giving up, rising from obscurity, or battling adversity to win the gold. Although Team USA did not fit into that narrative, the Olympics provided a series of indelible images of skateboarders and

skateboarding that seemed to charm the worldwide public: of competitors lifting one another up, literally and figuratively, after one of them fails to land a trick; of skaters wholeheartedly congratulating a rival competitor for his or her better performance; of profound joy even after failing to medal. For some skaters, these images confirmed to the world how they know and understand skateboarding—not as an athletic competition focused on winning but as a diverse community concentrating on friendship.

Although it is too soon to measure the effect Tokyo 2020 had, many hope that the Olympic branding of skateboarding as something that is happy and healthy will encourage more people to skate. Some skateboard shops have seen an uptick in demand for skateboards from young women, what James Hope-Gill, CEO of Skateboard GB, called "the Sky Brown effect." Community activists lobbying for more skateparks in their cities or neighborhoods are optimistic that public officials will see new parks as the training grounds for future Olympians. While more skateboarders and skateparks should have a healthy effect on the profits of the skateboard industry, others worry that the Olympics will overly emphasize skill and performance as definitions of "good" skating. This type of skating was evident in the Japanese women's Olympic team. Its members had clearly been working on mastering the hardest tricks to perform during

their competition runs to stack up the most points to win. This approach to producing a "winning" run was not as obvious during the American women's runs. Some Americans did nearly the exact same tricks they had been performing since their 2019 competitions and did not unleash any new, more technically difficult maneuvers to increase their scores. One could see, as the skaters would say, the Japanese and the Americans had two very different vibes.

Only time will tell if this different vibe of Olympic-grade competition, requiring year-round access to training facilities, coaches, nutritionists, physical therapists, sports psychologists, and more, will be something that other official IOC-recognized national governing bodies for skateboarding will provide for skateboarders. Many families may not be able to afford access to national and international qualifying competitions to produce an Olympic skateboarder. Even more unknown is how many skateboarders will want to undertake that sort of regimen for the chance of winning a medal. There is room for all sorts of skateboarding and skateboarders. Will skateboarding alter some of its creativity and spontaneity genes to continue to be an Olympic sport? Probably, but the overall community of skateboarders will continue to skate how and when and where they want. And ironically, No Skateboarding signs will continue to be posted, even at the entrance to Olympic skateboarding stadiums.

COLLECTING THE OLYMPICS

As a sports curator, one of the best aspects of my job is watching the Olympic and Paralympic Games every two years, deciding what objects would be a good fit for the sports collections. Collecting these contemporary objects in real time as history unfolds can prove challenging, as time adds perspective and collecting objects right after an event can be a bit of a gamble.

Record-breaking performances, firsts, or displays of great sportsmanship are obvious choices for inclusion in the collections. But what happens when the athletes you thought would win gold don't qualify for the finals or make the podium? Enter USA Skateboarding. Heavily favored to win gold in men's park and street events, Team USA took home two bronzes. The women failed to garner any medals. In this scenario, my first instincts were to collect Alexis Sablone's board, as I considered her grit and determination against athletes half her age an Olympic accomplishment. Although Nyjah Huston, the gold medal favorite in men's street, was an obvious pick, he failed to medal. Some of today's athletes succumb to the mounting pressure of competition, and seemingly laid-back skaters are no different. Huston's struggle to medal under immense pressure should also be chronicled.

Jagger Eaton's bronze medal win put him in that "first" category as the first American athlete to win an Olympic medal in street skateboarding. In addition, an eleven-year-old Eaton was the youngest athlete ever to compete in the 2012 X Games. Hence, both of those "firsts" earned him a place on the collecting wish list. Cory Juneau, the only American park skater to win a medal in Tokyo, places him on the "first" list as well. Bryce Wettstein failed to medal, but her extreme show of sportsmanship when a competitor fell became an Olympic highlight and shined a light on skateboarding's inclusive community. Curator's choices for collecting become easier when these "firsts" happen or records are broken, but it is often actions like Wettstein's, the unexpected moments, that transcend competition and provide the perfect object to tell an Olympic story.

—Jane Rogers

Top: *This 2019 Schmitt Stix skate deck was signed by each member of the inaugural USA Olympic skateboarding team, though not all members of this first team competed in Tokyo. Athletes had to compete in qualifiers to make the team, and with COVID-19 restrictions, there were only a few contests in which to earn points.*

Above: *Team USA's Jagger Eaton holds his bronze medal won in the 2020 Olympics Men's Street skateboarding final, the first medal won by an American in Olympic skateboarding competition.*

ACKNOWLEDGMENTS

We dedicate this book to our loving and supportive families and to the family of skateboarders around the globe.

We gratefully acknowledge the following individuals whose leadership, generosity, and vision made this book happen:

Secretary Lonnie G. Bunch III, Under Secretary for Art Kevin Gover, and directors Anthea Hartig, director of the National Museum of American History, and Cynthia Chavez Lamar, director of the National Museum of the American Indian, who boldly supported the idea of the Smithsonian Institution collecting skateboard culture and history and even allowed mini-ramps to be built on Smithsonian grounds.

Our publisher, Smithsonian Books, especially Jaime Schwender, Carolyn Gleason, and Matt Litts, who championed this book from concept to actuality with expertise, humor, and patience. Thanks for listening to our explanations about the critical significance of sticker packs. Sharon Silva, editor extraordinaire, was essential to the project and bravely accepted our spelling of griptape, halfpipe, and skatepark despite what *Merriam-Webster's* said. Our designers, Elise Crigar and Alex Barnes, who masterfully gave our words swagger and style and never once complained about having too many skateboards on a page. And to Gary Tooth, creative director of the project, who pushed the pages across the finish line.

Our donors who generously gave us treasured pieces of their legacy that tell the story of the history of skateboarding. Your confidence and faith in us are humbling.

Our colleagues at the National Museum of the American Indian and the National Museum of American History who tirelessly supported this book with photography, editorial advice, and enthusiasm. You were exceedingly kind to feign interest in our innumerable long-winded descriptions of the importance of the closed-bearing wheel as well as hundreds of others. Ellen Roney Hughes, sports curator extraordinaire, for having the foresight to collect those first bits of skateboard history and for fostering a relationship with the Brauchs, allowing the museum to begin its journey into the magical world of skateboarding. And to the Brauch family for selflessly sharing Tim's story with the world, providing us with the beginnings of a truly fabulous collection.

Our foreword author, Rodney Mullen, who continues to give an unparalleled gift of insight into and love for skateboarding. When this book was little more than an idea, you accepted without hesitation to contribute. We are honored to call you a friend.

Our contributors—Salman Agah, Brian Anderson, Leo Baker, Ted Barrow, Matt Bass, Cara-Beth Burnside, Bob Denike, Derrick Patrick "Skip" Engblom, Jim Fitzpatrick, Eli Morgan Gesner, Tony Hawk, Kevin Imamura, Eric Jentsch, Mimi Knoop, Catharine Lyons, Dan Mancina, Richard Novak, John O'Malley, Judi Oyama, Bryan Ridgeway, Alexis Sablone, Jack Smith, Rodney Smith, Miriam Klein Stahl, Elissa Steamer, C. R. Stecyk, Bryce Wettstein, Cindy Whitehead, and Neftalie Williams—who graciously allowed us to interview them, email them, text them, and endlessly query them for years about the content of this book. If this list appears like a Hall of Fame roster, it is. You are GOATs in our minds, and we will be forever indebted to you.

All of the artists, authors, researchers, inventors, foundations, company owners, advocates, writers, critics, photographers, historians, academics, and especially the skateboarders whose work, friendship, and passion have been a constant source of inspiration to us throughout this process of trying to understand skateboarding. Some of you are listed here: Robin Alaway, Christian Alexander, Jeff Ament, Jeff Atkinson, Neil Atkinson, Rhianon Bader, Larry and Louise Balma, Sal Barbier, Thomas Barker, Kyle Beachy, Becky Beal, Binckley-Gordon family, Iain Borden, Bod Boyle, J. Grant Brittain, Jeff Brodie, Glenn Brumage, Thom Callan-Riley, Dave Carnie, Carpet Company, Henry Chalfont, Bryant Chapo, Ron Chatman, Jeffrey Cheung, Mike Chino, Ryan Clements, Sean Cliver, Conner family, Contemporary Arts Center (Cincinnati), Terri Craft, Creative Urethanes, Bill Danforth, Garry Scott Davis, Barret "Chicken" Deck, Israel Dejene Malle, Ed Economy, Gustav Eden, Daniel Fedkenheuer, Morizen Foche, Katherine Fogden, Josh Friedberg, Anthony Friedkin, Jerome Gardner, Chris Gibbs, Jim Goodrich, Debbie Gordon, Marty Grimes, Keegan Guizard, Nick Halkias, Alexandra Harris, Chris Haslam, Barry Haun, Michael Hays, Eric Haze, Bruce Hazelton, Thomas Heitfield, Henry Hester, High Speed Productions, Jeff Ho, Hugh Holland, Sander Holsgens, Christian Hosoi, Todd Huber, Anthony Jabin, Miles Jackson, Tara Jepson, Bret Anthony Johnston, Randy Kilwag, Stevil Kinevil, Adrian Koenigsberg, Mark Lake, Todd Larson, Lee Leal, George Leichtweis, Christian Lepanto, Lerma family, Dan Levy, Logan family, Ian Logan, Oscar Loreto Jr., Stuart Maclure, Maddie Manson, Mike Mapp, Brian Maruca, Whitey McConnaughy, Neil McDougall, Patti McGee, Rob Meronek, Morro Bay Skateboard Museum, Hunter Muraira, Jim Murphy, Mark Nardelli, Frank Nasworthy, Mark Nickels, NMAH Lunch Crew, NMAI EPO, Nano Nobrega, Paul O'Connor, Steve Olson, Mike O'Meally, George Orton, Chris Overholser, Patti Paniccia, Tim Payne, Jimmy Pelletier, Stacy Peralta, Oliver Percovich, Stephanie Person, Tim Piumarta, Walt Pourier, George Powell, Jaime Reyes, Edie Robertson, Lizabeth Ronk, Aaron Rose, Di Dootson Rose, Jim Rugg, Michael Savage, Brian Schaefer, Adam Schatz, Paul Schmitt, Ted Schmitz, Scream Distribution, Steven Sebring, Lane Segerstrom, SHACC, Skateistan.org, The Skatepark Project, Dale Smith, Dylan Smith, Gary Smith, Steve Smith, Craig Snyder, Greg Snyder, Guy "Grundy" Spagnoli, Felix Spowage, Keith Stephenson, Andrew Stess, Minna Stess, StrangeLove Skateboards, Cher Strauberry, Zander Taketomo, Jim Thiebaud, Laura Thornhill, Tanya Thrasher, Sandy Tiger, Tony Hawk Inc., Mark Train family, Janet Tramonte, Chuck Treece, Winston Tseng, Unity Skateboards, USA Skateboarding, Steve Van Doren, Nora Vasconcellos, Tony Vitello, Miki Vuckovich, Vu Skateboard Shop and all BMore skaters, Matt Weber, Jocko Weyland, Raphaël Zarka, Adam Zhu, and Paul Zitzer.

And lastly, we remember those no longer with us but who live on in the pages of this book: Jay Adams, Harold Hunter, Andy Kessler, and Drew Mearns.

PHOTO CREDITS

Jacket: *front cover, from top left:* NMAH, Gift of Tony Hawk, 2011.0017.01; NMAH, Gift of the Binckley/Gordon Family, 2019.0133.04; NMAH, Gift of Cindy Whitehead, 2019.0092.01; *back cover, from top left:* NMAH, Gift of Jaime Reyes, 2018.0217.01; NMAH, Gift of Brian Anderson, 2019.0056.01; NMAH, Gift of Eli Morgan Gesner, Adam Schatz, and Rodney Smith, 2022.0056.07.

Case: *front cover, from top left:* NMAH, Gift of Sal Barbier, 2022.0066.03; NMAH, Gift of Mimi Knoop, 2013.0187.01; NMAH, Gift of USA Skateboarding, 2019.0134.01; NMAH, Gift of Scream Distribution LLC, 2021.0132.01; NMAH, Gift of Tony Hawk, 2019.0311.01; NMAH, Gift of Frank and Joan Brauch, 2000.0240.04; *back cover, from top left:* NMAH, Gift of Daniel Mancina, 2019.0122.02; NMAH, Gift of Chris Gibbs, 2021.0096.01; NMAH, Gift of Strangelove Skateboards, 2020.0020.02; National Museum of the American Indian, Gift of the Binckley/Gordon Family, 27/554; NMAH, Gift of Eli Morgan Gesner, Adam Schatz, and Rodney Smith, 2022.0056.03; NMAH, 2019.0133.06.

Title page, from top to bottom: NMAH, Gift of Sal Barbier, 2022.0066.03; NMAH, Gift of Strangelove Skateboards, 2020.0020.01; NMAH, Gift of the Binckley/Gordon Family, 2019.0133.04; NMAH, Gift of the Binckley/Gordon Family, 2019.0133.03; Gift of Jack L. Conner and William A. Conner Jr., 2019.0249.01; **5***l:* NMAH, Gift of Marty Grimes, 2022.0064.01; **5***r:* NMAH, Gift of StrangeLove Skateboards, 2020.0020.02; **8–9:** Photograph by Steven Sebring; **8:** NMAH, Gift of Rodney Mullen, 2013.0160.01; **9:** Photograph by Hugh Talman, National Museum of American History, Smithsonian Institution; **12***l:* NMAH, Gift of D. Sean and Robin S. Brickell, 2001.3087.25; **12***r:* NMAH, Gift of Stephanie Person, 2021.0176.03; 13*l:* NMAH, Gift of Oscar Loreto Jr., 2020.0008.03; 13m: NMAH, Gift of Oscar Loreto Jr., 2020.0008.02; **13***r:* NMAH, Gift of Oscar Loreto Jr., 2020.0008.01; **14***l:* NMAH, Gift of Powell Corporation, 1987.0737.001; **14***r:* NMAH, Gift of Frank and Joan Brauch, 2000.0240.20; **15***l:* NMAH, Gift of the Binckley/Gordon Family, 2019.0133.08; **15***r:* National Museum of the American Indian, Smithsonian Institution, Gift of the Binckley/Gordon Family, 27/554; **16***l:* Photograph by Lee Leal; **16***r:* Photograph by Richard Strauss, National Museum of American History, Smithsonian Institution; **17***l:* Photograph by Hugh Talman, National Museum of American History, Smithsonian Institution; **17***r:* NMAH, Gift of the Binckley/Gordon Family, 2019.3079.14.5; **18***l:* NMAH, Gift of Cher Autumn Straub, 2019.0038.01.2; **18***r:* NMAH, Gift of Sotheby's, 2019.3006.01; **19:** NMAH, Gift of Ian Logan and Cindy Whitehead, 2021.3001.07; **20:** GIDGET © 1959, renewed 1987 Columbia Pictures Industries Inc. All Rights Reserved. Courtesy of Columbia Pictures and Getty images; **22***l:* NMAH, Gift of

the Binckley/Gordon Family, 2019.0133.03; **22***r:* GIDGET © 1959, renewed 1987 Columbia Pictures Industries Inc. All Rights Reserved. Courtesy of Columbia Pictures; **23:** NMAH, Gift of Jerome Gardner, 2021.0036.01-02; **24***l:* NMAH, Gift of Neil Atkinson and Jack Smith, 2021.3038.01; **24***r:* Courtesy of the *Valley Times;* **25***l:* NMAH, Gift of Patti Villa McGee, 2013.0130.03; **25***r:* NMAH, Gift of Patti Villa McGee, 2013.0130.01; **28:** Courtesy of the Sherman Library; **29***t:* National Portrait Gallery, Smithsonian Institution, NPG.2007.195; **29***b:* National Portrait Gallery, Smithsonian Institution; Frederick Hill Meserve Collection, NPG.81.M704; **30***l:* NMAH, Gift of Sharon Ann Marshall in memory of William Michael "Mike" Marshall, 2015.0190.01; **30***r:* National Air and Space Museum, Smithsonian Institution, Photograph By Jason A. Smith, Donated by Miss Katherine M. Smart, A19710699439; **31***l:* NMAH, Gift of Karl Kogler in memory of David Paul Kogler, 2015.0189.01; **31***m:* Library of Congress, Prints & Photographs Division, LC-DIG-ggbain-34632; **31***r:* Toni Frissell, *Vogue,* ©Condé Nast; **32***t:* © Peterson Collection/Surfing Heritage & Culture Center; **32***b:* Courtesy of the Santa Monica Public Library; **33***t:* ©Bruce Brown Films/Surfing Heritage & Culture Center; **33***b:* NMAH, Gift of Dusters Skateboards/Dwindle Distribution, 2015.0240.01; **34***l:* NMAH, Gift of Fernando Aguerre, 2015.0186.01; **34***r:* NMAH, Gift of Keith Maynard and Christine Eshelman, 2015.0227.02; **35***t:* Courtesy of James Fitzpatrick; **35***b:* NMAH, Gift of Abe Cohen, 1991.0317.01; **36***l:* NMAH, Gift of Michael Savage, 2010.0149.01; **36***r:* Courtesy of James Fitzpatrick; **37:** NMAH, Gift of James Fitzpatrick, 2018.0269.01; **38***t:* Courtesy of James Fitzpatrick; **38***b:* Courtesy of *The Independent;* **39***t:* Courtesy of John O'Malley; **39***b:* Bettmann/Getty; **40:** Photograph of Chaz Bojórquez's pictographic tag Señor Suerte, 1973. Charles "Chaz" Bojórquez papers, 1956–2017. Archives of American Art, Smithsonian Institution; **41***t:* Photograph by Castro Frank; **41***b:* NMAH, Gift of Vans, 2010.0052.01 and 2010.0052.03; **42:** NMAH, Gift of Phyllis Diller, 2003.0289.01.01; **43:** NMAH, Gift of Phyllis Diller, 2003.0289; **44:** Courtesy of *SkateBoarder* magazine and Six Stair Productions; **46***l:* NMAH, Gift of Robin Logan, 2013.0186.02; **46***m:* NMAH, Gift of Robin Logan, 2019.0196.05; **46***r:* NMAH, Gift of Tracker Trucks, 2015.0239.01; **47:** NMAH, Gift of Di Dootson Rose, 2013.0163.33; **48:** Photograph by Warren Bolster, courtesy of Janet Tramonte; **49:** Photograph by J. Grant Brittain; **50:** NMAH, Gift of the Binckley/Gordon Family, 2019.0133.04; **51***l:* NMAH, Gift of G&S Surfboards and Skateboards, 2015.0263.03; **51***r:* Courtesy of *SkateBoarder* magazine and Six Stair Productions; **52***t:* NMAH, Gift of Nick Halkias, 2013.0185.02; **52***b:* NMAH, Gift of Mark Lake, 2011.0092.03; **53:** NMAH, Gift of Powell Corporation through Mr. George Powell, president, 1987.0738.01; **56:** NMAH, Photograph by Bruce Hazelton, Gift of Cindy

Whitehead, 2013.0165.09.2; **57***t:* Courtesy of the Whitehead Family archives; **57***b:* NMAH, Gift of Cindy Whitehead, 2013.0165.01; **58***l:* NMAH, Gift of Laura Thornhill Caswell, 2013.0162.01; **58***r:* NMAH, Gift of Cindy Whitehead, 2013.0165.05-07 **59:** Photograph by Warren Bolster, courtesy of Janet Tramonte; **60:** NMAH, Gift of Thomas G. Heitfield, 2021.0049.01; **61***t:* NMAH, Gift of Frank Nasworthy, 2021.0116.01; **61***m:* NMAH, Gift of Frank Nasworthy, 2021.0116.08.1, 2021.0116.09.1, and 2021.0116.10; **61***b:* NMAH, Gift of Frank Nasworthy, 2021.0116.03.1, 2021.0116.06.1, and 2021.0116.10; **62:** Photograph by C. R. Stecyk; **63***t:* NMAH, Gift of Russ Howell; **63***b:* Gift of Anthony Jabin, 2014.0022.01; **64:** Photograph by Hugh Holland; **65***t:* Photograph by C. R. Stecyk; **65***b:* Photograph by Anthony Friedkin; **66:** ©Bev Morgan/ Surfing Heritage & Culture Center; **67***l:* ©Hobie Collection/ Surfing Heritage & Culture Center; **67***r:* Photograph by Tim Piumarta, courtesy of Bob Denike; **68:** NMAH, Gift of Tony Hawk and Steve Hawk, 2013.0166.01; **69:** Courtesy of Jack Smith; **70***t:* Photograph by Warren Bolster, courtesy of Janet Tramonte; **70***b:* NMAH, Gift of Guy Grundy Spagnoli, 2014.0121.01 and 2014.0121.03; **71–72:** Courtesy of Bryan Ridgeway; **73***t:* Courtesy of Jack Smith; **73***m:* NMAH, Gift of Jack Smith and Dylan Smith, 2013.0161.01; **73***b:* Courtesy of Jack Smith; **74:** Courtesy of Tony Hawk Inc. **75***t:* NMAH, Gift of Tony Hawk and Steve Hawk, 2013.0166.01; **75***b:* Courtesy of Tony Haw, Inc.; **76:** NMAH, Photograph by Dan Devine, Gift of Judi Oyama, 2013.0128.04; **77***t:* Photograph by John Krisik, Gift of Judi Oyama, 2013.0128.02 **77***b:* Gift of Judi Oyama, 2018.0270.01; **78:** Courtesy of the Conner Family; **79:** NMAH, Gift of Jack L. Conner and William A. Conner Jr., 2019.0249.01, 2021.0118.01, 2021.0118.03, and 2021.0118.02; **80***t:* NMAH, Gift of John O'Malley, 2015.3048.02; **81***t:* NMAH, Photograph by Warren Bolster, Gift of John O'Malley, 2015.3048.05; **81***b:* NMAH, Gift of John O'Malley, 2015.3048.03; **82:** Photograph by Hugh Holland; **83***l:* NMAH, Gift of John O'Malley, 2015.3048.01; **83***r:* Photograph by Mike Chino; **84:** NMAH, Gift of Nick Halkias, 2013.0185.03; **86***t:* Courtesy of *Thrasher* magazine; **86***b:* Photograph by J. Grant Brittain; **87:** Photograph by J. Grant Brittain; **88:** NMAH, Gift of Nick Halkias, 2013.0185.07; **89***l:* NMAH, Gift of the Binckley/Gordon Family, 2022.0065.01; **89***r:* NMAH, Gift of Mark Lake, 2011.0092.04; **90:** NMAH, Gift of Scream Distribution LLC, 2021.0132.01; **91***l:* NMAH, Gift of Steve Smith, 2017.3155.01; **91***r:* NMAH, Gift of Stephanie Person, 2021.0176.01; **94:** Photographs by Lee Leal; **95:** NMAH, Gift of Tony Hawk, 2011.0017.01; **96:** Courtesy of Bryan Ridgeway; **97***l:* Courtesy of Bryan Ridgeway; **97***r:* NMAH, Gift of Bryan Ridgeway, Rick Summerfield, John Wittpenn, Tim Cline, and Chris Carter, 2021.3012.01; **98:** NMAH, Photograph by Bruce Hazelton, Gift of Cindy Whitehead, 2013.0165.09.1; **99***t:* NMAH, Courtesy of Ed

Economy and Cindy Whitehead; **99b:** NMAH, Gift of Cindy Whitehead, 2013.0165.04; **100l:** Photograph by Bruce Hazelton, courtesy of Cindy Whitehead; **100tr:** NMAH, Gift of Cindy Whitehead, 2019.0095.01; **100br:** NMAH, Gift of Cindy Whitehead, 2013.0165.03; **101:** NMAH, 2021.3035.01; **102l:** NMAH, Gift of the Binckley/Gordon Family, 2022.0065.03; **102r:** Courtesy of *Thrasher* magazine; **103:** Courtesy of Salman Agah; **104l:** NMAH, Gift of Michael Alan Hays and George Leichtweis, 2013.3045.01; **104r:** Courtesy of Salman Agah; **105:** Courtesy of Jack Smith; **106:** Courtesy of SkateOne Corporation; **107t:** Courtesy of NHS Inc.; **107m:** NMAH, Gift of Jack Smith and Neil Atkinson, 2021.3038.07; **107bl:** NMAH, Gift of Chris Gibbs, 2021.0096.01; **107br:** NMAH, Gift of Christian Hosoi, 2016.0349.01; **108l:** NMAH, Gift of Christian Lepanto, 2021.0181.02; **108r:** NMAH, Gift of Christian Lepanto, 2021.0181.01; **109l:** NMAH, Gift of Paul Schmitt, 2013.0224.07; **109r:** NMAH, Gift of Eli Morgan Gesner, Adam Schatz, and Rodney Smith, 2022.0056.10; **110:** Photogaph by Todd Laffler; **111t:** Courtesy of SHUT Skates; **111b:** NMAH, Gift of Eli Morgan Gesner, Adam Schatz, and Rodney Smith, 2022.0056.54.01–.02; **112:** NMAH, Gift of Eli Morgan Gesner, Adam Schatz, and Rodney Smith, 2022.0056.01, 2022.0056.03, and 2022.0056.02; **113t:** Photograph by J. Grant Brittain; **113b:** NMAH, Gift of the Binckley/Gordon Family, 2022.0065.02; **114:** Photograph by Tim Piumarta, courtesy of Bob Denike; **115:** Courtesy NHS Inc.; **116:** Photo by Lizabeth Ronk; **118l:** NMAH, Gift of Frank and Joan Brauch, 2000.0240.01; **118r:** NMAH, Gift of Scream Distribution LLC., 2021.0132.02 **119l:** NMAH, Gift of Michael Alan Hays and George Leichtweis, 2013.3045.05; **119m:** NMAH, Gift of Nick Halkias, 2013.0185.01; **119r:** NMAH, Gift of Eli Morgan Gesner, Adam Schatz, and Rodney Smith, 2022.0056.53.04; **120l:** NMAH, Gift of Catharine Lyons, 2018.0271.02; **120r:** NMAH, Gift of Jimmy Rogers, 2019.0203.01; **121:** Photograph by Rob "Whitey" McConnaughy; **124:** Photo by J. Grant Brittain; **125l:** NMAH, Gift of Mark Lake, 2011.0092.02 **125r:** Gift of Bill Danforth, 2014.0075.01; **126:** NMAH, Gift of Nick Halkias, 2013.0185.08; **127:** NMAH, Gift of Jim Thiebaud, 2019.0225.02 and 2019.0225.01; **128:** Photograph by Elska Sandor, courtesy of Catharine Lyons; **129:** NMAH, Gift of Jaime Reyes, 2018.0217.01; **130:** NMAH, Gift of Catharine Lyons, 2018.0271.05 and 2018.0271.10; **131:** Photograph by Christina Mack, courtesy of Catharine Lyons; **132l:** NMAH, Gift of Gnarhunters, 2020.0079.01; **132r:** NMAH, Gift of Leo Baker, 2020.0029.01; **133:** NMAH, Gift of the Binckley/Gordon Family, 2022.0065.04; **134:** Courtesy of Eric Haze; **135l:** Courtesy of Eric Haze; **135r:** Photograph by Matt Weber; **136–37:** Photograph by Henry Chalfont; **136b:** NMAH, Gift of Eli Morgan Gesner, 2022.0046.01; **138:** NMAH, Gift of Eli Morgan Gesner, Adam Schatz, and Rodney Smith, 2022.0056.20; **139:** NMAH, Gift of Eli

Morgan Gesner, Adam Schatz, and Rodney Smith, 2022.0056.05–.07 and 2022.0056.12, **140:** Photograph by J. Grant Brittain; **141:** NMAH, Gift of Vans, 2016.0351.04; **142:** Collection of the Smithsonian National Museum of African American History and Culture, 2014.221.1ab; **143, 144:** Photograph by J. Grant Brittain; **145l:** NMAH, Gift of John J. and Timothy J. Condon, 2002.0112.01; **145r:** NMAH, Gift of Sal Barbier, 2022.0066.01 **146:** Photograph by J. Grant Brittain; **147t:** NMAH, Gift of James Fitzpatrick, 2022.0084.01; **147b:** NMAH, Gift of James Fitzpatrick, 2019.0018.01; **148:** NMAH, Gift of Shannon Downing, 2021.0071.11.2; **149l:** NMAH, Gift of Cindy Whitehead, 2022.0067.01; **149r:** NMAH, Courtesy of *Thrasher* magazine; **150t:** Photograph by Mike O'Meally, courtesy of *Thrasher* magazine; **150b:** Courtesy of Dave Carnie; **151–53:** NMAH, Gift of George Orton, 2013.0154.05, 2013.0154.10, 2013.0154.01, and 2013.0154.12; **154–55:** NMAH, Gift of Brian Anderson, 2019.0056.01; **156t:** NMAH, Gift of the Binckley/Gordon Family, 2019.0133.01.1–.3; **156b:** Wikimedia Commons; **157t:** NMAH, Gift of William Sturgis Bigelow, TR.247884; **157b:** NMAH, Gift of the Binckley/Gordon Family, 2019.0133.02; **158:** Tony Hawk, born 12 May 1968, by Rick Chapman, born 1966. 2002, selenium-toned gelatin silver print. National Portrait Gallery, Smithsonian Institution; gift of the artist and ESPN.©2002 Rick Chapman **160:** NMAH, Gift of the Binckley/Gordon Family, 2022.0065.05; **161:** Installation view, *Beautiful Losers: Contemporary Art, Skateboarding and Street Culture.* Photograph by Tony Walsh, 2004. Image courtesy of the Contemporary Arts Center, Cincinnati, OH; **162–63:** Photograph by Mike Blabac/Quiksilver/DC via Getty Images; **164t:** NMAH, Gift of Skateistan.org, 2021.0098.05.03; **164b:** NMAH, Gift of Tony Hawk, 2019.0311.02.1; **165:** Courtesy Walt Pourier, Stronghold Society; **168–71:** NMAH, Gift of Vans, 2016.0351.07, 2016.0351.08, 2016.0351.01, and 2016.0351.03; **172:** NMAH, Photograph by Lance Dalgart, Gift of Frank and Joan Brauch, 2000.0240.27.1; **173:** NMAH, Gift of Frank and Joan Brauch, 2000.0240.01, 2000.0240.02, 2000.0240.08, and 2000.0240.24; **174:** Photograph by Zander Taketomo; **175l:** NMAH, Gift of Daniel Mancina, 2019.0122.01; **175r:** Photograph by Zander Taketomo; **176:** NMAH, Gift of Daniel Mancina, 2019.0122.02; **177l:** NMAH, Gift of Daniel Mancina, 2019.0122.02; **177m:** NMAH, Gift of Christian Alexander, 2019.0076.01; **177r:** NMAH, Gift of Christian Alexander, 2019.0076.01; **178:** Stephen Dunn/Getty Images; **179:** NMAH, Gift of Alexis Sablone, 2020.0007.01; **180:** Photograph by Kevin Knoop; **181l:** Photograph by Kevin Knoop; **181r:** NMAH, Gift of Mimi Knoop, 2013.0187.01; **182:** NMAH, Gift of the Binckley/Gordon Family, 2019.0133.05; **183:** Photograph by C. R. Stecyk; **184–85:** National Museum of the American Indian, Gift of the Binckley/Gordon Family, 27/551, 27/556, 27/552, and 27/553; **186–87:** NMAH, Gift of Leo Baker,

2018.0276.11, 2018.0276.03, and 2018.0276.04; **188:** NMAH, Gift of Ian Logan and Cindy Whitehead, 2021.3001.19; **190:** NMAH, Gift of Aaron "Wheelz" Fotheringham, 2020.0009.01; **191tl:** NMAH, Gift of the Binckley/Gordon Family, 2019.3079.12.2; **191ml:** NMAH, Gift of the Binckley/;Gordon Family, 2019.3079.14.3; **191bl:** NMAH, Gift of the Binckley/Gordon Family, 2019.3079.14.2; **191r:** NMAH, Gift of Scream Distribution LLC, 2021.0132.03; **192tl:** NMAH, Gift of Judi Oyama, 2021.0010.01; **192bl:** NMAH, Gift of Cindy Whitehead, 2021.3001.01; **192r:** NMAH, Gift of Unity Skateboards, 2018.0162.01; **193tl:** NMAH, Gift of Tara Jepsen and Miriam Klein Stahl, 2018.0145.03; **193tm:** NMAH, Gift of Unity Skateboards, 2018.0162.03; **193tr:** NMAH, Gift of Leo Baker, 2020.0029.02; **194:** NMAH, Gift of Ian Logan and Cindy Whitehead, 2021.3001.04; **195:** NMAH, Gift of the Binckley/Gordon Family, 2022.0065.06; **198, 199:** Photograph by Neftalie Williams; **200tl:** Photograph by Neftalie Williams; **200tr:** NMAH, Gift of Sal Barbier, 2022.0066.03; **200mr:** NMAH, 2022.0066.02; **201, 202:** Photographs by Neftalie Williams; **203:** NMAH, Gift of Brian Anderson, 2019.0056.08; **204l:** NMAH, Gift of Brian Anderson, 2019.0056.01; **204tr:** NMAH, Gift of Brian Anderson, 2019.0056.04; **204br:** NMAH, Gift of Brian Anderson, 2019.0056.03; **205:** NMAH, Gift of Tony Hawk, 2019.0311.01; **206:** NMAH, 2018.0276.10; **207t:** NMAH, Gift of Leo Baker, 2018.0276.09; **207b:** NMAH, Gift of Leo Baker, 2018.0276.02; **208t:** Courtesy of Jack Smith; **208b:** NMAH, Gift of Jack Smith and Dylan Smith, 2013.0161.03; **209t:** NMAH, Gift of Jack Smith and Dylan Smith, 2013.0161.04; **209b:** NMAH, Gift of Jack Smith, 2018.0237.01–.03; **210:** NMAH, Gift of Brian Anderson, 2019.0056.06; **211l:** NMAH, Gift of Brian Anderson, 2019.0056.06; **211r:** NMAH, Gift of the Binckley/Gordon Family, 2019.3079.09; **212:** Courtesy of Miriam Klein Stahl; **213l:** Courtesy of Miriam Klein Stahl; **213r:** NMAH, Gift of Tara Jepsen and Miriam Klein Stahl, 2018.0145.01; **214:** NMAH, Gift of StrangeLove Skateboards, 2020.0020.03.02; **215l:** NMAH, Gift of StrangeLove Skateboards, 2020.0020.01; **215r:** NMAH, Gift of StrangeLove Skateboards, 2020.0020.01; **216:** NMAH, Photograph by Lanna Apisukh, Gift of Adrian Koenigsberg, 2022.0029.05; **217:** NMAH, Gift of Leo Baker, 2018.0276.05, 2020.0029.03, and 2018.0276.01; **218t:** Mario Tama/Getty Images; **218b:** NMAH, Gift of Judith L. Bazis, 2018.0259.01; **219:** NMAH, Gift of Nicholas Halkias, 2017.0325.01; **220:** Ezra Shaw/Getty Images; **221:** Photograph by Ian Logan; **222–23:** Jamie Squire/Getty Images; **224:** Photograph by Ian Logan; **225:** Imaginechina Limited/Alamy Stock Photo; **226l:** NMAH, Gift of Minna Stess and Andrew Stess, 2021.0095.01; **226r:** NMAH, 2021.3035.04; **227l:** Jaime Squire/Getty Staff; **227r:** Reuters/Mari Saito; **228–29:** NMAH, Gift of USA Skateboarding, 2019.0134.01; and **229b:** Mickael Chavet/Alamy Stock Photo.

CONTRIBUTORS

Salman Agah received a skateboard from his parents in the mid-1970s when he was just four or five years old and has been in love with skateboarding ever since. He was named Skater of the Year by *Thrasher* magazine in 1993, the most influential skater of the 1990s by *Transworld Skateboarding* magazine, and is credited with being the originator of switch stance skateboarding. Today, Agah operates Pizzanista! in Los Angeles and lives with his wife, Joan, and his children, Zephyr and Sabbath.

Brian Anderson began his professional skateboard career in 1998 with Toy Machine and was named Skater of the Year by *Thrasher* magazine the following year. During the past nearly quarter century, he has accumulated an impressive list of career and personal achievements, including riding for Girl and Antihero; launching his signature shoe, Project BA, for Nike SB; founding 3D Skateboards; and being one of the first pro skateboarders to come out publicly as gay. Anderson is also an artist; his first solo show was at New York's West Side Arts Coalition in November 2020.

Leo Baker has an extensive competitive professional skateboarding career, including first place finishes at the X Games, Street League Super Crown, Maloof Money Cup, and Mystic Sk8 Cup. In 2020, Baker resigned from the USA Skateboarding National Team for women's street after deciding that, as a nonbinary person, competing in women's sports was not viable. Baker's sponsors include Independent Trucks, Mob Grip, and Nike SB. In 2020, Baker founded the skateboard company Glue with fellow queer skaters Cher Strauberry and Stephen Ostrowski.

Ted Barrow is a youthful art historian, middle-aged writer, and ancient skateboarder currently living in San Francisco, California. In his skateboarding work, he has focused on the intersections of skateboarding, social media, graphics, fashion, and skate videos. He is currently finishing his doctorate in art history from The Graduate Center, City University of New York.

Matt Bass, an Emmy Award–winning filmmaker who focuses on historical and cultural documentaries, received film degrees from the Rochester Institute of Technology in Rochester, New York, and the School of Visual Arts in New York City. A member of the Directors Guild of America and the International Cinematographers Guild, Bass lives in Los Angeles.

Cara-Beth Burnside was the first woman skateboarder to be featured on the cover of *Thrasher* (1989) and the first woman to have a signature skate shoe (Vans, 1999). Her career in skateboarding includes more than sixteen titles in the X Games, All Girl Skate Jam, Vans Triple Crown, Slam City Jam, and Soul Bowl. She has also been a competitive snowboarder, finishing in fourth place in the 1998 Nagano Winter Olympics. Burnside was named Female Vert Skater of the Year in 2004 by World Cup Skateboarding, cofounded the Action Sports Alliance with Mimi Knoop and Drew Mearns in 2005, and was inducted into the Skateboarding Hall of Fame in 2015.

Robert "Bob" Denike is the CEO of NHS Inc., with a thirty-five-year history at the company. During his tenure, he helped make NHS the number one skateboard company in the world and was the project lead on the NHS Skateboard Museum, which is housed at the company headquarters in Santa Cruz, California. Denike was the editor of the 2004 coffee table book *Built to Grind*, which draws on the archives of the NHS-owned Independent Truck Company to tell the story of the brand from its inception.

Derrick Patrick "Skip" Engblom is a surfboard builder, owner of the skateboard brand Santa Monica Airlines, and was a co-owner of the Jeff Ho Surfboards and Zephyr Productions shop in Santa Monica, California. Long at the forefront of skateboarding, Engblom launched the careers of many influential skateboarders, including the Z-Boys, Natas Kaupas, Julien Stranger, Jim Thiebaud, Tim Brauch, Lizzie Armanto, and Jesse Martinez, among others.

Jim Fitzpatrick was born in 1948 and began surfing and skateboarding in La Jolla, California. He went on to work in documentary films in Hollywood and later, along with his wife, established the Santa Barbara Montessori School. He became the promotions director for the Bones Brigade at Powell-Peralta and later founded the nonprofit International Association of Skateboard Companies (IASC), where he directed successful campaigns to establish public skateparks. The author of several books about skateboarding and skateboarders and other action sports athletes, Fitzpatrick, a father of three and grandfather of five, lives in Austin, Texas.

Eli Morgan Gesner is a multidisciplinary artist born and raised in New York City. A key figure in the evolution of New York City's skateboarding, hip-hop, and street-wear cultures throughout the 1980s, 1990s, and 2000s, he helped to start such brands as Phat Farm and Zoo York. Today, Gesner works in film and television.

Tony Hawk is one of the all-time innovators and legends of the sport of skateboarding. He is a twelve-time world champion, sixteen-time X Games medalist, inventor of more than one hundred tricks, and inaugural member of the Skateboarding Hall of Fame. A philanthropist, entrepreneur, author, video game character, and dad, his accomplishments and contributions have transcended the sport.

Kevin Imamura, a native of Los Angeles, California, describes his life as divided into two chapters: before and after finding skateboarding. At age fourteen, the "after" life included purchasing the February 1987 issue of *Transworld Skateboarding*, which contained numerous images of skaters wearing Air Jordan 1s. That singularly defining moment led him to jobs at *Transworld* and Nike and to writing an essay on the shared DNA of sneaker culture and skateboarding for this book.

Eric Jentsch is the lead curator for entertainment and sports at the Smithsonian's National Museum of American History. In that role, he has worked on a number of projects—lectures, podcasts, exhibitions—that connect American history to its popular culture.

Mimi Knoop is a former professional skateboarder and cocreator of hoopla skateboards. A five-time X Games medalist, Knoop cofounded the Action Sports Alliance in 2005 with fellow skater Cara-Beth Burnside and Drew Mearns to bring pay equity for women to the Summer and Winter X Games. In 2015, she founded the Women's Skateboarding Alliance, a consulting and management company dedicated to representing women's skateboarding authentically in commercials, film, and at events worldwide. Knoop served as the women's head coach and team leader for USA Skateboarding at the 2020 Olympic Games in Tokyo, Japan.

Catharine Lyons cofounded Rookie Skateboards, a New York City skateboard company, with Elska Sandor and Jung Kwak in 1996. It was the first female-owned and -operated skateboard company. She lives in New York City with her husband, two children, and a variety of pets.

Dan Mancina is a blind advocate and skateboarder and holds a master's degree from Western Michigan University in vision rehabilitation therapy. He works to change the misconceptions about the blind through his skateboarding, social media, and his hands-on work with the visually impaired and blind community.

Rodney Mullen is known as Godfather of Modern Street Skating because he invented so many of the tricks that define its modern era. He's also the most dominant world champion in the history of the sport, defending his title thirty-five of thirty-six times. In 2019, he was named a director's fellow at the MIT Media Lab.

Richard Novak is the business brains behind NHS Inc. Known for his keen sense of timing and opportunity identification, he was instrumental in setting the foundation for the modern skateboard industry in the mid-1970s. When he is not surfing, mountain biking, traveling, or telling stories, he is hard at work as chairman and consigliere to the NHS management team, helping push the company into the future. In 2013, Novak was inducted into the Skateboarding Hall of Fame as an industry icon.

John O'Malley is a multimedia designer and the author of *Urethane Revolution: The Birth of Skate*. He resides in New York City.

Judi Oyama was born and raised in Santa Cruz, California, and is a Japanese American professional skateboarder and graphic designer. Inducted into the Skateboarding Hall of Fame in 2018, Oyama has had the longest professional skateboard career of any female skater, spanning more than forty-seven years, and was a pioneer in vertical, downhill, and slalom skateboarding.

Bryan Ridgeway was handpicked out of the hills of West Virginia at the age of nineteen by some of skateboarding's most iconic industry leaders and relocated to California. For the past forty years, he has been an integral part of the strategic teams that created both an infrastructure and a road map to ensure the sport thrives for decades to come.

Alexis Sablone is a professional skateboarder sponsored by Alltimers Skateboards, Converse shoes, Orchard Skate Shop, Thunder Trucks, and Dial Tone Wheels. A member of the 2020 USA Skateboarding National Team for women's street, she placed fourth at the 2020 Summer Olympics in Tokyo, Japan. She has won multiple gold medals at the X Games, has a master's degree in architecture from MIT, and is currently the head coach for the USA Skateboarding National Team for women's park and street.

Jack Smith began skateboarding in 1964 on a clay-wheeled board built by his father. In 1974, he discovered Cadillac urethane wheels and has never stopped skateboarding. A slalom and downhill racer, he competed in the 1975 Bahne-Cadillac National Championships and thirty years later played the part of the contest announcer in the film *Lords of Dogtown*. In 1976, he and two friends were the first to push a skateboard across America. He made three more cross-country pushes with friends, in 1984, 2003, and 2013, and then, in 2018, became the first person to ride an electric skateboard across America.

Rodney Smith is an entrepreneur and former professional skateboarder. Known as the Godfather of East Coast Skateboarding, he cofounded SHUT Skates with Bruno Musso in 1986, the first street skateboard company on the East Coast. Seven years later, he cofounded Zoo York with Eli Morgan Gesner and Adam Schatz, pioneering the skate lifestyle brand. In 2018, Smith cofounded the New York–based All One, an eco-friendly, action sports apparel brand.

Miriam Klein Stahl is a San Francisco Bay Area artist, educator, and activist and the illustrator of two *New York Times* best sellers, *Rad American Women A–Z* and *Rad Women Worldwide*. As an artist, she follows in the tradition of making socially relevant work, creating portraits of political activists, misfits, and radicals. Stahl is also the co-owner of Pave the Way Skateboards, a queer skateboarding company formed with Los Angeles–based comedian, actor, writer, and skateboarder Tara Jepsen. Stahl lives in Berkeley, California, with her wife, artist Lena Wolff, and their daughter and two dogs.

Elissa Steamer started skateboarding as a young girl in Fort Myers, Florida. In 1996, Toy Machine invited her to be in its *Welcome to Hell* video, making her the first woman street skater to be featured in a skate video. Three years later, she was the only woman skater featured in *Tony Hawk's Pro Skater* video game. Her competition record includes numerous gold medals at the X Games, Slam City Jam, Vans Triple Crown, and World Cup Skateboarding. In 2014, Steamer started her own brand, Gnarhunters, and in 2015, she was inducted into the Skateboarding Hall of Fame.

C. R. Stecyk is an artist and writer who has chronicled surfing, skateboarding, and auto culture. He was cowriter and production designer on the film *Dogtown and Z-Boys*, which won two awards at the Sundance Film Festival. A surfboard designed and painted by Stecyk is in the permanent collection of the Smithsonian, and he is also a member of the Skateboarding Hall of Fame.

Bryce Wettstein is a professional skateboarder, riding for Stereo Skateboards, and is currently a student at the San Dieguito Academy in Encinitas, California. She was a member of the USA Skateboarding National Team in women's park at the 2020 Tokyo Summer Olympics and is on the 2022 USA Skateboarding team. She enjoys playing the ukulele, art, surfing, and beach volleyball.

Cindy Whitehead is a professional skateboarder, writer, and activist. At fifteen years old, she was the first girl to have a two-page article and centerfold in a skateboarding magazine, where she spoke out about the impact of being one of the only females in the male-dominated sport. Inducted into the Skateboarding Hall of Fame in 2016, Whitehead is the author of three books and is the founder of Girl is NOT a 4 Letter Word, a multi-platform movement that supports and encourages girls and womxn to skateboard.

Neftalie Williams is a sociologist who investigates global issues of race, diversity, and youth empowerment through the lens of action sports culture, a University of Southern California provost's postdoctoral scholar at the Annenberg School of Communication and Journalism, and a Yale Schwarzman Center visiting fellow in race, culture, and community. He is the chair of diversity, equity, and inclusion for USA Skateboarding, on the board of The Skatepark Project (formerly the Tony Hawk Foundation), and on the advisory board of Skateistan and of the McKinnon Center for Global Affairs at Occidental College. Williams has two upcoming books, with Artisan Books and University of California Press, on skateboarding culture.

INDEX

A

Action Sports Retailer (ASR), 147
Adams, Jay, 32, 64
Adolph Kiefer McNeil Corp., 24
aerospace 14, 21, 28, 30, 54
Agah, Salman, 103–4, 172
Agnew, Mike, 111
airplanes, 21–22
Airwalk, 93, 142
Ali, Muhammad, 15
All '80s All Day Vert Challenge, 16, 94
Alter, Hobart "Hobie," 26, 66, 67
Alltimers Skateboards, 234
Alva Skates, 124
Alva, Tony, 52, 64, 77, 124–27, 169
Amateur (AM) contests, 186
Anderson, Brian, 101, 154, 193, 203–4, 210–11
Andrecht, Dave, 72, 74
Antihero Skateboards, 203
Apache Skateboards, 182
Apollo 11, 214
Apple Skatepark, 71–72

B

baby boomers, 22
Bahne Skateboards, 46, 54
Bahne-Cadillac Del Mar Nationals, 63
Baker, Leo, 132, 186, 216–17
Balma, Larry, 86, 87
banana board, 4, 50
Barbier, Sal, 4, 122, 145, 200, 230
Barrow, Ted, 124, 168
Bass, Matt, 106
Beach Boys, 21, 22, 57
Bearer, Wendy, 24–25
Bennett Hijacker, 46
Bennett, Ron, 46, 68
Bergthold, Dave, 82
Berryman, Ellen, 56, 69
Bertlemann, Lawrence "Larry"
    Kaaua Mehau, 15
Best of Skate Fate (zine), 91
Big Brother magazine, 119, 150
Big Three, 90, 91, 118, 124. *See also*
    Powell-Peralta; Santa Cruz; Vision
Bigfoot magazine, 193
BIPOC, 190, 193
    racial inequality, 21–22
    photography, 198–202

Black Hill, 69–70
Blake, Tom, 29–30, 31
blindness, 174–77
boardslide, 119
Bojórquez, Charles "Chaz," 40–44
Bolster, Warren, 48, 59, 70, 81, 164, 170
Bones Brigade, 55, 82, 88–89, 93, 102, 110,
    113, 132, 138, 140, 160, 233
Bones Brigade Video Show (film), 89, 93
Booney Ramp, 86
bowl, type, 45, 47, 50–51, 58, 82–83, 87–88,
    98, 106, 138, 159, 180, 212, 233
Bowman, Brad, 98
Boyd, Colleen, 24
brands, 46–47, 89–90, 108, 118–20, 125–27, 138,
    141–42, 145–47, 160–61, 171, 182, 184, 187, 189
Brauch, Tim, 14–15, 172–73
Brittain, J. Grant, 49, 86, 113, 124, 140, 142,
    145–46, 230
Breeden, John, 81
Brewer, Art, 48
Brodie, Jeffrey, 16, 60
Brown, Terry, 76
Bryggeriets Gymnasium, 83
Burnett, Mike, 168
Burnside, Cara-Beth, 76, 120, 148, 180

C

Caballero, Steve, 72, 85–88, 93–94, 102, 113,
    168–69
Cadillac Wheels, 46, 60–61
California Amateur Skate League (CASL), 186
Carlsbad Skatepark, 80–81, 82
Carter, Chris, 97, 123
Cassimus, James, 48, 50
Caster Skateboards, 78–79
catalogs, 71–73
Cave Homo (magazine), 203–4, 211, 217
Cespedes, Kim, 57, 69, 76
Chaplin, Charlie, 29
Chicago magazine, 41
Chin Ramp, 86–87, 140
Civil Rights Act of 1964, 27
Clark, Gordon "Grubby," 66
Cline, Tim, 97
Cliver, Sean, 106
Comme des Garçons, 189
Conner, William, Jr., 78
Consolidated Vultee Aviation, 30
Converse, 41, 141, 145, 161, 167, 189, 234

counterculture, 33–34
COVID-19, 189–91, 193–4, 224,
    226, 229
Cozens, Peggy, 86
Creative Urethanes, 60

D

Danforth, Bill, 97, 124–25
DC, 142
decks, 50–51
    development of, 47
    signature, 18, 48, 63, 89–90
Dee, Sandra, 22
Del Mar Skate Ranch, 85
DeSota, Freddie, 72
Diller, Phyllis, 12, 43
DIY, 91, 97, 106, 119, 211
    aesthetic, 126
    boards, 174, 212–13
    skate ramps, 13
    skateboard parks, 17
    zines, 97
Dogtown, 62–65
"Dogtown Chronicles," 49
Dootson Rose, Di, 17, 48, 57, 69
Douglas Aircraft's Project Engineering
    Group, 30
downhill racing skateboarding, 46–47,
    50, 56
due air, 50
Duerr, Jeff, 50

E

Earhart, Amelia, 29
East Coast, skateboarding on, 39
Eaton, Jagger, 227, 229
Ebeling, Kristin, 193
Eden, Gustav, 83
Edmonds, Mark André "ALI," 134
eighties, 85–91
    mail-order skateboards, 101–2
    personal stories, 103–4
    Powell-Peralta deck donation, 94
    sexism toward women, 98–100
    SHUT skateboards, 110–12
    skateboard crash of, 114–15
    zines, 96–97
Element, 160
Elguera, Eddie, 72

El Vatos Bandidos De Vario X, 86
The Endless Summer (film), 33–34
Engblom, Skip, 32, 62
Eppridge, Bill, 134
ESPN, 120, 151–52, 180–81
Estes, 172
Etnies, 93, 133, 142, 145, 173
Europe, skateboarding in, 37–39
Everlast, 189
Extreme Games, 120. *See also* X Games

F

Falcon skate shop, 71
Falcon Skatepark, 71–72
Fairbanks, Douglas, 29
Fédération Internationale de Roller Sports
    (FIRS), 225
Fender, 189
Fibreflex, 26, 68
fiberglass, 14, 21, 26, 30, 33, 39, 45–47,
    51, 54–55, 66, 57, 73, 76, 152
Filben, Mike, 73
Fitzpatrick, Jim, 35, 37, 113, 147
5Boro, 120
flat-ground ollie, 88
411 Video Magazine, 119, 137, 161
Free Former, 4, 50–51
freestyle skateboarding, 113
Friedkin, Anthony, 65
Freidman, Glen E., 48
French, Jeff, 73
Frissell, Toni, 28, 31
froSkate, 193

G

Garry Scott Davis (GSD), 90–91
Gelfand, Alan "Ollie," 50
gender discrimination
    facing sexism, 98–100
    fighting for fair play, 180–81
    pay gap, 58
George Cooley Co., 25
Gesner, Eli Morgan, 134
Gidget (film), 22
Gidget Grows Up (film), 28
Girl is NOT a 4 Letter Word, 4
Gnarhunters, 217
Godfrey, Jami, 72
Gold Cup Series, 85, 98–99

Goldsworthy, Brandt, 30
Graham, Jack, 80
graphics, 106–9
    graffiti art, 40–41
    style and substance correlation, 124–27
Gravity Skateboards, 15
Guerrero, Tommy, 102, 113, 123, 126 , 142, 146
Gullwing Trucks' Inside Out (film), 101

H

Hafke, Dana, 73
half cab, 113, 169
Hamersveld, John Van, 34
Hamm, Mia, 15
Haslam, Chris, 16
Haut, Doug, 67
Hawaii, 26–30, 61, 67, 129, 131, 184, 194
Hawk, Tony, 12, 17, 113, 118, 120, 151, 160,
    164, 205
    donating skateboards, 94–95
    first skateboard of, 74–75
Hawk, Steve, 74
Hays, Michael, 104
Heitfield, Tom and Vernon, 60
Hester Series, 51, 58
Hiraki, Kokona, 227
Ho, Jeff, 49, 54, 62–65, 233
Hobie
    skateboard team, 67
    Skateboards, 24, 67
    Super Surfer 24, 26
    Surfboards, 34
Hokus Pokus (film), 101
Holland, Huge, 64, 82
homemade ramps, 50, 86
Hope-Gill, James, 228
Huck magazine, 217
Hurley, Bob, 77
Huston, Nyjah, 227

I

Imamura, Kevin, 140
Innoskate, 9, 11, 16–17
International Association of Skateboard
    Companies (IASC), 147
International Olympic Committee
    (IOC), 224–28
International Skateboarding Federation
    (ISF), 225–26

J

Jeff Ho Surfboards and Zephyr
    Productions, 49, 54, 63, 65, 233
Jefferson, Atiba, 193
Jentsch, Eric, 33
Jimenez, Marty, 97
Juice magazine, 122

K

Kahanamoku, Duke, 21, 28–29
Kanoa Surf, 71
Kendall, Jeff, 97
Kennedy, John F., 21, 23, 27
Kessler, Andy, 134, 138
kickflip, 88, 119
kicktail, 45, 47
King, Billie Jean, 15
Knoop, Mimi, 17, 180
Kruger, Barbara 138
Kryptonics wheels, 105

L

La Jolla Shores, 36
leapfrog relay system, 73
Lake, Mark, 52, 89, 124–25, 230
Lemelson Center for Invention and
    Innovation, 16
LGBTQ, 204
    binary gender definitions, 216–17
    coming out, 211
    Paisley Grabs Back, 218–1
    Pave the Way Skateboards, 212–13
    safe spaces, 206–9
Life magazine, 24–25, 27, 134
localism, 56–57
Logan, Bruce, 80
Logan, Robin, 56
Logan Earth Ski, 46–47, 51, 55, 58, 69
Loreto, Oscar, Jr., 13, 230
Losi, Allen, 72
Louis Vuitton, 197
LOVE Park, 83, 119
Lucero, John, 108

M

magazines, 48, 58, 71, 76,88, 101, 111, 119–20,
    164, 172, 182
    and graphics, 106–7

print, 119, 164
   in seventies, 72–73
   skateboard, 22, 48, 51, 111, 120, 182
mail-order skateboards, 101–2
Makaha skateboards, 24, 37–38, 87, 113
Makaha surfboards, 24, 37
Malmö, Sweden, 82–83
Mancina, Dan, 174
Marc Ecko Enterprises, 160
McGee, Patti, 17, 24–25
McGill, Mike, 82
McSqueeb, 124
McTwist, 113
Mearns, Drew, 180
Meow Skateboards, 193
Mid-Eastern Skateboard Series
   (MESS), 96–97
Moore, Alyasha, 110
Moore, Carissa, 30
Mountain, Lance, 49, 102, 103, 113,
   132, 142
Murphy, Jim, 111, 164, 183
Musso, Bruno, 110, 136

N

Nash Manufacturing Inc., 24
Nasworthy, Frank, 45–46, 60
National Geographic (magazine), 30
National Skateboard Championships
   (NSC), 24, 26–27
National Skateboard Review
   (magazine), 48
Native Americans, 15, 182–85
NBC, 224–28
NHS Inc., 46, 67, 114–15
Nike, 40, 120, 132, 140–42, 145, 187, 189,
   203, 216–17
900, 113, 120, 151, 205
nineties, 117–21
   personal stories, 132–33, 154–55
   Rookie Skateboards, 128–31
   sneaker culture, 140–47
   snowboarding, 148–49
   style-substance correlation, 124–27
   X Games, 151–52
   Zoo York, 134–39
Novak, Richard, 66, 76

O

O' Connell, Jack, 147
O' Mahoney, James, 47, 69
O' Malley, John, 80, 82
O' Neill Surf Shop, 67
O' Connell, Jack, 147
Oki, Peggy, 56
ollie, 50
Olson, Steve, 77
Olympics, summer 2020, 12–13, 18, 30, 194
   collections, 229
   Olympic dream, 223
   post-Olympic future, 224–28
   skateboarding in, 220–21
Oneal, Ellen, 56
Orton, George, 151–52
Outlaw Ramp, 134–35, 138
Oyama, Judi, 56, 76, 99

P

Pacific Coast Surfboard Championships, 28
Palm, Mike, 82
Paramount Studios, 77
Pave the Way Skateboards, 193, 212–13
Peralta, Stacy, 14, 30, 50, 52, 64, 111, 159, 160
Person, Stephanie, 12, 91–92, 198
personal stories
   two-thousands, 174–77
   seventies, 74–79
   nineties, 132–33, 154–55
   eighties, 103–4
Peters, Duane, 26, 30, 32, 72, 107
Peterson, Preston "Pete," 30
photography, 198–202
Placa/Rollcall (painting), 41
politics, 124–27
Powell Corporation, 14, 51, 54
Powell, George, 30
Powell-Peralta, 30, 47, 71, 86, 97, 101,
   106, 113, 115, 118, 124, 126, 160
Poweredge magazine, 119
professionalism
   pro-skater living, 186–87
   turning pro,154–55
Proline Skateboards, 73
Puma shoes, 100
Push to Heal, 17
Pushead (Brian Schroeder), 52
Pushing Boarders conference, 82, 170, 189, 202

Q

Queen Emma, 29, 30
Quicksilver (Powell Corporation), 30, 52
Quiksilver All '80s All Day Vert Challenge,
   15, 95

R

racial inequality, 21–22
*Ramp It Up: Skateboard Culture in
   Native America* (exhibition), 15
ramps, 49–50, 87–88
"Rapper's Delight," 45
Reeves, Bobby, 72
Roderick, Tony, 46–47, 67
Ream, Gary, 225
Ridgeway, Bryan, 71, 96
Road Rider wheels, 47, 67–68
Robertson, Edie, 56
Rocco, Steve, 88, 108, 119, 212
Rock, Chris, 43
Roderick, Tony, 46
Roller Derby, 24
roller skate 15, 21–26, 35, 39, 45–46, 60,
   66–68
Rookie Skateboards, 120, 128–31, 138
Roskopp, Rob, 97, 107
Rowley, Geoff, 168
Ruth, Babe, 15

S

Sablone, Alexis, 150, 178, 220, 227
safe spaces, 206–9
Sandor, Elska, 128
Santa Cruz, 30, 66, 76, 77, 90, 107, 115,
   118, 160, 173
Santa Monica Airlines, 233
Schmitt, Paul, 142, 147
The Search for Animal Chin (film), 101
720, 113
Seinfeld, Jerry, 43
seventies, 45–52
   Carlsbad Skatepark, 80–81
   Creative Urethanes, 60
   Dogtown, 62–65
   magazines, 71–72
   personal stories, 74–79
   pushing skateboards, 73
   shops, 66–68
   Signal Hill Runs, 69–70

skateboarding heritage, 82–83
women's skateboarding, 56–58
Shackle Me Not (film), 101
Shaft (film), 40
Sherwood, Kent, 30
shops, 66–68
The Shredder (zine), 96–97, 103, 124
Shuirman, Jay, 66–67, 68, 76
SHUT Skates, 110–12, 120, 136–37
sidewalk surfing, 24, 25, 28, 45, 156
Signal Hill Runs, 69–70
Sims Skateboards, 47, 92
single lens reflex (SLR) camera, 48
sixties, 21–25
    Charles "Chaz" Bojórquez, 40–44
    counterculture, 33–34
    personal stories, 32, 35–36, 37–38, 39
    skateboarding on East Coast, 39
    skateboarding in Europe, 37–39
    surf-to-skateboard genetic transfer, 28–32
SK8FACE (film), 106, 109
Skateboard Action (book), 101
SkateBoard World (magazine), 48, 57–58, 71,
SkateBoarder (magazine), 45, 48–50, 85–86
skateboarding
    as career, 178–79
    in comedy, 43
    donations, 94–95
    on East Coast, 39
    in Europe, 37–39
    expatriating heritage, 82–84
    first contests, 24
    graphics, 106–9
    homophobia in, 190, 204
    mail-order skateboards, 101–2
    Native American history and culture, 182–85
    Native American skate decks, 15, 182–85
    in new millennium, 168–70
    in Olympics, 220–29
    as part of American narrative, 12–13
    pro-skater living, 186–87
    professionalism, 154–55
    pushing, 73, 105, 208–9
    Rookie Skateboards, 128–31
    Smithsonian collection, 14
    and sneaker culture, 140–47
    style-substance correlation, 124–27
    skateboards, collecting, 13–14, 16, 78, 95, 172
Skateistan, 164
Skateism magazine, 211

Skate Fate (zine), 88, 90–91, 96–97
skateparks, 71–73
    decline of, 96–97
    and sexism, 98–100
Skate Rags, 91
skate videos, 90, 102, 119–20, 122, 126,
    159, 161, 168, 233
Skee-Skate, 25
Sky Brown effect, 228
slalom skateboarding, 24
SLAP magazine, 119
Smith, Lance, 81
Smith, Rodney, 110, 136–37
The Smothers Brothers Comedy Hour
    (TV show), 25
sneakers, 140–46
snowboarding, 148–49
Sotheby's, 18
Soul Artists of Zoo York magazine, 135, 138
Spagnoli, Guy "Grundy," 69
Spalding, 189
Stahl, Miriam Klein, 212
Steamer, Elissa, 132, 178
Stecyk, C. R., 12, 14, 28, 48, 62, 64, 135, 182
Stephenson, Keith, 60
Stevenson, Larry, 24, 37, 45, 87
Strauberry, Cher, 18, 207, 230, 233
Stranger, Julien, 126–27
StrangeLove Skateboards 4, 214–15, 230
street skateboarding, 110, 125, 229
Street Survival (film), 104
Strople, Chris, 78
Sugarhill Gang, 45
Summerfield, Rick, 71, 97
Supreme Skateboards, 120, 197
surfboards, 4, 14–15, 21–22, 26, 28–34, 36,
    38–39, 54, 60, 62–63, 66–67, 233, 235
Surf Guide (magazine), 25, 37, 87
surfing, 21–25
    counterculture, 33–34
    name origins, 32
    surf-to-skateboard genetic transfer, 28–32
Syndicate, 41

T

Team USA. *See* Olympics, summer 2020
Texas Backyard Series, 87
Thornhill Caswell, Laura, 17, 56
Thrasher (magazine), 77, 85–86, 90, 92–93,
    96–97, 111, 125, 147, 149, 155, 168, 190, 193,

196–97, 202–3
360, 113
Tillman, Joi, 213
Tokyo 2020. *See* Olympics, summer 2020
Tony Hawk Foundation, 15, 95, 164
Tony Hawk's Pro Skater (video game), 120
Toy Machine, 133, 154–55, 203
Tracker trucks, 69, 78, 86–87, 103, 115
Tracker wheels, 78, 103
Transworld Skateboarding (magazine), 86, 88,
    90, 120, 133, 164
Treece, Chuck, 90, 93
tricks, 8–9, 12, 17, 25, 39, 4, 50, 56, 58, 72, 88
    heel flip, 88
    impossible, 88
    kickflip, 88
    kicktail, 45
    900, 113, 120, 151, 205
    ollie, 50
    720, 113
    360, 113
    vert tricks, 87
trucks, 47, 50–51
    Signal Hill Runs, 69–70
Turner, Laurie, 24, 25
Turner, Peggy, 69
twenty-tens, 189–95
    coming out, 210–11
    interacting with Leo Baker, 216–17
    Olympics, 220–29
    Pave the Way Skateboards, 212–13
    photography, 198–202
    safe spaces, 206–7
two-thousands, 159–65
    fighting for fair play, 180–81
    Native Americans in, 182–85
    personal stories, 174–77
    skate collection beginnings, 172–73
    skateboarding as career, 178–79
    skateboarding in new millennium, 168–70

U

Underhill, Ray, 97
Union Cycliste Internationale (UCI), 225
United States Olympic & Paralympic
    Committee (USOPC), 226
United States Skateboard Association
    (USSA), 47, 69
Unity, 193
University of South California (USC), 202

Urethane, 30, 45, 46, 56, 60–61, 63, 66, 67, 68, 73, 88, 140, 159, 234
UT pads, 110

V

Val Surf, 24, 71
Vallely, Mike, 102, 113, 118, 169
Vans, 41, 120, 141, 145, 148–49, 160, 168–73, 181, 186
Vernon Courtland Johnson (VCJ), 107
vert skateboarding, 51, 58, 76, 87–88, 91, 118–20, 151
Vickers, Vicki, 56, 58
video games, 120
videos, 88–89
    mail-order skateboards, 101–2
    video days, 125
    YouTube, 161
Vision, 90, 97, 103, 107–8, 113, 115, 118, 124, 135, 160–62
Vitello, Fausto, 85
Vogue (magazine), 28, 31, 183, 200
Void Skateboards, 13
Von Essen, Desiree, 76
Vultee, Gerard "Jerry," 29

W

Walker Skateboards, 52, 89, 157
Weaver, Gregg, 80
Weingartner, Briel, 19
Welcome Skateboards, 197
Welcome to Hell (film), 203
wheels, 45–47, 67–68
    Cadillac Wheels, 60–61
    Kryptonics wheels, 105
    Road Rider wheels, 47, 67–68
    Tracker wheels, 78, 103
White, Alex, 193
Whitehead, Cindy, 56, 76, 98
Wild World of Entertainment (magazine), 69
Wild World of Skateboarding (magazine), 48
Wide World of Sports (magazine), 25
Williams, Neftalie, 198
Wilson, Buster, 35–36
Winnie Mae (airplane), 29
Wittpenn, John, 96–97

women, 132–33
    lack of bias against, 24–25
    seventies skateboarding, 56–61
    skateboarding as career, 178–79
    skateboarding pride, 150
World Skateboard Association (WSA), 47

X

X Games, 69–70, 120, 151–52, 179, 180

Y

YouTube, 161
Yun Chung Chiang, 40

Z

Z-Boys, 49
Z-Flex, 64
Zephyr, 62–64
zines, 90–91, 107, 217
    rise of, 96–97
    proceeds from selling, 211
Zoo York, 120, 134–39, 160